THE BURDEN
OF
VICTORY

Also by Laird Kleine-Ahlbrandt

The Policy of Simmering, A Study of British Policy during the Spanish Civil War 1936-1939

Appeasement of the Dictators, Crisis Diplomacy

La Tosca, The Drama behind the Opera

Twentieth-Century European History

Europe Since 1945, From Conflict to Community

THE BURDEN OF VICTORY

France, Britain and the Enforcement of the Versailles Peace, 1919-1925

Wm. Laird Kleine-Ahlbrandt

University Press of America, Inc.
Lanham • New York • London

Copyright © 1995 by
University Press of America,® Inc.
4720 Boston Way
Lanham, Maryland 20706

3 Henrietta Street
London, WC2E 8LU England

Library of Congress Cataloging-in-Publication Data

Kleine-Ahlbrandt, W. Laird (William Laird)
The burden of victory : France, Britain, and the enforcement of the
Versaille peace, 1919-1925 / Wm. Laird Kleine-Ahlbrandt.
p.   cm.
Includes bibliographical references and index.
1. Paris Peace Cenference (1919-1920). 2. Treaty of Versailles
(1919) 3. World War, 1914-1918--Peace. 4. France--Foreign
relations--Great Britain. 5. Great Britain--Foreign relations--France.
I. Title.
D645.K54   1995   940.3'141--dc20   95-33189   CIP

ISBN 0-7618-0068-9 (cloth: alk ppr.)
ISBN 0-7618-0069-7 (pbk: alk ppr.)

⊖™The paper used in this publication meets the minimum
requirements of American National Standard for Information
Sciences—Permanence of Paper for Printed Library Materials,
ANSI Z39.48—1984

TO TREVOR

For the glass of the years is brittle. . .

CONTENTS

Appendices

ILLUSTRATIONS

THE FRENCH PRESIDENT desired to speak privately with the British prime minister. Germany, after 44-years of political division, was about to be reunited, thereby again threatening a daunting domination of European political and economic affairs; and François Mitterand was alarmed. The meeting was easily arranged. Both leaders were in Strasbourg, attending the December 1989 sessions of the Council of Europe.

At the talks, Mitterand suggested that he and Margaret Thatcher find a common policy on how to deal with the impending reunification. He remarked that the Germans were "a people in constant movement and flux." He reminded the prime minister that "at moments of great danger in the past France had always established special relations with Britain." The president felt that "such a time had come again."

Thatcher welcomed the proposal. A new Anglo-French entente could not only counterbalance German power, to prevent the Germans having "things all their own way," but could also forestall the strengthening of an already existent French and German axis in which France was junior partner and Britain was odd-man-out. Thatcher observed that both France and Britain had the will to contain German power, but had yet to develop the way—much less agree on what way was best.

Mitterand believed German power could be contained through strengthening the European Union, welding Germany even more tightly to the interests of the member states, making an independent course impossible. Thatcher, though, felt such an association would only give Germany a stronger platform on which to develop greater power and influence. She preferred a loser, more balance-of-power style arrangement, not unlike the Europe of nations, which Charles de

Gaulle had proposed earlier. European economic integration could continue and would be strengthened, but not at the expense of basic

national sovereignty and closer Anglo-French relations. While accepting, as Mitterand, the sad inevitability of reunification, she nonetheless wanted to slow it down, giving Europe more time to readjust, thus avoiding destabilization. In the end her policy failed. And the reunification of Germany proceeded without the presence of any Anglo-French entente. This was hardly surprising. Since the beginning of the twentieth century British and French efforts to develop a common security policy had persistently fizzled, providing little optimism that things would be any different now.

With the timid formation of the *Entente Cordiale* in 1904, the British and French had begun a century-long quest to find a means to brake the "German juggernaut." But their intention to reach agreement always seemed outstripped by events. Even immediately before and during the First World War, a high point of cooperation, differing Anglo-French concerns, influenced and transmogrified by tradition, geography, and political economics, pulled against the gluing of lasting ties. In the face of the German military threat they had abandoned their traditional animosity, but their new founded cooperation did not endure. As their relations in the decade following the First World War showed, they were associates, but not partners.

I WOULD like to gratefully acknowledge those who assisted me in the research and preparation of this book for publication. The British Public Record Office is surely one of the easiest and most comfortable places to do research despite that daily commute from London and the schlepp from the Kew tube station. The PRO's system of buzzing the arrival of documents through portable, personal radio receivers—audible anywhere in the building even the W.C.—is a delight of efficiency. Its staff always handled my inflated appetite for documents with professionalism and aplomb. (Do they still have those metal detectors at the entrance?) Working at the French Ministry of Foreign Relations was also an agreeable experience, if for no other reason than its archives are still located in the same building where the nation's foreign policy is decided—the foreign minister's office is on the next floor down from the reading room. More to the point, though, the Quai d'Orsay's pleasant archival staff, small and overworked, went out of its way to help get the materials I requested, even bending the rules on occasion to retrieve more than the daily 4-volume limit and to facilitate use of the reference library of the professional staff of the foreign ministry.

Colleague and friend Walter Forster helped me shape and formulate my ideas on foreign policy, especially in the dynamics of the balance of power system. We agreed on Wilson, but not Clemenceau. And my weekly lunches with old buddy Joseph Haberer, *science politicien en retraite*, were a pleasant and painless way to refine concepts and shape attitudes. Sheila Hégy Swanson, *confidante et femme époustouflante*, provided valuable criticism of the text and suggested the title. Courtenay Kleine-Ahlbrandt was an estimable lynx-eyed editor of the manuscript copy. I am also indebted to the gracious and indulgent office staff from the Purdue University history department. I especially want to recognize Nancy Cramer, Amy Cox, and Susan English. And I again pay tribute to Julie Mántica, Eleanor Gerns, and Judy McHenry, all who helped finish my previous book. I was delighted and gratified in being able to count on their assistance once more. This book I have dedicated to my son of whom I am justifiably proud.

Wm. Laird Kleine-Ahlbrandt
Oak Park, Illinois

THE FORMATION OF AN ALLIANCE

SHORTLY PAST NOON, 1 May 1903, the train carrying King Edward VII pulled into the Bois de Boulogne station. French President Émile Loubet, wearing sombre morning attire and the cordon of the grand commander of the Legion of Honor, was waiting on the platform to greet him. The British monarch, resplendent in the scarlet uniform of a field marshal, descended from the carriage to shake Loubet's hand. The formalities over, Loubet escorted the monarch outside to a waiting carriage for the journey to the British embassy on the Rue St-Honoré where Edward would be staying the days he was in Paris.

The carriage bearing the French and British chiefs of state was part of a six-vehicle cortege, flanked by mounted *gardes républicaines* in plumed Napoleon III helmets and polished-steel breastplates. People crowded the sidewalks to watch the procession pass. Some spectators had the bad manners to shout derogatory slogans as *"Vive les Boers"* and *"Vive Fashoda"*, alluding to recent examples of Anglo-Imperial realpolitik, but mostly they were friendly and cheered and waved. Edward enthusiastically returned their greetings. His pleasure was genuine.

Paris was Edward's last stop on a grand tour which had left Portsmouth five weeks earlier and had visited Lisbon, Gibraltar, Malta, and Rome. The king had suggested the trip, helped plan its itinerary, and arranged many of its details. This was his first time abroad since he had succeeded his mother, Queen Victoria, on the throne two years before. He had brought with him 70 trunks of personal luggage, enough clothes to change many times a day—as custom required.

Edward adored Paris: its free and easy atmosphere and elegant cuisine. As prince of Wales, he had visited many times, escaping the stuffiness of the Victorian court and the moral rectitude of his mother. On this trip, royal nostalgia could be indulged, but not at the expense of more serious business. Foreign Secretary Lansdowne, knowing the king's popularity with the Parisians, hoped to use it to promote the British policy of detente with France. The two nations had recently begun negotiations to resolve their colonial differences, but these talks were presently mired in "all sorts of ignoble ruts." Lansdowne had assigned Under-secretary Charles Hardinge to the king's retinue as "minister plenipotentiary," charging him with public relations, especially the task of writing the monarch's public speeches. Hardinge could produce one of these in less than an hour. The second day of his visit Edward addressed the local British Chamber of Commerce:

> The days of conflict between [our] two countries are, I trust, happily over, and I hope that future historians, in alluding to Anglo-French relations in the present century, may be able to record only a friendly rivalry in the field of commercial and industrial developments, and that in the future, as in the past, England and France may be regarded as the champions and pioneers of peaceful progress and civilization and as the homes of all that is best and noblest in literature, art, and science.[1]

The speech was hardly a stylistic masterpiece—this 85-word sentence was strung together with nine "ands", several of them serving to garland clauses—but it covered all the necessary policy bases and elicited praise from the Paris newspapers, which gave full credit to the king for the message of good will. Lansdowne was impressed by the response:

> The French nation saw in His Majesty's words and actions a guarantee that the adjustment of political differences might well prepare the way for bringing about a genuine and lasting friendship, to be built up on community of interests and aspirations.[2]

Edward had a feel for foreign affairs, but little taste for the routine work and studious conceptualization necessary to formulate policy. Moreover, his status as constitutional monarch precluded his exercising much control. The success of the Paris visit was due in no small measure to his conviviality and flair for ceremony, but his congeniality could not alone wipe away centuries of ill-will and conflict. Despite periods of peace and cooperation in the 18th and 19th centuries, the two nations had engaged in one of the longest and most persistent national rivalries in European history.

THE BRITISH had refrained from joining alliances in times of peace, keeping their hands free to throw their weight against whatever country or coalition threatened their security. This role of "holder" of the balance of power was predicated on will almost as much as strength. By the end of the nineteenth century, however, Britain was no longer Europe's paramount power.[3] In the generation following 1888, when Wilhelm II had ascended the German throne, the Reich had assumed that position, leading Europe in the production of iron ore, crude steel, electrical energy, sulfuric acid, copper, tin, zinc, potassium. Between 1900 and 1913, its industry expanded by 64 percent while Britain's went up only 25 percent. Britain was ahead only in the production of coal and in the monetary value of its foreign trade.[4] And, though still one of the world's leading industrial nations, it was less capable of maintaining the economic edge on which its traditional foreign policy had depended.

The British seemed willing to adjust to German ascendency, such accommodation being an important component in balance of power politics. They even emphasized that increased German economic strength created a better market for British goods. The British also did not seem particularly threatened by the German alliances with Austria-Hungary and Italy, believing that the Triple Alliance promoted stability and peace. Sir Edward Grey, secretary of state for foreign affairs from 11 December 1905 to 11 December 1916, reasoned in his memoirs:

> only when the dominant power becomes aggressive and [Britain] feels her own interests to be threatened that she, by an instinct of self-defense, if not by deliberate policy, gravitates to anything that can be fairly described as a Balance of Power.[5]

If true, Britain had abandoned one of the cardinal assumptions of realpolitik: that capabilities were more important than perceived intentions.

Before Edward's visit to Paris, the British had seemed less concerned about their position in Europe than about their status in Africa, in the Near East, and in the Far East—parts of the world where Germany was less an adversary than France or Russia. British policymakers tended to regard the European equilibrium as self-fulfilling, an attitude that would soon change, considering the lack of moderation of Kaiser Wilhelm the Second.

Otto von Bismarck once said Wilhelm was "like a balloon, if you don't keep fast hold of the string, you never know where he'll go off to." But Bismarck was of another age; he was 44 years older than Wilhelm, born in 1815, the same year as the Battle of Waterloo. "If Frederick the Great had this sort of chancellor, he would not have been great," Wilhelm sneered.[6]

After Bismarck's resignation in March 1890, Wilhelm proceeded to dismantle the Iron Chancellor's diplomatic system. He encountered little opposition because the imperial constitution, written by Bismarck, gave the sovereign great personal power. Moreover, Bismarck had so feared talented men in high office that he had left no really qualified successors, allowing Wilhelm a clear field to appoint whatever mediocrity he chose.

The Wilhelmian era began with the alienation of Russia, when the German foreign ministry refused to renew the Reinsurance Treaty, which gave German diplomatic support to Russia in exchange for a more significant Russian pledge to remain neutral in the event of a Franco-German war. It was a bad time to cut Russia loose.

By 1890, France had recovered sufficiently from its defeat by Germany in 1871 to be considered a serious power. It had the means to give Russia financial assistance to build factories, construct railways, offset budgetary deficits, and equip armies. French aid did not come without a price. In August 1891, France got Russia to agree to mutual consultations, if either were threatened by aggression. The following October, France advanced Russia an important loan.[7] The next year, France insisted that the Russians sign a military convention. Two years later, the convention was upgraded into a formal alliance.

The Franco-Russian treaty of January 1894 was an important step in the realignment of European politics. Each country promised to support the other, if either were attacked by any country of the Triple Alliance.[8] Furthermore, if any Triplice member were to mobilize, then France and Russia would also mobilize and move their forces as near to the enemy frontiers as possible. Thus mobilization became a declaration of war, and any conflict between Russia and Austria could trigger a clash between France and Germany.

The British looked on this realignment with concern, but their concern was primarily naval. Britain still operated under the two-power standard, that the Royal Navy had to be stronger than a combination of the world's next two navies. The Franco-Russian Alliance appeared especially dangerous because it grouped together the second and third largest world fleets. (The fear was heightened by the fact that the British kept only about one-third of their fleet in home waters.) The British were soon weighing the alliance's implications when they discovered that the French intended to gain control of the Sudan, a territory the British considered within their own sphere of interest.

The British informed the French that they would consider this an "unfriendly act," but the French ignored the warning and commissioned Major Jean-Baptiste Marchand to head an expedition to move into the Upper Nile. Marchand's small army left the French Congo, in May 1896, heading towards the fortress town of Fashoda. The British ordered General Herbert Kitchner to take a force of his own north from Egypt to intercept the French. Kitchner arrived at Fashoda in September 1898, two months after Marchand. The two field commanders were too sensible to shoot it out and referred the question of ownership to their respective capitals.

The Fashoda crisis almost brought the two nations to blows before being resolved in Britain's favor. However, as steamed as the French were over their loss, they realized that they could no longer afford the luxury of having Britain as their enemy. The British were coming to the same conclusion about France.

ON 28 MARCH 1898, the Reichstag voted credits to construct, over the next seven years, 19 battleships, 8 armored ships, 12 heavy cruisers, 30 light cruisers, and almost 50 destroyers. Wilhelm II embraced the doctrines of Captain Alfred Thayer Mahan of the American Naval War College, who preached that successful foreign policy was determined by the control of the seas with capital ships. This meant that the Germans had to build a navy whose strength surpassed that of the British Royal Navy. Admiral Alfred von Tirpitz, the head of the Reich naval office,[9] planned to accomplish this in stages, the first being the construction of a fleet of sufficient power that no other navy would dare attack it without suffering serious losses. The "risk theory" period would ultimately and inevitably be followed by German mastery of the North Sea.

In 1900, the Reichstag took a significant step in that direction by providing monies for 38 battleships, 14 heavy cruisers, 34 light cruisers, and 96 destroyers. This program, upon completion in 1915, would give Germany a fleet which, ship for ship, would equal or surpass any in the world. The Press Bureau of the German Foreign Office had promoted the bill's passage by encouraging newspapers to play up the British threat.

The British had once considered signing some sort of treaty of friendship with Germany. But the Germans wanted a full-scale, global commitment with colonial concessions, British recognition of their possession of Alsace-Lorraine, and support against Russia. Prime Minister Salisbury believed these demands carried more liabilities than benefits. In his mind, a British promise to help Germany against Russia was hardly equivalent to the dangers run by poisoning relations with France, especially if Britain were to recognize German ownership of Alsace-Lorraine.[10] But a more serious stumbling block to reaching an agreement was Germany's aggressive naval policy. Britain's main line of defense was the Royal Navy while Germany without a High Seas Fleet was still the strongest power on the continent. Any challenge to Britannia ruling the waves was a dagger pointed at Britain's heart. Britain went shopping for allies.

On 20 January 1902, Britain concluded a treaty with Japan that promoted resolution of areas of conflict in the Far East. The two powers promised to give each other diplomatic, and, under certain circumstances, military support.[11] The alliance allowed Britain to concentrate more on European affairs and to repatriate some of its Far Eastern naval units, but it did little to offset Britain's differences with France. The British judged that the most sensible way of dealing with these was through direct negotiations "to smooth away and remove possible sources of conflict."[12]

FRANCE had lived in Germany's shadow since its defeat in the Franco-Prussian war in 1871. The treaty, signed at Frankfurt on 10 May, had given the Germans virtually all they had demanded: most of Lorraine and all of Alsace, except Belfort, whose garrison had successfully withstood a 15-week German siege. France was required to pay an impressive indemnity of five billion francs (roughly one billion dollars) and to support an army of occupation until the debt was acquitted. Taking Alsace-Lorraine encouraged the instability and impermanence it was supposed to prevent and produced the spirit of revenge it was supposed to suppress. The French regarded the Germans no different from those barbarians who had once crossed the Rhine to seize the lands of northern Gaul and bring home trophies to admire in their tribal lodges. France never forgot the loss of its "sacred soil."

In Paris, the statue to the city of Strasbourg in the Place de la Concorde was draped in black. French maps, published after 1870, were always careful to remind viewers that the lost departments of the Upper and Lower Rhine (Alsace) and the Moselle (Lorraine) were still part of the Nation. A stable Europe depended on the reconciliation of France and Germany. But, isolated and humiliated, France nursed a passion for revenge. To rebuild its strength, it turned to overseas expansion.

In twenty years, it patched together the world's second largest empire. The Germans encouraged this expansion as a means of diverting French attention from Europe and poisoning French relations with Great Britain. The Fashoda crisis of 1898 seemed to justify the strategy. The showdown in the Sudan, however, proved to be a turning point, a high-water mark of Anglo-French rivalry. Foreign Minister Théophile Delcassé worked hard to put Anglo-French enmity to rest, especially after the signature of the Anglo-Japanese treaty. Delcassé feared that a war between Japan and Russia might trigger a conflict between France and Britain. To avoid this happening, he pushed to regulate Anglo-French relations with an agreement of his own. But, at the same time, he had to see what he could do to change traditional French attitudes.

French anglophobia was so deeply rooted that it had even found its way into the songs mothers sang to their children. All classes were involved in Britain bashing, but it was particularly fashionable among the intellectuals. In his *Essay on the Political Psychology of the*

English Nation in the Nineteenth Century, Émile Boutmy, the head of the École Libre des Sciences Politiques in Paris, wrote:

> No man who has lived long in England can dispute the bestiality of the great majority of the [British] race. To-day, as of old, sport, betting, intoxication count among the pleasures most appreciated by Englishmen. To-day, as of old, they need the overloading of a full stomach to stimulate their genius.[13]

Boutmy called the English a race of pirates with a passion for oppressing, exploiting, and destroying subject peoples. Delcassé hoped that such propaganda stunts, like Edward's visit to Paris, would soften these attitudes. He intended to do what he could to maintain its momentum.

On 7 July 1903, he and President Loubet embarked on a return visit to England. The king met them at London's Victoria Station. From their arrival until they left three-days later, the French leaders' schedule was so crammed with activities they had little time to rest. Their first stop was The City, London's financial district, where the Loubet first proposed the conclusion of an *Entente Cordiale* between the two peoples. He said that

> their common interests should inspire them with a spirit of conciliation and accommodation....[and] of the value which the whole French government attaches to the development of...friendship between our two countries.[14]

That evening, he hosted a banquet at the French embassy. Edward attended wearing again his British field marshal's uniform. A gala performance at Covent Garden followed dinner. Two of the world's most renown divas, Emma Calvé and Nellie Melba, did scenes from *Carmen*, *Rigoletto*, and *Roméo et Juliette*.[15] The next morning, the French statesmen visited Windsor Castle and then Frogmore to lay a wreath at Queen Victoria's tomb. In the afternoon, they witnessed a military parade at Aldershot. On display were the Horse Artillery, the 1st Life Guards, the 13th and 18th Hussars, the London Guards, the Scots Guards, the Royal Fusileers, the Cheshires, the Yorkshires, the Lancasters. No one could have asked for a better demonstration of British nineteenth-century-style panache, even though the correspondent from *The Times* regretted that Britain had not shown its "French guests 60,000 men from the Indian establishment."[16]

That night, Lord Lansdowne gave a state ball at his townhouse on Berkeley Square, inviting 2,220 guests, including American Ambassador Joseph Choate and 30 officers from the American naval squadron which had docked at Portsmouth earlier in the day. (The British never passed up an opportunity to remain on the best possible terms with the United States.) A complete list appeared in the next edition of *The Times*, together with descriptions of the most elegant ball gowns.

Loubet and Delcassé returned home exhausted, but to great acclaim. The Paris press, not without official encouragement, hailed the trip as an important step in eliminating Anglo-French animosity. But the two foreign offices were still as far apart as ever in their search for an agreement.

The British and French understandably had enormous difficulty sorting out their imperial baggage: how to adjust claims in West Africa, how to establish commercial duties in Madagascar, how to share control of the New Hebrides, how to settle spheres of influence along the frontiers of Thailand, and how to regulate fishing rights off Newfoundland. Furthermore, Paris wanted an alliance, similar to the one signed with the Russians; the British envisaged only an informal and general "cordial understanding." In the end, the British had their way. Delcassé was willing to settle for something less than he wanted in anticipation that more would come later.

In the *Entente Cordiale*, signed on 4 April 1904, France promised to allow Britain freedom of action in Egypt in exchange for a British promise to respect French interests in Morocco.[17] The two also pledged to give each other diplomatic support in other areas of importance, settling their differences in a range of disputed areas. The understanding contained nothing in it that was anti-German, and the British continued to pretend that splendid isolation still existed. Establishing cordial relations with France seemed its own reward. Even years later, Edward Grey, one-time foreign secretary, maintained:

> The gloomy clouds were gone, the sky was clear, and the sun shone warmly.... To see what is pleasant, where we have seen before only what was repellent; to understand and to be understood where before there had been misrepresentation and misconstruction; to be

friends instead of enemies—this, when it happens, is one of the great pleasures of life.[18]

The Entente, though, was an important step in pulling Britain and France together. The British might extol the virtues of Platonic friendship, but the powerful and aggressive presence of Germany worked to move the Entente towards a formal alliance. The French would soon discover how far the British were willing to go. In January 1905, the French pressured the sultan of Morocco to put his country under their protection despite recognition of the sovereignty of Morocco by all the major European nations and the United States in the 1880 Madrid Convention.

UNDER THE GUISE of upholding the sanctity of international agreements, German chancellor, Bernhard von Bülow, decided to sow mistrust and disagreement into the newly formed Entente, to, as he explained,

> break the continuity of aggressive French policy, knock the continental dagger out of the hands of Edward VII and the war group in England and, simultaneously, ensure peace, preserve German honor and improve German prestige.[19]

He, therefore induced the kaiser, who was taking a Mediterranean cruise, to land at Tangier, on 31 March, and make a speech, at the local German consulate, in which Germany promised to guarantee the independence of the sultan's government. Bülow anticipated that the French would back down and the British think twice before the signing any more agreements, like the Entente Cordiale, without first looking to Berlin for permission. The rightness of this course of action was confirmed on 27-28 May 1905, when the Japanese destroyed Russia's entire Baltic Naval Squadron in action in the Straits of Tsushima. After such a debacle, the Russians could no longer give effective support to their French ally.

Bülow figured that Britain would hardly risk war over Morocco and sensing victory insisted on the convocation of a conference of the great powers. Had Britain, and, to a lesser degree France, been the imperial powers they pretended to be, the conference would never have been held. At this meeting which took place at Algeciras, Spain, in

January 1906, the issue of Moroccan independence and sovereignty was not directly considered; it appeared on the agenda only in the discussions over which country should run the Moroccan police force and control the state bank. In both matters, the rights of the French were confirmed. Austria alone supported German interests. Italy, the other partner of the Triple Alliance, remained neutral.

THE MATCH-MAKER MALGRÉ ELLE.

Mlle. La France (aside). "IF SHE 'S GOING TO GLARE AT US LIKE THAT, IT ALMOST LOOKS AS IF WE MIGHT HAVE TO BE REGULARLY ENGAGED."

The match-maker inspite of herself. Punch *rarely passed up an opportunity to critizize or make fun of the kaiser and his government. In this Bernard Partridge cartoon, published on 12 April 1905, a week and a half after the kaiser made his dramatic landing at Tangier, "Germania" appears in 16th century garb as a bossy, domineering old shrew, a female stereotype to which the male-dominated political society of Britain could easily relate.*

The Germans might have suspected that they would be outvoted—status quo powers usually had more votes at such meetings, or did before the existence of the United Nations—but that they, with all their bullying, were able to exert enough pressure to succeed marked an important alteration of the current balance of power. This though was not enough to satisfy the Germans, and they went home convinced that the only way they could, henceforth, achieve their goals was through a policy of force. Such truculence convinced the British that the Germans had wanted a port on the Moorish coast as a first step to establishing control in the Mediterranean. The French exploited these fears and pressed the British into deciding where their forces should be stationed in a war with Germany.

British statesmen seemed unaware of the change that was occurring in their relations with France and considered that staff talks would constitute no departure from previous policy.[20] Since the Entente Cordiale contained no military clauses, they did not see how discussions in fact established a peacetime commitment to go to war. Even if British politicians and diplomats were reluctant to admit to the existence of such an alliance, the generals and admirals had no problems in doing so.

FIRST SEA LORD Sir John Fisher always assumed the Entente Cordiale carried a military commitment. He was convinced that the Germans would never stop building ships until they had the power to destroy the Royal Navy. Late in 1904, he told Edward VII that the Royal Navy should make a surprise attack on the German fleet to destroy it before it got too strong. The king was unreceptive. "My God, Fisher, you must be mad" he replied.[21]

Fisher, therefore, prepared a more conventional response. He worked to ready the British navy for instant action—mobilization was now tantamount to a declaration of war—while improving the quality of his ships. He pushed the construction of a superbattleship: the *H.M.S. Dreadnought*, which could cruise at 21 knots and mounted 10 twelve-inch guns with a range of 14,000 yards, nearly 8 miles.[22] Fisher hoped that dreadnoughts would put an end to German dreams of nautical splendor. *Au contraire.* With all other existent battleships now obsolete, the British advantage was reduced to the time it took the Germans to produce an all-big-gun ship of their own, or just 18 months.[23] The prospect of bringing an end to the naval race was more remote than ever.

The Germans regarded any brake on ship building as a limitation on their status as a great power. "I have no desire for a good relationship with England at the sacrifice of the increase of Germany's navy," the kaiser wrote.[24] And Tirpitz declared that he would rather resign than agree to slowing down German naval construction. There could be no successful negotiations as long as Germany's leaders believed they had a right to a navy as fearsome as their army. The Germans felt that building as many ships as they wanted was their sovereign right. It was, but the policy was not wise.

In the context of this frenetic arms race, the British were unable to maintain their old two-power standard and now predicated "command of the seas" on exceeding the strength of their nearest competitor, Germany, by at least one-third.[25] Recent advances in nautical technology convinced them of the necessity of working out detailed military plans prior to the start of hostilities. And, at the beginning of 1906, British military chief joined their French counterparts in detailing how their forces should be deployed. They decided that the French concentrate their navy in the Mediterranean, while the British place theirs in the Atlantic and the North Sea. "Our drill ground should be our battle ground", Fisher exclaimed as he began holding war games in the areas designated for the Royal Navy.[26] The British would also create an expeditionary force—six infantry divisions and one cavalry division—to send to the continent as soon as hostilities began. Disembarkation ports, transport facilities, soldier billeting were decided with the French insisting that the British take up battle positions on the left flank of their forces near the Belgian frontier. On the diplomatic front, the French pushed the British to improve their relations with Russia. This led to the signature of a Anglo-Russian Entente in 1907.[27] Although the agreement was not a formal alliance, it solidified the emerging anti-German coalition. To maintain the balance of power, however, Britain had to do more than compete in an arms race.

The British Foreign Office developed the rationale for the change of policy. In a memorandum published on 1 January 1907, Senior Clerk Eyre Crowe stated that Germany was determined to establish its primacy in international politics at the cost and at the expense of other nations. He doubted the Germans recognized that such a goal was doomed to fail. German policy, he speculated, was either "the expression of a vague, confused, and impractical statesmanship," or a result of the "erratic, domineering, and often frankly aggressive" personality of the Kaiser. Britain, however, had to remain committed to maintaining the European balance of power and to keeping strong militarily because:

> nothing is more likely to produce in Germany the impression of the practical hopelessness of a never-ending succession of costly naval programs than the conviction...that for every German ship England will inevitably lay down two, so maintaining the present relative British preponderance.[28]

Crowe cautioned against a one-sided policy of appeasement, asserting that graceful British concessions would never improve relations with Germany—

> concessions made without any conviction either of their justice or of their being set off by equivalent counter-services.[29]

That Germany could be conciliated and become more friendly was, according to Crowe, a vain hope.

The transformation of the Entente into an alliance, via specific military obligations, was kept from the public eye. It was not even discussed in the cabinet. Grey minimized the new commitments, calling them procedural.[30] The government continued to insist that it had retained freedom of action, with Grey arguing that promises of military support had been intended to apply only to the Moroccan crisis.

When news of the military conversations leaked beyond the Imperial Committee of Defence, the government tried to cover itself by insisting—in a letter Sir Edward Grey sent to Paul Cambon, the French ambassador to London—that

> such consultation does not restrict the freedom of either Government to decide at any future time whether or not to assist the other by armed force... and is not, and ought not to be, regarded as an engagement that commits either Government to action in an contingency that has not arisen and may never arise.[31]

Cambon replied in kind. The letters, however, were more than a simple clarification of policy between diplomats. In them, each country recognized its pledge to go to war on the behalf of the other. Cambon said:

> in the event of one of our two Governments having grave reason to fear either an act of aggression from a third Power, or some event threatening general peace, that Government would immediately examine with the other the question whether both Governments should act together to prevent the act of aggression or preserve peace. If so, the two governments would deliberate as to the measures which they would be prepared to take in common; if those measures involved action, the two Governments would take into immediate consideration the plans of the General Staffs and would decide as to the effect to be given those plans.[32]

By 1912, military planning had assumed its own dynamic and its own independence. The French and British peoples found out about the existence of this "secret treaty" only when war broke out in 1914.

As long as the German threat remained, the Anglo-French military alliance flourished. The defeat of Germany in the First World War, however, brought about significant reevaluation and change. France wanted to continue the Entente Cordiale as a guarantee against German aggression and an alliance through which the integrity of the peace settlement could be protected. The British, however, wanted a return to the Entente's original spirit: as a means of resolving differences in a conciliatory and neighborly spirit, not the military alliance it had become. Britain longed for the days when it had acted as the holder of the balance of power, a role which, in the postwar world, would make Britain a mediator between France and Germany.

The difference of approach between Britain and France was basic and led to continuous disagreements over how the peace settlement should be written, how it should be enforced, and whether it should be revised. Different readings of national interest produced different prescriptions for European security. The Entente partners disagreed over how strong Germany should become before it would be considered a threat. They differed in their policies concerning other countries, like Turkey and the Soviet Union. Even those leaders, who believed cooperation was devoutly wished, chose different paths to salvation.

The burden of victory made France and Britain ill-at-ease with their friendship. When Germany again tried to destroy the European balance of power such Anglo-French division almost proved fatal.

Team Work. *The handshake between a Tommie and a Poilu, celebrating their cooperation during the Battle of the Somme, glorified the spirit of friendship and unity between the partners of the Entente Cordiale, (Cartoon of Louis Raemaekers, July 1916.)*

Notes and Sources:

1. Sidney Lee, *King Edward VII* (New York: Macmillan, 1927), II, 237.

2. *British Documents on the Origins of the War*, III, Appendix A, 398.

3. Paul Kennedy, *The Rise and Fall of the Great Powers, Economic Change and Military Conflict from 1500 to 2000* (New York; Random House, 1987), 209-215.

4. In 1913, British imports amounted to $3.4 billion, exports of British products were $2.6 billion; Imperial Germany had $2.7 billion in imports and $2.5 billion in exports. If foreign trade alone determined industrial power rank, the industrial colossus of the United States would have come in only third. In 1913, the Americans imported only $1.7 billion worth of goods and exported $2.4 billion worth. J. Scott Keltie, ed., *The Statesman's Year Book 1915*, 73, 950, 459.

5. Viscount Grey of Fallodon, *Twenty-Five Years 1892-1916*, (New York: Frederick A. Stokes, 1925), I, 8.

6. Michael Balfour, *The Kaiser and His Times* (Boston: Houghton Mifflin, 1964), 127.

7. The intimate relationship between French foreign and financial policy was also evident in the persistent denial of the Paris money market to Germany. The *bourse* even refused to list German securities, and the government threatened any French banking institution with sanctions should it advance Germany credits.

8. Thus Russia would attack Germany, if France were attacked by Germany, or attacked by Italy supported by Germany, or attacked by Austria supported by Germany. Likewise, France would help Russia, if Russia were attacked by any member of the Triple Alliance.

9. He was Chief of Staff of the Supreme Naval Command in 1892 and in 1897 Secretary of State for Naval Affairs.

10. Norman Rich, *Great Power Diplomacy 1814-1914*. (New York: McGraw Hill, 1992), 389.

11. Japan and Britain agreed to remain neutral should either become involved in a war with a third power, except if the third power had the support of an ally. Then, Britain and Japan would wage war together. The treaty further provided that the British and Japanese navies would cooperate in times of peace, and that their fleets in Far East waters would together exceed that of any third power.

12. Viscount Grey of Fallodon, 47.

13. "England Viewed through French Spectacles", *The Quarterly Review*, vol. 195, January and April 1902 (London: John Murray, 1902), 506.

The quote is from Boutmy's *Essai d'une psychologie politique du peuple anglais au XIXème siècle*. (Paris: Armand Colin, 1901).

14. *The* (London) *Times*, July 8, 1903, 9.

15. "A Very Grand Opera Night," *Punch or the London Charivari*, July 15, 1903, 34.

16. *The* (London) *Times*, July 9, 1903, 10.

17. The Japanese attack on the Russian base at Port Arthur in February 1904 gave added urgency to the search for an agreement. Although the treaties that Britain had with the Japanese, and the French with the Russians, avoided pledges of specific military support, the fear that relations might become severely strained and divert attention from the main concern of security in Europe strengthened their resolve to bring their negotiations to a positive conclusion. The French were determined to get a British commitment. They had promised to use their influence in St. Petersburg to better Anglo-Russian relations and were willing to abandon completely any claims that they had in Egypt, fully recognizing those of the British.

18. Viscount Grey of Fallodon, 50.

19. Quoted by Luigi Albertini, *The Origins of the War of 1914* (London: Oxford University Press, 1952), I, 154.

20. *British Documents on the Origins of the War, III, The Testing of the Entente, 1904-6*, 87.

21. In Arthur Marder, *From Dreadnought to Scapa Flow* (London: Oxford University Press, 1961), I, 113. Edward got used to the idea. When Fisher brought it up again early in 1908, the king agreed that the prospect of "Copenhagening" (blowing apart in a sneak attack) the German fleet had considerable merit.

22. The *Dreadnought's* keel was laid in 1905. It could engage two older battleships, which at the most had only four 12 inch guns each. Although the dreadnought's keel plate was laid down during the Anglo-German naval race the ship's new conception on weaponry had really come from lessons learned from the Russo-Japanese war. See: Robert K. Massie, *Dreadnought, Britain, Germany, and the Coming of the Great War* (New York: Random House, 1991), 468-497.

23. While Tirpitz developed the German dreadnought, he also ordered the widening of the Kiel Canal and the reconstruction of the country's main naval ports, proceeding in this task at a faster rate than the British had anticipated. The Germans also outpaced their rivals in the construction of submarines. Meanwhile, Fisher pushed the big-gun principle into the construction of cruisers. The result was the *H.M.S. Invincible*, a ship mounting the dreadnought's 12-inch guns, but faster in speed by five knots.

24. Albertini, I, 322.

25. By 1914, Britain had 29 dreadnoughts and 9 battle-cruisers; Germany had 17 dreadnoughts and 7 battle-cruisers. Among the other nations possessing dreadnoughts; the United States had 10; France, 4; Austria-Hungary, 3; and Russia, 2. The cost for such build-ups was enormous. From 1905 to 1914, Britain's yearly naval expenditures increased from 33,151,841 pounds sterling to 51,551,000 pounds sterling. In Germany, during the same period, the yearly amounts rose from 11,301,370 to 23,444,129 pounds.

26. Arthur Marder, *Fear God and Dreadnought* (London: Jonathan Cape 1956), II, 63.

27. The British and Russians settled their differences in various parts of the world. They divided Persia into three areas: a Russian zone of influence in the north, a British zone in the south, with an area of mutual penetration in between. The Russians agreed to recognize British interests in Afghanistan and in the Persian Gulf; and the British promised to support the Russians in the revision of the Straits Agreement, to allow free passage of their warships into the Mediterranean.

28. *British Documents on the Origins of the War*, III, Appendix A, 418.

29. *Ibid.*, 419.

30. Viscount Grey of Fallodon, 83-84.

31. *Ibid.*, 95.

32. In his letter to Cambon on November 22, 1912, Grey had specified "an unprovoked attack" as well as "something that threatened the general peace." Cambon's reply the next day somewhat broadened the circumstances. *Ibid*, 96.

CHAPTER 1

THE CEREMONY AT VERSAILLES

IN THIS GREAT ROOM, Louis XIV had once danced the gavotte, seen his grandchildren baptized, and received the homage of Europe's rulers. On 28 January 1871, the Hall of Mirrors had also seen Prussian King Wilhelm I proclaimed the German Emperor. Now, on 28 June 1919, 48 years and another war later, the French intended to avenge that insult by rubbing the Germans noses in the shame of their own defeat.

Georges Clemenceau had taken personal charge of the arrangements. He had selected the Louis XV writing table on which the peace treaty would be signed, insisting that it be an "important" piece of furniture without previous historical associations. He had chosen the opulent rococo ink-well, making sure that it matched the table in style and age. He had scheduled the ceremony for mid-afternoon so the delegates would witness the humiliation of Germany after they had eaten lunch.

The Versailles palace had suffered badly during the war. Lack of maintenance, rather than battle damage, had resulted in leaky roofs, cracked plaster, and warped parquet floors. The damage seemed less in the Hall of Mirrors, but only because today there were more important things to catch the eye.

Clemenceau arrived at 2:30 p.m., half an hour before the ceremony began. The room was already crowded. Allied statesman, government officials, and other dignitaries impatiently milled around, stepping over furniture, chatting with friends and acquaintances, circulating, getting each other's autographs.   A couple of dozen officers of the *gardes municipaux* hovered around the conference tables to prevent souvenir hunters from pinching the pens, ink wells, or other seductive memorabilia. It was noisy and very hot.[1]

GHOSTS AT VERSAILLES.

The 1871 Versailles ghosts *are those of Helmut von Moltke, Wilhelm I, and Otto von Bismarck. The scene, conjured up by Bernard Partridge for* Punch *(May 7, 1919), disregards Wilhelm I's abdication and exile and the existence of a successor republican government to which fell the shameful duty of signing the peace treaty. The Allies believed that this new German government was spiritually little different from the old.*

Clemenceau had become premier in November 1917, when faith in an allied victory was feeble. He had vowed to fight the Germans before, behind, and inside Paris until, as he said, the last quarter-hour

But, while galvanizing the nation for its final, grand effort, he tried to keep a "perfect entente" with Britain and the United States, the other two nations most responsible for today's triumph. But in victory the solidity of this alliance could no longer be taken for granted.

The Americans, separated from the French by an immense expanse of water, appeared increasingly willing to retreat into isolationism. And the British were again becoming preoccupied with imperial affairs and their days of "splendid isolation." A Treaty of Guarantee, pledging Britain and the United States to come to the aid of France, if it were attacked, would be signed the same time as the Treaty with Germany, but, nonetheless, France felt alone and dreaded bearing the brunt of peace enforcement.[2]

Before taking his place, Clemenceau chatted briefly with a group of combat veterans, invited as living symbols of the sacrifice and heroism of the French soldier. These *poilus*, their chests amplified with medals of valor, had come here on empty stomachs, their sandwiches tucked aside until after the proceedings were over.

The chief delegates of the Allied and Associated powers would sit at baize-covered straight tables arranged in a rectangular horseshoe around the *bureau plat* on which the treaty would be signed. The table had been placed midway down the hall, beneath Le Brun's famous ceiling, depicting the Sun King's coming of age. "*Le roi gouverne par lui-même*," (the king rules by himself), said the inscription. Small, flat desks, assigned to secretaries and aides, hovered around the center group and were followed by rows and rows of chairs and benches for other officials, diplomats, politicians, high-level bureaucrats, wives, and special guests.

After Clemenceau had seated himself at the center of the head table, American president Woodrow Wilson entered. The crowd greeted him with polite applause. Next came British Prime Minister David Lloyd George. When these and the other delegates were in place, Clemenceau signaled the ushers to hush the crowd (a difficult proposition) and ordered the two German plenipotentiaries, Dr. Hermann Müller and Dr. Johannes Bell, escorted into the room. Müller was foreign secretary, Bell the minister of colonies—for a country with no more colonies. The two bowed slightly, then took their seats. "The one is thin and pink-eyelidded....the other is moon faced and suffering," wrote a member of the British delegation.[3]

Clemenceau called the meeting to order: *"La séance est overte."* It was exactly twelve minutes past three. The premier addressed the German delegates. Your signatures, he said, constitute

> an irrevocable engagement to carry out loyally and faithfully in their entirety all the conditions that have been decided upon.

He then invited them to come forward and inscribe their names.

Clemenceau despaired that the German and the French people could ever live in harmony. Since the end of the Franco-Prussian war, he had visited Germany almost every year and come away convinced that the German character was essentially flawed, deficient in a basic sense of justice.[4] Clemenceau had once feared that the Germans would not sign this treaty unless the Allies marched on Berlin.[5] This fortunately had not proved necessary, and allied military power could now be concentrated on making sure the Germans fulfilled the agreement's obligations.

Demobilization, however, had proceeded at an alarming pace. When the Armistice was signed in November 1918, the allied army had 198 divisions, but in six months that number had fallen to 39 divisions (18 French, 10 British, 5 American, and 6 Belgian). Generalissimo Ferdinand Foch knew that the Allies no longer had sufficient forces to carry out any significant military action against Germany.

> They would have to detach so many men to safeguard the position in his rear that only a very enfeebled Army would reach [Berlin], and its Southern flank would be seriously menaced.[6]

If Germany had failed to accept the treaty, Foch could offer only limited action, perhaps by chopping off the provinces of Baden, Württemberg, and Bavaria.[7]

Clemenceau doubted that the agreements signed today would be worth much unless the wartime alliance could be preserved. He especially worried over the weakened status of the Anglo-French Entente. He and Lloyd George had serious disagreements on security. The British prime minister did not favor taking any action that might induce Germany to put "her vast organizing power at the disposal of the revolutionary fanatics."[8] Lloyd George thought that the threat of Bolshevism was more dangerous than German militarism, and he would agree only to limited military action. Fortunately, the Germans as yet lacked the skills to exploit these disagreements.

AFTER FOUR MONTHS of often bitter and confusing negotiations, the Allied powers had assembled the Versailles treaty with such haste and confusion that Maurice Hankey, the British *rapporteur*, claimed:

> no one in the Conference, not even the Council of Three nor their Secretary, myself, had the slightest idea of its size, shape or total contents up to the eve of its presentation to the Germans.[9]

The text was 80,000 words and contained 440 separate articles. It made Germany a weaker and smaller power, taking away 27,000 square miles of European territory, including Alsace-Lorraine claimed by France, parts of Pomerania and Prussia given to the new Poland, the northern part of Schleswig returned to Denmark, and the areas of Eupen, Malmédy, and Moresnet awarded to Belgium. Germany received no compensation for all the public property in the areas ceded to Belgium, Denmark, and Poland and none for all the "public and private" property in the lands ceded to France. Germany also forfeited its entire overseas empire.

All German territory west of the Rhine with a 50-kilometer (31-mile) zone following the river on the east was demilitarized and subject to control. The Allies would occupy the Left Bank for fifteen years, effecting an earlier evacuation only if the Germans behaved themselves and honored their obligations.[10] Should Germany violate the treaty, the withdrawal could be suspended and the Rhineland reoccupied. This loss of sovereignty inflamed the Germans, but it was still less than what the French considered necessary for their own security.

Clemenceau had pushed for the total separation of the Rhineland, creating some sort of Rhenish Republic. However, Wilson and Lloyd George were opposed. Indeed, less than a month before the treaty was signed, the British prime minister had confessed that *any* occupation of Germany was dangerous, "doubly so in the case of peoples who hated one another for centuries."

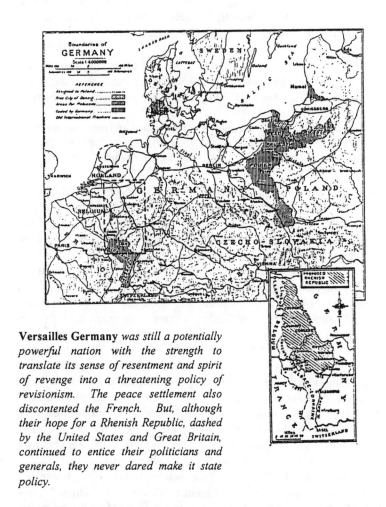

Versailles Germany *was still a potentially powerful nation with the strength to translate its sense of resentment and spirit of revenge into a threatening policy of revisionism. The peace settlement also discontented the French. But, although their hope for a Rhenish Republic, dashed by the United States and Great Britain, continued to entice their politicians and generals, they never dared make it state policy.*

Lloyd George feared that such occupation could eventually result in "an incident which would necessitate Great Britain coming to the assistance of France." He questioned its purpose, since Germany posed no danger to France for thirty, possibly fifty, years.[11]

Clemenceau doubted this was the time to be lenient and to forsake control over Germany. He knew that Germany had no intention of carrying out the treaty, and without the guarantee provided by the occupation of the Rhineland, the "whole Treaty would go by the board."[12] Clemenceau had also demanded total annexation of the coal-rich Saarland as compensation for the wartime destruction of French factories and mines. But the treaty gave France economic control of the mineral resources for only fifteen years with the League of Nations taking charge of the area's political administration. In 1935, the Saarlanders would be allowed to decide whether to join France, rejoin Germany, or become independent.

The treaty reduced the once powerful German army to the size of a domestic police force: 1,000,000 volunteers with a minimum enlistment of twelve years for the ranks and twenty-five years for officers. This was supposed to prevent the Germans from training a larger force through annual recruitment. But Marshal Foch had argued that the more frequent the turnover, the less effective would be the training of the troops and the weaker their enterprise.

It would be better to have an army of sheep commanded by a lion than a number of lions commanded by an ass.[13]

The treaty also forbade the Germans to possess heavy artillery and more than 288 pieces of light artillery. It prohibited them from building armored ships larger than 10,000 tons, possessing submarines or military airplanes It prevented their constructing new fortifications, manufacturing poison gas, or erecting high-power telegraph stations. It obliged them to pay the entire costs of the Allied Control Commission and the army of occupation.

In Article 231 the Germans shouldered all responsibility for the damage that they and their allies had caused in their "war of aggression" and undertook to pay reparations to the Allied and Associated governments and their nationals.[14] The "war quilt clause" avoided specifying that Germany *alone* was to blame, but that was its clear intention. Clemenceau stated:

it is only possible to conceive of such an obligation if its origin and cause is the responsibility of the author of the damage.[15]

The treaty contained more whimsical clauses. The British, for example, demanded the return of the skull of Sultan Mkwawa, which the Germans had removed from their protectorate in East Africa and taken to Berlin.[16] The Germans were at a loss to know to what this referred until a member of their delegation recalled

> the mighty battle which the wild black hero of the Wahene fought...[and] the overwhelming end which the once powerful sultan found in the forest with the last of his servants.[17]

THE ALLIES first handed the terms of the peace to the Germans, on 7 May 1919, in the grand salon of the Trianon Palace, a deluxe hotel located at the entrance to the Versailles gardens, and instructed them to make only written comments. The treaty's harshness was no surprise. Three weeks earlier, German Foreign Secretary Count Ulrich von Brockdorff-Rantzau had found out its general terms from Ellis Dresel, a representative of the Supreme Council, and had already prepared his responses: one was defiant the other conciliatory.[18] He decided to give the defiant response shortly after his arrival in Paris, when he saw a newspaper report on the seating arrangements of the allied and German delegates.

The paper had labeled the seats reserved for the Germans the *"banc des accusés"* (prisoners' dock). Few could doubt that this was done at the bidding of the French government. Since 1915, the Quai d'Orsay had routinely, through its propaganda and information division, supervised and directed rapportage in the French press. Brockdorff determined to refrain from appearing before the allied representatives like a criminal before his judges, and he read his reply seated, compounding the insult by lighting a cigarette as he left the hall. Lloyd George was so enraged that he felt like punching the German foreign secretary in the face.[19]

Dr. Walter Simons advised Brockdorff to avoid all further provocation. He felt that by appearing conciliatory the Germans could gain valuable time to make a case for revision. He reasoned:

> Every week that we gain will weaken the position of our opponents. The better this treaty becomes known, the more impossible will it be to put into effect.[20]

But Brockdorff preferred to present blanket objections to almost every clause—a tactic that made the Allies fear that Germany might refuse to sign.[21]

On 16 June, the Supreme Council rejected all the German counterproposals, except for allowing certain plebiscites to be held in land originally earmarked for Poland and Denmark. They threatened to take military action unless the Germans approved the treaty within five days. Brockdorff resigned, and a new German government presented the treaty to the Reichstag. Konstantin Fehrenbach, the assembly president, swore that the legislators would rather die like Roman senators than submit to such disgrace.[22] But the final vote showed a different mood: 237 favored ratification, 138 were opposed, and 5 abstained. The approval came just three hours before the Allies had planned to invade unoccupied Germany. There was, however, a final act of defiance.

On 21 June, the skeleton crews on the ships of the German High Seas Fleet interned at Scapa Flow opened the vessels' sea cocks and sent 10 battleships, 6 battle cruisers, 6 light cruisers, and 50 destroyers to the bottom of the harbor—the bulk of that force which had seen action at the great battle of Jutland.[23]

The Allies now demanded that the Germans surrender most of their remaining warships: 8 dreadnoughts, 8 light cruisers, 42 destroyers, and 50 torpedo boats. These, plus a few that had survived the scuttling, were distributed among the Allies. Britain got seventy percent of the confiscated German fleet, France and Italy got ten percent, Japan got eight percent, and the United States two percent.[24]

The British had reason to celebrate. The settlement maintained their current naval advantage. The sinking at Scapa Flow meant that Britain averted the ticklish prospects of distribution and an increase in other nation's navies.[25] Clemenceau even suspected that the British had deliberately orchestrated this nautical *Götterdämmerung* (twilight of the gods) to avoid giving France its share of the naval spoils.

WHEN MÜLLER AND BELL had finished their thankless task, the representatives of the other countries, following a precise order, came forward to sign: the United States first, then came Italy, Japan, Belgium and so forth. The seals had already been affixed and the procedure took less than an hour. Clemenceau watched with seeming indifference. When all the ink had been blotted, Clemenceau had the ushers attempt to bring the crowd once more to silence and announced the end of the meeting.

"La séance est levée."

Outside, a battery of guns roared a salute. The delegates rose and began to congratulate each other. Some asked for the autographs of the German delegates. Clemenceau invited Wilson and Lloyd George to come outside to see the chateau's magnificent fountains which had just begun to play.

The peacemakers were exhausted. Wilson still felt the effects of his bout with "influenza" two months before.[26] He looked tired and bedraggled and much older than his 63 years. The virus had most likely attacked his brain, a particularly serious development for one with a history of cerebral-vascular disease, and had caused swelling, resulting in mood changes that alternated between euphoria and paranoia. He gave contradictory orders and suspected—no doubt with some justification—that his French servants were spies, overhearing everything he said.[27] He was determined to continue his full schedule, although at the end of each day he had trouble remembering what had just been discussed.

At 78, Clemenceau was the oldest of the Big Three, but he also seemed to be running out of steam. In February, a would-be assassin had emptied a revolver at him, two bullets hitting home, lodging near his spine. The bullets were never removed. Clemenceau bravely dismissed the *attentat* as an accident and said that his assailant should be punished only for the "careless use of a dangerous weapon and for poor marksmanship."[28] Lloyd George, though, noticed a profound alteration in the premier's behavior. Clemenceau "just comes to the Conferences and has not the energy to take part in the Debates or give any decisions," he said.[29]

The British prime minister, a relatively young 56, seemed to have survived the ordeal the best, but he complained of malaise and on occasion stayed in bed to recuperate. On the day of the signing, he was out of sorts and particularly grouchy.

The moment the Big Three appeared outside, a wildly cheering crowd pushed boisterously forward. A file of soldiers cleared a path to keep them from being crushed. Photographers took thousands of pictures; newspapermen scribbled notes and hustled interviews.

Frances Stevenson, Lloyd George's personal secretary and mistress, wrote disapprovingly:

> The Press is destroying all romance, all solemnity, all majesty.
> They are as unscrupulous as they are vulgar.

Clemenceau viewed the occasion differently. He had participated in the formation of the Third Republic, had been on hand for the important deliberations of the national assembly at Versailles following the defeat to Prussia in 1871. Now, a half a century later, he was back in the same building. It seemed very appropriate. On this same day, five years ago, Gavrilo Princip's bullets had felled Archduke Franz Ferdinand at Sarajevo.

As Clemenceau had made his way outside, former premier Paul Painlevé grasped the old man's gloved hand in congratulation. Clemenceau's voice was hoarse and his eyes glistened with tears, "Yes," he said, "it's a fine day.

"C'est une belle journée."[30]

Notes and Sources:

1. See: Ferdinand Czernin, *Versailles 1919: The Forces, Events, and Personalities that Shaped the Treaty* (New York: Putnam, 1964); John Maynard Keynes, "The Treaty of Peace" in *Essays in Persuasion* (New York: Harcourt, 1932).

2. *Foreign Relations of the United States, The Paris Peace Conference*, 1919, III, 142.

3. Harold Nicolson, *Peacemaking 1919*

4. Paul Mantoux, *Les délibérations du Conseil des Quatres* (Paris: Centre National de la Recherche Scientifique, 1955), I, 44.

5. *Foreign Relations of the United States, The Paris Peace Conference*, VI, 549.

6. *Ibid.*, 502-3.

7. *Ibid.*, 544.

8. David Lloyd George, *The Truth about the Peace Treaties I*, 408.

9. Lord Hankey, *The Supreme Council at the Peace Conference* (London: Allen and Unwin, 1963), 134.

10. That is, after five years, they could leave the northern sector centered on Cologne, after ten years the middle area around Koblenz, and after fifteen the southern district around Mainz.

11. *Foreign Relations of the United States, The Paris Peace Conference*, 1919, III, 142.

12. *Ibid.*, III, 144.

13. *Foreign Relations of the United States, The Paris Peace Conference*, IV, 217.

14. David Lloyd George, *History of the Peace Conference of Paris*, III, 214.

15. Alma Luchau, *The German Delegation at the Paris Peace Conference* (New York: Howard Fertig, 1971), 254.

16. *A History of the Peace Conference of Paris, III*, 233-4.

17. Remarks of Dr. Walter Simons. Simons said he never imagined that he would meet "this black ghost in the park of the Trianon." Alma Luchau, *The German Delegation at the Paris Peace Conference*, 120.

18. Ulrich Brockdorff-Rantzau, *Dokumente* (Charlottenburg: Deutsche Verlagsgesellschaft für Politik und Geschichte, 1919); *Comments by the German Delegation on the Conditions of Peace* (New York: American Association for International Conciliation, 1919).

19. Frances Stevenson, *Lloyd George, A Diary* (New York: Harper and Row, 1971), 183.

20. Alma Luchau, *The German Delegation at the Paris Peace Conference*, 120.

21. *Reply of the Allied and Associated Powers to the Observations of the German Delegation on the Conditions of Peace* (New York: American Association for International Conciliation, 1919).

22. Many politicians, like Centrist Fehrenbach, denounced the Treaty of Versailles for its severity but had seen nothing wrong with the way Germany had handled its own vanquished, namely the French in the Treaty of Frankfort 1871, and more recently the Russians in the Treaty of Brest-Litovsk 1918.

23. Arthur J. Marder, *From the Dreadnought to Scapa Flow, Victory and Aftermath* (New York: Oxford University Press, 1970), 270-96.

24. According to the agreement, reached on 9 December 1919, these ships were to be sunk or rendered useless as fighting ships within eighteen months. Marder, 294.

25. The British had suggested that the German fleet be shared among the Allies in proportion to the naval losses suffered during the war, giving them the largest chunk. The Americans proposed that the allotment be done according to a formula which took into account the size of the national forces that had participated in the defeat of Germany. The French wanted a more even split.

26. Rear Admiral Cary T. Grayson, *Woodrow Wilson, An Intimate Memoir* (New York: Holt, Rinehart and Winston, 1960), 85.

27. Edwin A. Weinstein, "Woodrow Wilson's Neurological Illness", in John M. Cooper, Jr., ed., *Causes and Consequences of World War I* (New York: Quadrangle Books, 1972), 334.

28. Stephen Bonsal, *Unfinished Business* (New York: Doubleday, Doran and Company, 1944), 19.

29. Francis Stevenson, *Lloyd George, A Diary* (New York: Harper and Row, 1971), 174.

30. The description of the signing of the treaty of Versailles is based on the accounts of Lord Hankey, *The Supreme Council at the Paris Peace Conference;* Harold Nicolson, *Peacemaking 1919;* Ray Stannard Baker, *Woodrow Wilson and World Settlements;* Harry Hansen in *Source Records of the Great War*, Volume VII; *Lord Riddell's Intimate Diary of the Peace Conference and After;* and Frances Stevenson, *Lloyd George, A Diary.*

CHAPTER 2

SECURITY IS EVERYTHING

ALONG THE ENTIRE line of the march—10-kilometers from the northern edge of the Bois de Boulogne past the Arch of Triumph to the place de la Concorde, up the rue Royale to the church of the Madeleine, and down the *Grands Boulevards* to the place de la République—people jammed the sidewalks. By all accounts, the *grand défile* the French held on the 14th of July 1919 was the most glorious and impressive pageant any of the victors gave to commemorate the end of the Great War.[1]

Those who had arrived the night before had appropriated the best places near the curb, waiting out the dark hours, by singing, playing cards, picnicking, and passing around bottles of wine. Late arrivals had to be content with standing on boxes or benches, or looking through periscopes. Children sat on parents' shoulders. Some people climbed trees, others perched precariously on the decorative ledges of buildings, or rented office or apartment windows. The prefect of police tried to discourage crowding on balconies by warning property owners that they would be liable for any accidents. One balcony did collapse, injuring eighteen people. The humanity was so dense that those with tickets for the main reviewing stands had difficulty getting to their places. If the French people were dissatisfied with the treaty recently signed at Versailles, fearful that it gave them inadequate protection against Germany, if they were concerned about the ability of their country to recover from the worst war in its history, that certainly did not show today. Georges Clemenceau watched the procession from the main reviewing stand at the Rond-Point des Champs-Elysées in the company of President Raymond Poincaré. From the common front these two displayed today, it would have been difficult to imagine how seriously they had disagreed over the terms of peace with Germany. In addition to a celebration, the parade was also a reminder of the high price the French nation had paid for victory. Men whose lives the war had so wantonly and conspicuously shattered—one thousand *grands mutilés*, the horribly disfigured and maimed harvest of the battle field, representing all branches of service, classes of society, and areas of the country—occupied the place of honor. Bunched in loose columns, making no effort to keep in formation or walk in step, these wrecked souls were first to pass underneath the Arc de Triomphe and shuffle down the Champs-Elysées as best they could with their bandaged heads, their dark glasses, and plaster casts. Some were led, some hobbled with the help of crutches or artificial legs, some walked with canes, and some were pushed in wheel chairs like babies in perambulators.

PRESIDENT POINCARÉ had attacked Clemenceau for endangering French security by compromising in the Rhineland settlement. He argued that, if Clemenceau had pressed French claims more tenaciously, Clemenceau would have succeeded in separating the territory from Germany. Poincaré was also bitter that he had been excluded from all major conference decisions. In the past, presidents of the Republic had not been sent to their rooms when foreign policy was being decided.

The Rhineland settlement had also antagonized many French generals, beginning with Marshal Foch, who, despite his official obligation to stay away from partisanship, had actively taken up the cudgels against the peace settlement by forcefully campaigning for the Rhineland's total political and military separation from Germany.[2] Foch also wanted the League of Nations organized as a league of victors to protect Europe against future German aggression.[3]

Clemenceau had endeavored to keep Foch in the dark about the Rhineland compromise until the Germans received the treaty, but Foch found out anyway and grumbled that the Germans were only waiting for an opportunity to move their troops into the demilitarized zone to prepare for a thrust into Belgium and northern France. Foch said that the French army, to avoid total defeat, would have to retreat behind the

Somme, the Seine, or even the Loire rivers.[4] Foch dismissed the possibility of France receiving any effective help from Britain or the United States. When he failed to alter government policy through private protest, he complained to the press. He also refused to make travel arrangements for the German delegates to come to Paris to accept the treaty, telling Clemenceau that he should do it himself since Clemenceau was minister of war.

Clemenceau felt he had endured enough of Foch's subversive tactics. He summoned him before the cabinet and gave him a dressing down. In these surroundings even Poincaré, Foch's strongest supporter, refused to come to his support. Humiliated and isolated, Foch later could only gripe to veteran diplomat Jules Cambon, "We shall all be accused of treason because the nation will never understand that from our victory bankruptcy is likely to come."[5] Clemenceau, however, did not dismiss Foch, a step that Foch's insubordination clearly justified—certainly had their roles been reversed, Foch would not have hesitated for a moment. Clemenceau feared that getting rid of the generalissimo might have a dreadful effect on public morale and encourage more German obstreperousness. Besides, Clemenceau admired Foch's military talents.

Resistance from the French military was not confined to Foch. In May 1919, a cabal of Rhineland commanders, led by generals Charles Manguin, Émile Fayolle, and Augustin Gérard, plotted with German separatist leaders to establish an "independent" Rhenish republic by seizing control of the local governments in Speyer and Wiesbaden, a move the native populations failed to support. The British and Americans protested, referring to the provisions of the Treaty of Versailles in which the signatories promised to respect Germany's post-war frontiers and political unity. The venture ended almost as quickly as it had begun, but Clemenceau waited before reassigning the unruly officers to less important posts. Then the Rhineland command was unified and placed under the more obedient General Jean-Marie Joseph Degoutte.

At the peace conference, Clemenceau had wanted to separate as many Germans as he could from Germany, but not because he believed in the Rhenish "self-determination" dreams of French nationalists. His desire had come in large part from fears of Germany's large population.[6] Even before the war, a rapid increase in the German birth rate had alarmed French leaders. In 1913, the National Assembly tried to offset the greater size of the German army by voting to increase the standard period of military service from two to three years. But this hardly compensated for Germany's ability to field more soldiers or have more workers available for its factories. The Germans had one and a half times more people employed in industry and agriculture than did France.[7] The reacquisition of Alsace-Lorraine had barely replaced France's wartime losses in production and population and, with the French people showing no inclination to produce more babies, the numbers gap between the two countries began to widen.[8]

Clemenceau was also deeply concerned about his country's social and ideological divisions, many of which dated back to the French Revolution, but were now envenomed by the current controversy over the peace treaty. He feared these persistent internecine quarrels could undermine all the gains of victory, and he chose *fraternité* as his theme in presenting the Treaty of Versailles to the National Assembly on 26 August 1919. He said that peace would be only a mirage unless we are capable of living at peace with ourselves, that is, unless we are able to make the domestic harmony of our country the foundation of peace abroad.[9]

The debate over ratification of the Versailles treaty dragged on for six weeks. Many legislators, who had demanded French expansion to its "natural frontiers" on the Rhine, lambasted Clemenceau for failing to separate the entire West Bank from Germany. Some wondered how that Catholic, wine-loving area of Germany, once part of France, could ever have been Prussianized; and a senator claimed that France had a "moral duty" to help these Celtic peoples achieve independence.[10] He was hardly alone in believing that Rhenish self-determination needed only a little encouragement to succeed. Many more, though, agreed with Foch that a permanent military presence in the Rhineland was necessary to guarantee French security, and they questioned the worth of a guarantee that the American Senate was unlikely to approve.[11] On the other hand, the Socialists argued that the Versailles treaty was too harsh to be imposed on a democratic Germany.

In his closing arguments, given before the Senate, Clemenceau said that France had to use its superiority with moderation if future generations would be spared from the mistakes of the past. He said that an Anglo-American guarantee to protect France against attack was necessary to make up for the deficiencies of collective security. He expressed alarm over the fall in the French birth rate and warned that, even were Germany completely disarmed, France would decline because without large families "there will no longer be any more French." The treaty, he said, "does not specify that the French are committed to have many children, but that would have been the first thing to include."[12]

The treaty, presented *en bloc* without the possibility for amendment, passed the Chamber of Deputies 372 to 53, with 72 abstentions; the Senate accepted it unanimously "for the record."[13] The lopsided votes did not bring an end to doubt. Clemenceau knew that Germany was bound to recover from its defeat and that France would eventually have to become reconciled with its stronger neighbor. "The conqueror is a prisoner to her conquest; that is the revenge of conquered nations," he later told Lloyd George.[14] Clemenceau recognized that the Versailles agreement would someday be revised. In a letter written on the occasion of the submission of the treaty's final draft to the Germans on 16 June 1919, Clemenceau pointed out that the settlement could be "modified from time to time to suit new facts, new conditions, as they arise" provided that this process be accomplished peacefully "by discussion and consent."[15] But Clemenceau avoided expressing such an opinion publicly.

MOST FRENCH favored enforcement of the Versailles treaty, but not modification. In the elections to the Chamber of Deputies in November 1919, the voters gave a majority of the seats to those who were determined to make Germany pay for the war and who were most verbal in their desire to contain Bolshevism. The winning *Bloc national républicain* was an alliance of conservative nationalists, predominantly veterans of the war and practicing Catholics, many colorless and unimaginative with little political experience. So many of the newcomers wore their uniforms to the opening session that the legislature became known as the *bleu horizon* (sky blue) chamber. Over half of the old deputies lost their seats.[16] The National Bloc spoke for the prosperous middle class, opposing state monopolies but not private cartels, denouncing the progressive income tax but not protective tariffs. Its members protested loyalty to existing institutions, but aimed to alter the constitution by creating a strong executive. The National Bloc wore its anti-socialist, anti-labor, and anti-democratic colors proudly.

Clemenceau tried to combat this rightist drift by seeking election to the French presidency. (Poincaré, frustrated by the office's restrictions, had decided against running for another seven-year term.) Clemenceau's popularity was enormous, and his associates were sure he could win, but the French people did not elect the president—that was the job of the National Assembly (the senators and deputies voting together by secret ballot). Clemenceau did not want to finish his career with a political defeat and tested the waters by allowing his name put forward on a straw vote. The returns were discouraging: Paul Deschanel, the elegant, underwhelming speaker of the Chamber, received the majority of votes. Not only had the members of the National Bloc held Clemenceau responsible for the failings of the Treaty of Versailles, they also detested his agnosticism. Should he die in office—Clemenceau was now almost eighty—there would be a secular funeral!

Clemenceau withdrew his candidacy; and, on 17 January 1920, Deschanel was elected president, 734 to 154 votes. Clemenceau, bothered by frequent micturition, quipped that the presidency was as useless as the prostate gland but his disappointment was enormous. When Deschanel came to pay Clemenceau a courtesy call at the Ministry of War following his election, Clemenceau exclaimed, "Tell that gentleman that I'm not here."[17] The next day "the Tiger" announced he would resign his post.

ON 19 MARCH 1920, the United States Senate, on its second attempt, refused to ratify the Treaty of Versailles.[18] Most senators from both parties favored acceptance, providing the sovereign rights of the United States were protected. Senator Henry Cabot Lodge, chairman of the Foreign Relations Committee, had offered fourteen modifications underscoring Congressional prerogatives in the conduct of foreign affairs, including direct Senate approval for any League of Nations action that involved the use of American armed forces.[19] Wilson believed, however, that any change in the Covenant would only weaken the moral authority of the United States to protect other states from aggression.[20] He felt he had made all his concessions in Paris and refused to make any more to his fellow Americans.[21] Accepting Lodge's qualifications would have been an admission that the foreign policy of the United States was motivated by national self-interest—something that Wilson had tried his entire political life to conceal. He was determined not to appear to go back to the evil days of the balance of power system with its inevitable wars, and he urged his supporters to vote against any changes in the treaty. The treaty was thus killed because of his orders.

In a letter to Senate minority leader Gilbert Hitchcock, he said that he had become convinced during the proceedings of the Paris conference

> that a militaristic party, under the most influential leadership, was seeking to gain ascendancy in the counsels of France. They were defeated then but are in control now.[22]

Collective security, the president asserted, was intended as a bulwark against French militarism and imperialism, a choice between democracy and the right of people to govern themselves and between imperialism and the right of domination by force. The letter was published in the *New York Times* and touched off a storm of controversy.

Paris newspapers had a field day in whipping up old anti-American resentment among the French, who remembered a self-serving johnny-come-lately participation of the United States in the war, and the apparent hypocrisy, insensitivity, and naiveté of President Wilson. One commentator said that he was sorry that Americans were led by one so unhinged. French Ambassador Jules Jusserand delivered a formal protest over Wilson's imperious self-righteousness to which Wilson indignantly countered that Jusserand should be reprimanded.[23]

Not lost in the hubbub was the American Senate's refusal to bring the Treaty of Guarantee to a vote. Reluctance to underwrite French security against a resurgent, revisionist Germany was in keeping with traditional American political, but not commercial, isolationism. American refusal to act as holder of the European balance of power meant that once again the U.S. could be dragged into a war it had played no role in preventing.[24]

The death of the Treaty of Guarantee in the Senate Foreign Relations Committee allowed the British to use the escape clause of their guarantee to excuse themselves of any further obligations, thereby leaving the French with no formal pledge of assistance against a German attack. The British had no regrets. They believed that, since Germany could not possibly be a threat for the next twenty or thirty years, they could significantly reduce their military establishment, and that the French should follow suit. The British believed that they had not defeated German power only to make the world safe for French hegemony.

The British "desertion" was particularly painful to the French, who felt that policing the postwar world required the same joint effort as fighting the war. Great nations were supposed to enforce treaties they signed. The failure to get a Treaty of Guarantee prompted French leaders to seek alternatives. Some favored revision, still pushing for the separation of the Rhineland from Germany; others concentrated on maintaining the strength of the French army while looking elsewhere for allies. The search was frustrating because such support could now only come from the lesser powers. Nonetheless, something was better than nothing, and France began with Belgium, a country disenchanted with neutrality.[25]

IN SEPTEMBER 1918, the Belgian government denounced the 1839 neutrality guarantee agreement and began searching for a policy that would better protect the country's security and national honor, claiming its right to seek "additional guarantees" through specific alliances.[26] The Belgians considered concluding security agreements with the Dutch, the British, the Americans, and the French. They pressed the Dutch for a military agreement to provide for the common defense of the area between the Reichswald and the northern tip of the Ardennes due west of Cologne, the area known as the Limburg Gap through which the Germans were most likely to attack, arguing that the Dutch should not expect a repetition of the 1914 Schlieffen-Moltke Plan, which had avoided the violation of Dutch neutrality by bringing the First Army around south of Aachen. The Dutch, however, still believed that neutrality had saved their country from invasion and rejected the offer.

The Belgians discovered that the British, and especially the Americans, were also unwilling to commit themselves. The Americans even refused to sign a commercial agreement because they feared Belgium's industrial recovery might worsen their own trade deficit. New York bankers had protested to Washington that their profits were being undercut when the British had loaned Belgium money with credits from American capital transfers.[27] And the American government had dutifully influenced the British to curtail such lending. Thus through a process of elimination, Belgium was reduced to an alliance with France—a country with which it had more historical, cultural, political, economic, and strategic ties than any other.[28]

Belgian Foreign Minister Paul Hymans, despite his anger at being excluded from the great decisions made at Paris, remembered the lessons of 1914 and the need to secure French protection against a German attack. Hymans wanted to make sure, however, that Belgian independence would be affirmed.[29] He also needed French help in the annexation of Luxembourg, one of his country's war aims. Failing that, since the Luxembourgeois strongly opposed rule from Brussels, Hymans would seek French blessing in creating a Belgian-Luxembourg customs union.[30]

Franco-Belgian negotiations began less than two months after the signing of the Treaty of Versailles and almost broke down over the question of control over the 128-mile Guillaume-Luxembourg Railroad, which had crucial importance for the economies of both countries. This line linked the main coal producing regions of Belgium, Luxembourg, France, and Germany, stretching from Lorraine to the Ruhr.[31] The French War Ministry was currently running the company from its Paris headquarters, and Clemenceau told Hymans that he expected this arrangement to continue.[32] Hymans put off concluding an alliance until Belgium's rights concerning the railroad line were recognized.

After a year of bickering, the two countries agreed on a compromise: France would hold on to the railway lines south and east of Luxembourg City, and Belgium would get those to the north and west. France also approved a customs union between Belgium and Luxembourg. The agreement cleared the way for the signing of a treaty designed to protect Belgium and France against further German aggression.

The Military Agreement against Non-provoked German Aggression, on 7 September 1920, provided for a common response to German mobilization. The signatories pledged to coordinate the defense of their countries' eastern frontiers, including the protection of Luxembourg. The French agreed to protect the Belgian coastline, and the Belgians agreed to cooperate with France in the occupation of the Rhineland.[33] To protect themselves against any automatic involvement in French military adventures, the Belgians insisted, however, that the treaty affirm their sovereign rights

in respect to the imposition of military burdens [and] in regard to determining each case whether the eventuality contemplated by the present undertaking has in fact arisen.[34]

The escape clause appeared more significant than it actually was.[35] In effect, France could use Belgium as a battle ground to meet a German attack and could launch an offensive directly from Belgian soil into the lower Rhineland and the Ruhr.

In Belgium, the pact touched off a debate between those who believed that it was necessary for the nation's security and those who feared that it would provoke the very attack it was intended to prevent.[36] The disagreement was frequently ethnic with the Walloons in favor and the Flemish against. This unsettled question of national security made the French connection tenuous.[37] Furthermore, in an egregious act of bad faith, the French never did give Belgium its share of the Guillaume-Luxembourg railways.

THE FOLLOWING YEAR, the French concluded an alliance with Poland. Even before the treaty was signed, however, the French had been actively defending Polish interests—at least as these coincided with their own. At the Paris Peace Conference, Clemenceau had pushed for the reestablish of as much of Poland's old pre-1772 frontiers as possible, despite opposition from Lloyd George, who feared that giving the new Poland large alien minorities would only encourage German revisionism.[38] In a prophetic debate over the fate of Danzig, whose annexation by Poland he had prevented, the British prime minister said,

> That I ask is that we do not put any articles in the treaty for which we are not prepared to go to war to defend. France would fight tomorrow to defend Alsace, if that were in dispute. But would we wage war for Danzig?[39]

Consequently, Danzig became a "free city". Still, the French had reason to be satisfied.

The Poles received considerably more land than they were ethnically entitled to have.[40] And Marshal Józef Pilsudski, in the process, had made Poland the greatest military power in East.[41] In 1919-1920, France had provided him with military aid and assistance during Poland's bitter six-month war with Communist Russia, enabling his armies to push the Red Army back into Russia. Checking the westward spread of Communist Russia, insured the liberty of the Finns and established the independence of the Baltic states.[42] Poland emerged as the largest state in East Europe, with over 155,000 square miles of territory and a population of 27 million.[43] Nonetheless, with its large ethnic minorities, Poland became a hostage to fortune.[44] Yet Poland seemed a bulwark against revisionism and the spread of Communism.[45]

The Franco-Polish treaty, signed on 19 February 1921, provided for political, economic, and military cooperation, whose purpose was the implementation of the Paris peace treaties, the containment of Communist Russia, and the economic reconstruction of Europe. France and Poland would take joint action in the event "either or both" should be attacked.[46] As spelled out in a secret military convention signed two days later, this meant that the two countries would come to each other's aid in the case of German aggression, but not in the case of Soviet aggression. Should the latter occur, France promised only aid, support, and assistance in keeping the lines of communication open. In short, France had avoided a promise to protect Poland's eastern frontiers, nor had it even committed itself to send soldiers to fight on Polish soil.[47]

Furthermore, the Poles agreed to build a peacetime army of 30 infantry divisions and 9 cavalry brigades, organized on the model of the French army. The secret agreement and the treaty would come into force after the conclusion of a commercial agreement in which the French promised to lend Poland 400 million francs for armaments, providing the money was spent in France.[48] France received additional advantage in the agreement's economic provisions. Poland accorded France most-favored-nation status, granted special tariff reductions on certain French products, and tax benefits for French-controlled petroleum companies, which could sell all oil above state quotas on the open market.

Although many French statesmen viewed the Franco-Polish alliance as essential for French security, others agreed with Lloyd George's assertion that Poland was too exposed and too geographically distant to be much of an asset. The prime minister had remarked:

> When we have gone home, the Poles will stay there alone, isolated
> in the midst of enemies which surround them on all sides.[49]

Marshal Foch had little regard for Polish military leadership, contemptuously dismissing their generals as amateurs. Philippe Berthelot, the recently appointed Secretary-General of the Quai d'Orsay, found Marshal Pilsudski too adventurous and believed "Polish Catholicism [to have] less of a chance of promoting stability than Czech empiricism."[50]

In their treaties with France, the Belgians and the Poles gave better than they got. The lack of reciprocity did not seem to worry the French, who considered security treaties with smaller powers essentially short-term agreements. A treaty with Poland might offer France some compensation for Britain's willingness to appease Germany, but it could hardly take the place of a Russian alliance.

Nonetheless, the search for allies continued, extending to the succession states of the Austro-Hungarian empire, where two possibilities existed. The French could try to promote some sort of federal union of states, with Hungary as the pivotal power (possibly coupled with a Habsburg restoration), or they could attempt to form an alliance with the newly-created and enlarged states of Czechoslovakia, Romania, and the Kingdom of the Serbs, Croats, and Slovenes (Yugoslavia). For a time, the French, anxious to stabilize this potentially explosive area of Europe, explored the merits of both policies.

In the spring of 1920, the Quai d'Orsay suggested that Hungary might obtain a realignment of the Treaty of Trianon frontiers, if the Hungarians were to grant special concessions to French banking and business interests.[51] The war between the Russians and the Poles was still in progress, and the French, desperate for a counterbalance to the gaining strength of the Red Army, informed Budapest that they were willing to equip four Hungarian divisions to protect eastern Slovakia and Ruthenia from Bolshevism.[52] Some diplomats favored an outright alliance that would promote Hungarian rearmament.[53] The Hungarians appeared eager to conclude an alliance. Indeed, they would have considered treaties with any powers that supported their policy of revisionism.[54]

Rumors of the French initiative prompted Czechoslovakia and Yugoslavia, who were already alarmed about Hungarian ambitions, to negotiate an alliance with each other. This agreement, signed 14 August 1920, pledged to maintain the integrity of the eastern settlement and provide mutual support and aid in case of an "unprovoked attack by Hungary." The following April, Czechoslovakia signed a similar treaty with Romania, and, in June 1921, Romania signed one with Yugoslavia.[55] The Romanian-Yugoslavian treaty also included a provision against Bulgarian revisionism of the Treaty of Neuilly.

The Czech-Romanian-Yugoslav alliance, known as the Little Entente, owed its existance to the effort of Karl I, in March 1921, to regain his lost Hungarian crown.[56] The three states considered the ex-king's presence in Hungary a casus belli and mobilized their armies. The Hungarian government immediately forced the pretender to leave and agreed to respect the territorial and military clauses of the Treaty of the Trianon. Hungarian leader Admiral Miklos Horthy, the former commander of the Austro-Hungarian navy, told the would-be king that, without a French guarantee against an attack from the states of the Little Entente, he would withhold his support.[57] Karl made another attempt in October 1921. The Entente went on alert, and again Horthy refused to cooperate, even handing Karl over to the British, who exiled him to Funchal in the Madeira Islands.[58]

In fact, French Premier Aristide Briand had encouraged the aspirations of the ex-emperor and had given him verbal assurances that France would recognize him as king of Hungary should he succeed. Briand had further promised that France would give Hungary economic and military aid and diplomatic support in readjusting its boundaries "to some extent."[59] But now Briand blandly denied it all.[60]

The willingness of the Little Entente countries to resort to arms had demonstrated its worth to the French as an ally, souring a connection with Hungary. The French realized that continued encouragement of Hungarian revisionism could weaken their enforcement of the Paris settlement.

During the first half of the twenties, the direction of French foreign affairs seesawed between the two temperamentally different personalities of Raymond Poincaré and Aristide Briand. Poincaré, a northerner, was cold, aloof, and suffered fools badly. His stern gaze concentrated on a vision of his country's past power that he was determined to resurrect. Aristide Briand, although born in Nantes, had the warm spirit of a meridional. He also had a great talent for obfuscation and a suspicion of historical precedent. He once said that history was like a cemetery: all right to visit occasionally, provided one did not stay too long. He was by nature a compromiser, a talent that explained his durability in office: he held the Third Republic's record for forming governments, being premier ten times between 1909 and 1929.[61] Their political styles were dramatically different. Nonetheless, the two agreed that Germany should be made to pay for the war. Poincaré was prepared to carry out his policy of strict enforcement, even if that meant that the French army had to act alone. Briand, however, had always envisaged treaty enforcement with the close cooperation of Great Britain.

Notes and Sources:

1. *New York Times*, 15 July 1919, 1

2. Note du Maréchal Foch, 10 January 1919, *Papiers d'Agents* 141 (Pichon Papers), volume 7 (1919), 11-13.

3. *Ibid.*, 14-15.

4. Note from Commandement en Chef des Armées Alliées (31 March 1919), *Papiers d'Agents* 141 (Pichon Papers), volume 7 (1919), 22-26.

5. Jere King, *Foch versus Clemenceau, France and German Dismemberment, 1918-1919* (Cambridge: Harvard University Press, 1960), 62.

6. Lloyd George suspected as much. David Lloyd George, *The Truth about the Peace Treaties*, I, 402.

7. By 1925, France had 3.9 million men and 2 million women engaged in manufacturing and industry, and 4.8 million men and 3.4 million women in agriculture. Germany had 7.4 million men and 2.8 million women in manufacturing and industry, and 4.8 million men and 5 million women in agriculture. *European Historical Statistics*, 20, 155, 156.

8. As a result of the peace settlement, France increased its population by nearly two million, Germany lost around ten million. This still gave Germany over a third more people as France. *Statesman's Year Book, 1920*, 827, 899. French population in 1921 was 39.2 million; in 1926, it was 40.2 million; in 1931, 41.2 million. In the decade and a half since WWI, the German population rose from 59.9 million in 1919 to 63.2 million in 1925 to 66 million in 1933. Ibid., 1925, 871, 947; *European Historical Statistics*, 20.

9. Georges Clemenceau, *Discours de guerre* (Paris: Presses Universitaires de France, 1968), 239.

10. Walter A. McDougall, *France's Rhineland Diplomacy, The Last Bid for a Balance of Power in Europe* (Princeton, N. J.: Princeton University Press, 1978), 87.

11. Édouard Bonnefous, *Histoire politique de la troisième république, L'après-guerre 1919-1924* (Paris: Presses Universitaires de France, 1959), 53.

12. *Journal officiel, Débats, Sénat*, 12 October 1919.

13. Édouard Bonnefous, *Histoire politique de la troisième république, L'après-guerre 1919-1924*, 56-7.

14. Clemenceau recalled this being said during the Peace Conference when he and the British prime minister were reviewing a parade of American troops before the statue of George Washington in Paris at the Place des États-Unis. When Clemenceau wrote down his recollections he was still embroiled in a face off with Foch and the remark probably reflects the need for further justification. Georges Clemenceau, *Grandeur and Misery of Victory* (New York: Harcourt, Brace, 1930), 200.

15. *British and Foreign State Papers* (1919), vol 112, 244-53.

16. The right-wing parties also took better advantage of a new voting procedure, the *scrutin de liste*, which gave additional seats on the basis of proportional representation to parties that had been able to form alliances. The parties of the Left, divided and radicalized by the issue of allegiance to the new Communist International and Moscow's repudiation of the tsarist bonds in which many French had invested considerable sums, were in disarray and fought each other for the same seats.

17. Jacques Chastenet, *Histoire de la troisième république*, (Paris: Hachette, 1955), V, 62.

18. Ralph A. Stone, ed., *Wilson and the League of Nations, Why America's Rejection* (New York: Holt, Rhinehart and Winston, 1967); John Chalmers Vinson, *Referendum for Isolation: Defeat of Article Ten of the League of Nations Covenant* (Athens: University of Georgia Press, 1961)

19. The Senate also had to approve any new expenses or resolutions to defend the territorial integrity and political independence of any other state. The League would be specifically forbidden to meddle in American domestic affairs, including the regulation of private debts and property rights; the United States would have the right to increase its armaments, no matter what manner of disarmament agreement that the League formulated. Furthermore, American withdrawal from the League need only be accomplished with a joint congressional resolution. *Congressional Record*, 66th Congress, First Session, 8773.

20. Thomas A. Bailey, *Wilson and the Great Betrayal* (Chicago: Quadrangle Books, 1963), 157.

21. Hamilton Foley, ed., *Woodrow Wilson's Case for the League of Nations* (Princeton: Princeton University Press, 1923).

22. *New York Times*, March 9, 1920, 1.

23. Thomas Bailey, *Wilson and the Great Betrayal*, 261.

24. Hamilton Armstrong called the death of the Treaty of Guarantee, "the first step towards the world of Hitler." Hamilton Fish Armstrong, *Peace and Counter Peace, From Wilson to Hitler* (New York: Harper and Row, 1971), 99.

25. Henri Pirenne, *La Belgique et la guerre mondiale* (New Haven: Yale University Press, 1928).

26. Sally Marks, *The Illusion of Peace, Europe's International Relations 1918-1933* (New York: St. Martin's Press, 1976), 29-30.

27. *Ibid.*, 325.

28. Ernst Heinrich Kossmann, *The Low Countries, 1780-1940* (New York: Oxford University Press, 1978).

29. In a speech to the Chamber of Deputies 4 March 1931, quoted in David Owen Kieft, *Belgium's Return to Neutrality* (Oxford: Clarendon Press, 1972), 2.

30. *Survey of International Affairs, 1920-1923* (London: Oxford University Press, 1925), 68.

31. At the peace conference France had tried to get the British and Americans to include Belgium in their guarantee treaty against German aggression. Robert Lansing, *Peace Negotiations*, 179-80.

32. *Ibid.*, 245-7.

33. Académie Royale de Belgique, *Documents diplomatiques belges, 1920-1940. La politique de sécurité exterièure, 1920-1924* (Brussels: Commission royal d'histoire, 1964), I, 405-8.

34. *League of Nations Treaty Series* (1920), II, 128-30.

35. Although the Belgians worried about becoming too dependent on France, they had no qualms about undermining the independence of the Grand-Duchy of Luxembourg. An agreement between the two countries was ratified in May 1921. It provided for the free exchange of goods and services, the circulation of Belgian currency in Luxembourg, and Belgian consular representation for Luxembourg abroad. It was intended to last for fifty years.

36. David Owen Kieft, *Belgium's Return to Neutrality*, 4.

37. The Belgians in 1936 decided to return to a policy of neutrality. Jane Kathryn Muller, *Belgian Foreign Policy between Two Wars, 1919-1940* (New York: Bookmann Associates, 1951); J. Armand Wullus-Rudiger, *La Belgique et la crise europeénne, 1914-1945* (Paris: Berger-Levrault, 1945).

38. Zygmunt L. Zaleski, *Le dilemme russo-polonais, L'alliance franco-russe et la Pologne, Les deux conceptions de l'ordre et de la liberté* (Paris: Payot, 1920).

39. Paul Mantoux, *Les délibérations de Conseil des Quatres*, I, 112. Danzig became a free city, included in the Polish customs area, but its people would direct their own political affairs, under the supervision of the League of Nations. The Poles would have the right to develop the city's docks and wharfs and regulate traffic on the Vistula. See: John Mason Brown, *The Danzig Dilemma, A Study in Peacemaking by Compromise* (London: Oxford University Press, 1946) and Christoph Kimmich, *The Free City, Danzig and German Foreign Policy, 1919-1934* (New Haven: Yale University Press, 1968).

40. The British favored drawing a ethnic/religious boundary between the Catholic Poles and the White Russian Slavs of the Uniate faith (those that practiced the Orthodox faith but accepted the authority of the Pope). The so-called Curzon-line was an educated guess, though it did attempt to apply objective standards to a very difficult problem. James T. Shotwell and Max E. Laserson, *Poland and Russia 1919-1945* (New York: Carnegie Endowment for

World Peace, 1945), 7-8. See also: M. K. Dziewanowski, *Joseph Pilsudski, A European Federalist, 1918-1922* (Stanford: Hoover Institution Press, 1969).

41.   Vlacav Benes, *Poland* (New York: Praeger, 1970), 180.

42.   The war ended with the Treaty of Riga, signed on 18 March 1921. The Lithuanian city of Riga was Pilsudski's boyhood town. The boundary between the two countries was basically where the two warring armies had stopped fighting. See: Norman Davies, *White Eagle, Red Star; The Polish-Soviet War, 1919-20* (New York: St. Martin's Press, 1972), and Józef Pilsudski, *Year 1920 and its Climax: Battle of Warsaw during the Polish-Soviet War, 1919-1920* (London: Pilsudski Institute of London, 1972).

43.   Titus Komarnicki, *Rebirth of the Polish Republic, A Study in the Diplomatic History of Europe, 1919-1920* (London: Heinemann, 1957).

44.   Of the roughly one-third who were not Polish, half were Ukrainians, one-fourth were Jews, and the rest were Germans, White Russians, Letts, and Czechs—none of these peoples became reconciled to Polish authority.

45.   Piotr S. Wandycz, *France and Her Eastern Allies*, 212-3.

46.   *League of Nations Treaty Series* (1923), XVIII, 12-13.

47.   But the French had promised to give the Poles diplomatic support. When the Council of the League settled the Upper Silesian question, the French managed to get the area partitioned instead of being awarded outright to Germany as the vote indicated and the British had desired because they believed that the overall recovery of Europe was dependent on the area's coal resources being exploited by an economically prosperous Germany. *Survey of International Affairs 1920-1923*, 267-70.

48.   Piotr S. Wandycz, France and Her Eastern Allies, 217-8.

49.   Paul Mantoux, Les déliberations de Conseil des Quatres, 48.

50.   Jules Laroche, *Au quai d'orsay avec Briand et Poincaré* (Paris: Hachette, 1957), 137.

51.   Piotr S. Wandycz, *France and Her Eastern Allies*, 188-9.

52.   Gyula Juhász, *Hungarian Foreign Policy, 1919-45* (Budapest: Akadémiai Kiado, 1979), 56.

53.   Mario Toscano, "Failure of the Hungarian-Rumanian Rapprochement of 1920", *Designs in Diplomacy* (Baltimore: Johns Hopkins Press, 1970), 22-3.

54.   In Britain, the Trianon treaty was roundly criticized for its harshness. Press lord Rothermere began what would become a 20-year lobbying effort on Hungary's behalf. Viscount Rothermere, *My Campaign for Hungary* (London: Eyre and Spottiswood, 1939).

55.   *Survey of International Affairs, 1920-1923*, 505-7.

56. Karl, unlike Wilhelm II, never formally abdicated. He merely renounced "all participation in the affairs of state." Gordon Brook-Shepherd, *The Last Habsburg* (New York: Waybright and Talley, 1968), 210.

57. Nicholas Horthy, *The Confidential Papers of Admiral Horthy* (Budapest: Corvina, 1965), 17-18.

58. Nicholas Horthy, *Memoirs* (New York: Robert Speller, 1957), 126. Karl lived on Funchal, isolated from any semblance of the world he had known, in poverty and broken health, until 1 April 1922 when he died of viral pneumonia. He was only thirty-five. His queen, Zita, was twenty-nine. She was left with eight children, the oldest of which, Crown Prince Otto, was just ten. The father had given them very little of himself except his name.

59. Gordon Brook-Shepherd, *The Last Habsburg* (New York: Waybright and Talley), 256-8.

60. Nicholas Horthy, *Memoirs*, 120-1.

61. Gordon Craig and Felix Gilbert, eds., *The Diplomats 1919-1939* (New York: Atheneum, 1963), I, 53.

CHAPTER 3

REDUCING THE CAUSES OF EXASPERATION

THE BRITISH had difficulty appreciating the tense anxiety the French felt over security. The German High Seas fleet, whose menacing presence had forced the British to end splendid isolation and seek allies, was being broken up for scrap. Germany's overseas empire was gone, and the German army had been downsized into little more than a domestic police force. German industry was expected to regain strength, but this would benefit all of Europe, especially Britain. By selling their goods on the German market, the British could boost their own productivity and cure unemployment, ensuring domestic harmony in the process. In fact, resumption of their role as holder of the balance of power obliged the British to help Germany again become prosperous and a contributing member of the European family of nations. Although the British certainly did not desire the re-creation of a Teutonic colossus, they hoped that concentration on making money would divert the Germans from more dangerous pursuits.

Even before the Versailles treaty was signed, Lloyd George said that the settlement should be considered the basis of accommodation and change rather than fulfillment and repression.[1] He informed Clemenceau and Wilson of his conclusions on 25 March 1919, after spending a weekend in a retreat with his advisors at the Hôtel France et Angleterre in Fontainbleau.

The British prime minister warned that, if Germany felt "she has been unjustly treated in the peace of 1919 she will find means of exacting retribution from her conquerors."[2] He feared that harshness

would drive the Germans into the hands of the Bolsheviks.   The
Communists might even seize power in Germany and

> all Eastern Europe will be swept into the orbit of the Bolshevik
> revolution and within a year we may witness the spectacle of
> nearly one hundred million people organized into a vast red army
> under German instructors and German generals equipped with
> German cannons and German machine guns and prepared for
> renewal of the attack on Western Europe.[3]

Although Lloyd George—at least at that time—affirmed a commitment
to the Treaty of Guarantee, he had no desire to see it play a major role
in Anglo-French relations.   That treaty had been concocted ostensibly
for reasons of French security.   Britain's real motive, however, had
been to get France to withdraw its demands for a permanent occupation
of the Rhineland.

Lloyd George claimed that the League of Nations should
eventually protect France against new German aggression.[4]   He also
said that reparations should "disappear if possible with the generation
which made the war."   But Lloyd George's commitment to a peace of
moderation had a hollow ring.   He believed that Germany had a right to
some territorial adjustment, but he still believed that Germany should
be required to make large "redemption payments".   The memorandum
made him seem more liberal than he, in fact, was.

Clemenceau had no trouble making this obvious by suggesting
that the prime minister might show the sincerity of his new
benevolence by renouncing reparations for Great Britain.   Clemenceau
further contended that the Germans would never accept another
people's concept of justice.   He insisted that the Allies had sacrificed
too much to compromise the result of their victory.

> The League of Nations is offered to us as a means of giving us the
> security we need: I accept the means, but if the League of Nations
> cannot enforce its decrees with military sanctions, we have to find
> sanctions somewhere else.

Clemenceau asked that France be ensured the same security on land
that Britain had achieved on the seas.

I have not decided how this will be accomplished. I beg you to understand my feelings, as I am trying to understand yours. America is far away, protected by an ocean. Britain could not be reached even by Napoleon himself. You are, both of you are, sheltered, we are not.[5]

Clemenceau argued that a peace of moderation could only lead to great dissatisfaction among the allied peoples and provoke the same revolutionary forces at home the Allies were trying to contain abroad.

AS THE MEMORIES of war began to fade, criticism of the Treaty of Versailles intensified. Especially in Britain many sections of society, regardless of party affiliation, social class, or occupation, raised voice against it. The British blamed the treaty for almost everything that was wrong with European politics. Such widespread opposition marked an important difference between the British and the French. In France, opposition to the treaty came largely from Socialists who feared that its harshness might be deleterious to the strengthening of German social democracy. But for the most part, Hun-bashing was still popular in France, becoming a handy device for politicians to win elections.

Despite vicious wartime propaganda, the British had not lost their respect for the German people and for German culture. They were prepared to forget earlier cries of vengeance and put their relations with their former enemy on a new plane so that both peoples could get on with their lives.[6] Most of the "hang-the-kaiser" types had either left the government or changed their tune. In his "Fontainbleau Memorandum" Lloyd George had anticipated such a reconciliation.

The impression, the deep impression, made upon the human heart by four years of unexampled slaughter will disappear with the hearts upon which it has been marked by the terrible sword of the great war. The maintenance of peace will then depend upon there being no causes of exasperation constantly stirring up the spirit of patriotism, of justice or of fair play.[7]

The absence of extensive wartime damage to the British isles contributed to this softening of attitude, as well as did the disappearance of the "Wicked Kaiser" from the world stage.

The ex-monarch was now comfortably installed in the small Dutch village of Doorn surrounded by personal possessions, including his beloved dachshunds, upon whose death he had lovingly buried under little marker stones in the garden near a path where he took his daily strolls. Staying carefully aloof from politics, as his host country insisted, the exile lived as an English country gentleman, pruning his roses and sawing firewood for the poor families in the nearby village.[8] He appeared more dotty than ferocious. He was, after all, a grandson of Queen Victoria.

Many intellectuals scorned Woodrow Wilson. Harold Nicolson, a member of the foreign office delegation at the Paris Peace Conference, wrote with adolescent resentment:

> We came to Paris confident that the new order was about to be established, we left it convinced that the new order had merely fouled the old. We arrived as fervent apprentices in the school of President Wilson: we left as renegades.[9]

Others had no illusions to destroy.

John Maynard Keynes, a delegate from the Treasury at the Paris Conference, mounted the most influential and devastating denunciation in his *The Economic Consequences of the Peace*, appearing at the end of 1919. The book, which sold an initial 140,000 copies and was translated into eleven languages, provided ammunition for much subsequent criticism of the treaty. Keynes said of Wilson that there was seldom a statesman of the first rank more incompetent than he "in the agilities of the council chamber."[10] Keynes believed the treaty was a massive economic blunder.

> The policy of reducing Germany to servitude for a generation, of degrading the lives of millions of human beings, and of depriving a whole nation of happiness should be abhorrent and detestable. ...Some preach it in the name of Justice. In the great events of man's history, in the unwinding of the complex fate of nations Justice is not so simple. And even if it were, nations are not authorized, by religion or by national morals, to visit on the children of their enemies the misdoings of parents or of rulers.[11]

The Economic Consequences of the Peace caused such a sensation that one almost wondered whether the treaty had any defenders left. *The Times* tried to put the treaty back in perspective when it called the book a clever product of an academic mind accustomed to metaphysical abstractions, but "against the facts and forces of actual political existence."[12] And The *Spectator* said:

> The world is not governed by economic forces alone, and we do not blame the statesmen at Paris for declining to be guided by Mr. Keynes if he gave them such political advice as he sets forth in his book.[13]

Nonetheless, the criticism proved significant, encouraging the Germans in their revisionism and increasing the insecurity of the French, who were already fearful, after the collapse of the Treaty of Guarantee, that the Entente was poised for further deterioration.

In truth, Keynes often appeared more magnetic when he was scoring debating points than when presenting a reasoned analysis of the dynamics of peacemaking. He was more even-handed in his next book. In it, he grudgingly and ambiguously praised Lloyd George for skillfully "protecting Europe from as many evil consequences of his own Treaty as lay in his power to prevent."[14] But this second work was much less popular than the first.

From Lloyd George's point of view, one of these evil consequences was sure to come over war crimes trials. Both the British and the French had initially favored putting German war leaders on trial. The French presented a list of 334 names, Hindenburg and Ludendorff heading it. The British list was shorter, but contained a higher percentage of naval personnel. Lloyd George soon began to fear, however, that the arrest of men considered national heroes might so provoke the Germans that the entire treaty could be jeopardized.

Despite the fears of Lloyd George, Alexandre Millerand,[15] Clemenceau's successor, was determined to bring the German officials to justice for their war crimes. Lord Chancellor Birkenhead tried to explain that it was impossible to expect that the German government would surrender its most prominent leaders to the Allies. But Millerand was adamant. Suppose, Birkenhead said, that the Germans had been victorious.

Can we for a single moment imagine that any of our peoples...would consent to hand over to hostile courts their countrymen of such high distinction?[16]

"But we wouldn't have signed the Treaty," Millerand replied. Millerand staunchly opposed leniency towards Germany because compromise would undermine enforcement of the entire treaty.

Lloyd George finally ended the dispute by leaking the British-French disagreement to the press. Millerand, fearing the harmful effects of a public airing of allied disunity, abandoned his demand for the trials. He assented that the Germans themselves could bring to trial those whom the allies considered had committed "crimes against the laws of civilized warfare."[17] Under this face-saving gesture, the Germans eventually tried a dozen men from the allied list, but their courts handed down meaningful judgements only in the case of two submarine officers who had sunk a lifeboat full of wounded British sailors and nurses. The men received four-year sentences, but shortly after the trial, they escaped confinement and disappeared.[18] No more trials were held. In a back-handed way, Lloyd George had won his first victory for appeasement.

The British prime minister also ran afoul his own foreign office professionals. The war over, he had difficulty adjusting to a less dictatorial style of leadership.[19] Many diplomats grew dissatisfied with his broad-brush approach to foreign policy and resented being excluded from his confidence.[20] As long as the conciliatory Arthur Balfour had been foreign secretary, friction was kept to a minimum. Balfour resigned in October 1919, however, and his successor, George Nathaniel Curzon, was not inclined to sit quietly while decisions were made elsewhere.[21] The prime minister and the new foreign secretary soon engaged in a turf battle.[22]

Curzon protested Lloyd George's appointment of an ambassador to Poland without first consulting the foreign office. Lloyd George countered that Curzon had kept him ignorant about negotiations with Soviet Russia.[23] Such divided counsels gave the impression that two foreign policies existed.[24] However necessity encouraged unity, especially when it came to the crucial relations between Britain and France concerning German treaty enforcement.

ON 19 MARCH 1920, German communists tried to seize control of the coal and steel industry in the Ruhr. Because the area was within the demilitarized zone outlined in the Versailles treaty, the German government appealed to the allied powers for permission to send in Reichswehr units to crush the uprising.[25] The British were eager to see the "Red Army" threat stamped out and readily agreed, but the French resisted because they suspected that the affair was merely a German ploy to further weaken the Versailles treaty. They believed that German officials in the Rhineland were Prussian agents dedicated to maximizing and exploiting discord.

The French agreed to the use of German troops, but only if the Allies could occupy certain areas of Germany as collateral. This demand made the British suspect that the French were really interested flexing their power over Germany. In fact, Marshal Foch was especially hot for action. He declared that if the Ruhr situation were serious enough to require the use of an army, then the allied governments should send in troops and restore order themselves.

Millerand continued to push for the occupation of the Ruhr and the virtual detachment of the Rhineland from Germany. He encouraged the French press to support this campaign, and even undertook negotiations himself with the Germans. Millerand aimed to establish conditions under which German troops would be allowed to enter the demilitarized zone only if the French army could occupy certain additional German towns. When Curzon threatened, however, to abandon the entire policy of cooperation and withdraw from the occupied area altogether, Millerand drew in his horns. He denied that France had ever intended to take action without British involvement, but the quarreling continued.

The situation in the Ruhr became more calamitous as the communist insurgents began terrorizing the local population. They let coal supplies dwindle. They confiscated private property and looted banks. The German government could no longer wait for the British and French to reach an agreement. On 3 April 1920, the Reichswehr was sent into the Ruhr. The French immediately charged Germany with treaty violations and, without consulting the British, ordered their army to occupy the Hessian cities of Frankfurt, Darmstadt, Hanau, and Dieburg, and the Saarland city of Bad Homburg. This *fait accompli* put British leaders in an embarrassing position.

Andrew Bonar Law, the leader of the House of Commons, remarked that the British would either have to "declare to the world that the unity of the alliance was broken, or express approval of, and assume responsibility for, a policy which they held to be wrong and dangerous."[26] Curzon denounced the action as incompatible with the mutual understanding and common action upon which depended the stability of the alliance and the security of Europe. Once viceroy of India, Lord Curzon was particularly distressed that the French had used troops from their colonies in the occupation.

The French promised to consult with Britain in the future, but continued to assert the legitimacy of their action. They declined to end their occupation until the Reichswehr units had left the Ruhr; and, even then, they evacuated those cities only east of the Rhine river, hanging onto Bad Homburg. Alexandre Millerand's desire to push around the Germans in the Rhineland was part of a larger policy that aimed at getting compensation for compromises made at the peace table. During his brief term in office (his government lasted until September 1920 when he was elected president of the Republic), Millerand showed that he was both in favor of the status quo and in favor of changing it. He pushed enforcement of the Treaty of Versailles while trying to weaken Germany's control of its western frontiers and to undermine its political unity. Thus Millerand kept alive the prospect of a separate Rhenish Republic. Millerand, however, never advocated the creation of a separate Rhenish Republic as "official policy," nor did any other French government, at least following signature of the Treaty of Versailles. To do so would have undermined all efforts to enforce the peace, and have left France more exposed and less secure than it was.

Lloyd George hoped that Millerand's successor would be more reasonable. Georges Leygues, however, feared making any move in foreign policy without first checking with Millerand. Only when Aristide Briand formed a government in January 1921 (Briand also assumed the post of foreign minister) did Lloyd George have a leader with whom he thought he could deal. In his congratulatory letter, he told Briand that all Britain wanted to do was to get on with business. Included in this desire was Lloyd George's determination to head off any potential deal between the French authorities in the Rhineland, and the local German industrialists.[27]

The prime minister knew most French leaders wanted Germany to pay for the war. Briand's desire for such became apparent when Briand proposed turning the Left Bank of the Rhine into a separate customs area, to make it easier to pressure Germany for reparations.[28] But Lloyd George also recognized that the French had a right to impose sanctions on Germany should a violation of the treaty take place. But he insisted that French policy must satisfy Great Britain that

> there was no intention to exercise force in order to bully or trample on Germany or to kick her when she was down. [The British people had to be convinced that the use of force would] commend itself to reasonable men as fair and practicable, without offending a great people or keeping it in servitude for forty or fifty years.[29]

Briand tested the limits of these cautionary words.

In March 1921, the Reparation Commission held Germany in default of three billion dollars. Briand demanded that French troops occupy the Rhineland ports of Düsseldorf, Ruhrort, and Duisburg. The French also wanted to seal off the zones of occupation from the rest of Germany, and hit all German exports into allied countries with a special tax. (Most of the reparations that Germany had paid was figured as occupation costs, leaving its indebtedness virtually unchanged anyway.) Lloyd George reluctantly approved Briand's aggressive tactics.

The Germans protested to the League of Nations and called upon the Americans for mediation. The appeal to the League got nowhere, since the French and the British controlled its agenda. And the United States was uninterested in helping settle a dispute to enforce a treaty the Senate had not ratified.

THE FRENCH wanted treaty enforcement to be handled by those special organizations that had been established at the peace conference. Such agencies included the Supreme Council, which supervised the activities of the Reparation Commission, the Conference of Ambassadors, which supervised the activities of the Rhineland Commission, and the Allied Control Commission, which monitored German disarmament. The British, on the other hand, wanted the authority of these organizations limited to supervision and only used as clearing houses for treaty administration. They would have no executive authority within Germany.[30] Lloyd George preferred dealing with German violations through ad hoc conferences—channels that would give him greater flexibility in achieving his real aim, which was to promote British recovery through general European recovery.

Lloyd George was the only one of the Big Three now left in office. This made him feel that he had a special responsibility for winning the peace.[31] Until his resignation in October 1922, he personally attended most of the twenty-two international conferences the Allies sponsored.[32]

Lloyd George had especially counted on the cooperation of the United States in solving the problems of reparations. Indeed, the whole peace settlement had been drafted with the assumption that the Americans would be active partners in carrying it out.[33] The British prime minister had expected the Americans to be a moderating influence on France, and he was dismayed when the world's most industrially developed state avoided assuming political responsibilities commensurate with its economic strength. American absence dealt a serious blow to European reconstruction. It made the British prime minister's efforts at conciliation more difficult, forcing him to change his focus. Now he insisted that the Europeans themselves had to take the initiative for their own political and economic recovery.

But Lloyd George knew that all his hopes would be dashed unless he proved able to satisfy the French need for security. The French government was still pushing for an unconditional Treaty of Guarantee. Briand argued that such a commitment, advantageous to the British, would enable France

> to reduce her forces, to make a long stride towards that military disarmament for which Great Britain in particular has pleaded, to relieve the burden upon her finances, and cooperate heartily with [Britain] and the other powers in bringing about the economic recovery of Europe.[34]

But Lloyd George would not give him any support.

Foreign Secretary Curzon feared an Anglo-French alliance would be a throwback to prewar days, entrapping Britain in a conflict in which the country had no direct interest. Curzon believed that the French connection had outlived its usefulness. He even doubted whether the French army could furnish any serious military assistance.

He remarked cuttingly that it was only capable of dispatching "abundant swarms of black troops let loose from the sands or swamps of Africa" to the north-west Indian frontier.[35]   Although, upon reflection, Curzon conceded that an Anglo-French alliance might guarantee "against the renewal of war for at least a generation", he confessed it was difficult to "anticipate what enemies we may be threatened by in the future or with whom we may find ourselves at war."[36]

> Peace must for the present rest on the execution of the peace treaties. These would hardly survive a breach between England and France at this moment.[37]

THE CHEERFUL GIVER.

Uncle Sam (to European Beggar). "TAKE THIS BAG OF GOLD. DID I SAY 'GOLD'? NAY. 'TIS SOMETHING FAR MORE PRECIOUS THAN THAT." [Collapse of Beggar.]

In his cartoon **The Cheerful Giver,** *Bernard Partridge reflects Lloyd George's attitude that the official commitment of the United States of European recovery was more talk than action. (Punch, December 27,1922) When American investment capital did flow to Europe, it was primarily private, the Coolidge administration opposing governmental aid packages.*

In short, the prime minister was willing to promise that Britain would aid France only in the event of a direct and unprovoked attack—something the French could reasonably count on anyway. Lloyd George said vaguely "Great Britain and France should march together for the economic and financial reconstruction of Europe."[38] To which Briand replied sarcastically,

> I hope the sun's rays will penetrate our spirits and create the disposition which will permit us to overcome in a spirit of reconciliation the difficulties that we will encounter.[39]

Francophile Harold Nicolson thought that Curzon failed to recognize the sincere pacifism that lay at the heart of French policy. "He should have realized that French security was at the basis of the whole European system."[40] Nicolson was echoing the sentiments of his boss, Sir Eyre Crowe, who touted the supreme importance of the French connection. But Curzon was deaf to the opinions of such diplomats. And he could count on support from officials at the British Treasury, who also advised Lloyd George to discount the French connection. The financiers look to the conclusion of a more promising business arrangement with Germany.[41ii]

Lloyd George was in a bind. He felt he should give the French something, but not much. He therefore promised Briand that Britain would stand by France "with all the forces of the Empire against a German invasion of her soil."[42] It was a hollow gesture, and it came with many qualifications. The prime minister, for example, specified that such a pledge would have to be included in an entente that resolved some of their outstanding differences, including those over the Greco-Turkish crisis in the Near East and over French naval armaments. In the latter context, Lloyd George deplored the recent increase in French submarine strength, which would, unfortunately, prompt the British to increase their own harbor defenses.[43]

Briand continued to insist on a specific technical convention for military cooperation and that Britain commit itself to the preservation of the boundary settlements of eastern Europe. But Briand feared that the British were more interested in talk than action. He knew that the British would never agree to guarantee the eastern frontiers. More distressing yet, Lloyd George had promised only mutual consultation should the Germans attempt to remilitarize the Rhineland.[44] The British were slipping back into their prewar frame of mind of splendid isolation, back to a time before the German threat had turned the Entente into an alliance.

THE CANNES CONFERENCE, which Lloyd George hoped would create a great momentum for European reconstruction, opened the first week of January 1922. It was the largest meeting of its kind since the Paris Peace Conference.[45]   Sessions were held in the swank headquarters of the local *Cercle nautique* (Yachting Club).

In his opening remarks, Lloyd George pledged to work for the complete economic reconstruction of Europe.   This included the stabilization of national currencies whose volatility contributed to unemployment.[46]   Monetary stability, he said, could be achieved through international cooperation at a future meeting at which all European powers would be represented, including Russia, but also the defeated powers of Germany, Austria, Hungary, and Bulgaria.[47]

In a move to put France at ease, the prime minister insisted that Britain would not violate any clauses of the Versailles treaty, and that Germany should "pay to the limit of its capacity...for the damage it caused."[48]   But he warned that the cost of exacting an indemnity be commensurate with its benefits.   The prime minister thought the problem of reparations could be solved by breaking down the barriers of German trade with eastern and central Europe.[49]   He proposed to invite the Germans to Cannes in order to, as he put it, ask them questions and arrive at an understanding.[50]

Briand had not come to Cannes to rework the economic structure of Europe.   He came to preserve the authority of the Treaty of Versailles whose lack of enforcement, he believed, had caused many of the problems now under discussion.[51]   Eliminating unemployment was not a goal of his foreign policy.[52]   Ever since the loss of Alsace-Lorraine, the French had restricted their trade with Germany and had no intention of changing that policy.   They feared the rebuilding of German industrial strength, because they believed that such power could only encourage the aggressive instincts of the German leaders. The restoration of German economic strength was tolerable only if it facilitated the payment of reparations and was not supposed to promote general European recovery.[53]   Briand also doubted that Soviet Russia could become a suitable trading partner. For France, recognition of the Soviet regime was out of the question until the Communists paid back the tsarist debts they had repudiated.[54]   Above all, Briand wanted Anglo-France cooperation to result in a security agreement to guarantee the European status quo.[55]

Briand was also hoping the Cannes conference would provide ways to get the Germans to pay reparations. (Currently in default, the Germans had used the convocation of the conference as an excuse to delay further payments.)   Briand believed that an invitation to Cannes would only encourage more German intransigence.   He feared that they would demand the removal of French troops from the Rhineland as the price for cooperation, thereby reducing French security and the ability to enforce the Treaty of Versailles.   An invitation would also weaken the Reparation Commission, and make the Germans arbiters of the allied powers.   "It is not possible to allow the Germans to discuss a situation whose origin is to be found in German bad faith," he said.[56] Briand demanded explanations, not dialogue.

Briand, however, did not want to threaten Germany with military force.   He hoped to get British support in order to exact German compliance.   He finally agreed to allow the Germans to come to Cannes, providing that it was accomplished in stages.   First, the Germans would come as far as Paris and await further allied orders.[57] Then they might be invited the rest of the way and meet the representatives of the Reparation Commission.   If they were able to explain adequately why they had failed to fulfill their obligations, they could be invited to participate in the conference itself.[58]

In his desire to enforce the authority of the Reparation Commission, Briand was no different from his arch-rival, Raymond Poincaré.   Yet, no matter how strongly Briand defended French interests, his conservative political opponents were convinced that he was prepared to sell out to the British.   They also demanded immediate reparations to avoid another devaluation of the franc.[59] Alexandre Millerand, assuming the authority of those days before the turn of the century when the president of the Republic was the main force in foreign policy, ordered Briand to accept no moratorium on German payments unless he got adequate guarantees.[60]   Millerand believed that France, if need be, should act without British support and warned that the Germans should answer to no other authority than that of the Reparation Commission.[61]   He and his nationalist supporters were willing to use any excuse to turn Briand out of office and replace him with Poincaré. They soon got their chance.

ON 8 JANUARY, Lloyd George suggested Briand try his hand at golf before the start of the afternoon session. Briand had little experience at the game, but he nonetheless agreed and, in a stroke of beginners luck, putted his first ball into the cup. But things went less smoothly from then on. Briand's unorthodox technique soon had the others laughing.[62] Photographers recorded the awkward encounter and some of their pictures appeared in the Paris papers.

Had Briand stuck to *boules*, he would have been better off athletically and politically. Briand's enemies found the golf game to be a symbol of the confusion and absence of purpose of the Cannes conference. Poincaré, the chairman of the Senate's Commission for Foreign Affairs, feigned shock.[63] And Millerand dispatched another warning. Briand found the criticism so alarming that he hurried back to Paris to address the Chamber of Deputies.

In his speech of 11 January, he refused to give an inch, defying others to do better than he had. Then, without bothering to wait for a formal vote of confidence, he walked out of the room, followed by his cabinet, and immediately submitted his resignation. The measure was unnecessary. Briand's opponents would have had difficulty rounding up the necessary support for a no-confidence vote. (A few days before in a vote of 312 to 199, the nationalists had already failed to force his recall from the Cannes Conference).[64] But Briand felt that he had temporarily outlived his effectiveness, and that it was best to go while he was still ahead. He calculated that he still retained sufficient support on which to stage a comeback. His departure was a judicious, temporary, retreat. People called him "the India-rubber man" with good reason.

While Briand was facing his critics in Paris, the Germans had their hearing before the Reparation Commission and then the Cannes conference. Walter Rathenau, their chief delegate, came well-prepared. Speaking in German and then switching to French "to save time", he insisted that Germany desired to pay the sums demanded of it, but said it was unable to do so unless it were to achieve financial stability. He "proved" his case metaphorically by saying that Germany was like a boat that was expected to go fast, but at the same time save coal.[65]

Without giving details, Rathenau claimed that Germany had saved the world against Bolshevism.[66]

The news that Briand and his whole cabinet had resigned cut Rathenau's presentation short. It made no sense to continue; and with nothing decided, the Reparation Commission agreed to a "provisional postponement" of the installments due for January and February, a moratorium that would end as soon as the allied governments reached a further decision.[67]

The Germans could rejoice at the apparent worsening of relations between France and Britain. On the surface, it seemed that the Entente was too far gone to be revived, and that the Germans might take advantage of the rupture to strike some sort of deal directly with the British or, failing that, with the other pariah power, Communist Russia.[68]

The French dreaded the consequences of any break with Great Britain, but, by continually insisting on their treaty rights, they insured that the breach between the two countries would get larger. France's contention that the Germans were deliberately provocative to show contempt for the Versailles treaty, however, had merit. No German government could have lasted politically had it advocated or practiced a policy of compliance.

Most of the center and right-wing German political parties—those that the French collectively labeled as Prussian—routinely favored the restoration of German territory lost at Paris and vigorously opposed paying any reparations. Many of these groups were also outspokenly anti-democratic. The cohesion of the old liberal German middle class was collapsing into extremism, anti-Semitism, and völkish nationalism. The series of fragile coalitions running the Weimar government no longer seemed to determine the nation's important political life. Patriotic, para-military groups, youth movements, and league-type organizations, many of which were preoccupied with the concept of a "new awakening" and the solution of problems through authoritarianism, seemed to be in control.[69] The French recognized the danger of this phenomenon, and they feared for the future.

Notes and Sources:

1. Martin Gilbert, *The Roots of Appeasement* (London: Weidenfeld and Nicolson, 1966), 68-80.

2. David Lloyd George, *The Truth About the Peace Treaties*, I, 405.

3. *Ibid.*, 405. Lloyd George sought to strengthen his position by leaking the memorandum to the press. Clemenceau countered by hinting that he was willing to discuss concessions, but only after the Germans had signed the treaty. The Germans doubted the premier's sincerity and did not bother to respond.

4. *Ibid*, 411.

5. Mantoux, I, 44-5. Clemenceau's written answer, containing much the same points, can be found in André Tardieu, *La paix* (Paris: Payot, 1921), 129-32, and in David Lloyd George, *The Truth About the Peace Treaties*, I, 416-20.

6. Lord Vansittart, *Lessons of My Life* (New York: Alfred A. Knopf, 1943), 8-9.

7. Lloyd George, *Memoirs of the Peace Conference*, I, 267.

8. *The Diaries of Sir Bruce Lockhart*, ed., Kenneth Young (New York: St. Martin's Press, 1973), 75.

9. Harold Nicolson, *Peacemaking 1919*, 187. See also Vera Brittain, *Testament of Youth* (New York: Macmillan, 1934), 469-70.

10. John M. Keynes, *The Economic Consequences of the Peace* (New York. Harcourt, Brace and Rowe, 1920), 32, 43.

11. *Ibid.*, 225.

12. *The Times*, 5 January 1920.

13. *Spectator*, 20 December 1919.

14. John M. Keynes, *A Revision of the Treaty: Being a Sequel to the Economic Consequences of the Peace* (New York: Harcourt, Brace, 1922), 2.

15. Millerand, personally backed by Poincaré, became head of the French government on 20 January 1920. He also took the portfolio of foreign affairs.

16. *Documents on British Foreign Policy*, first series, IX, 657.

17. Millerand's fairly brief ministry (from 20 January to 20 September 1920) before he became President of the Republic contained none of the men who had been in Clemenceau's cabinet.

18. Erich Eyck, *A History of the Weimar Republic* (Cambridge, Mass.: Harvard University Press, 1962), 187-8.

19. See: John Turner, *Lloyd George's Secretariat* (New York: Cambridge University Press, 1980).

20. George Buchanan, *My Mission to Russia*, II, 261.

21. British Prime Ministers and Foreign Secretaries, 1919-1924: David Lloyd George, and Arthur Balfour (until October 1919) then George Curzon (January 1919-October 1922); Andrew Bonar Law and Lord Curzon (October 1922-May 1923); Stanley Baldwin and Lord Curzon (May 1923-January 1924); J. Ramsay MacDonald, also foreign secretary. (January-December 1924).

22. Kenneth O. Morgan, "David Lloyd George" in John P. Mackintosh, ed., *British Prime Ministers in the Twentieth Century* (New York: St. Martin's Press, 1977), 137-8.

23. This was a gratuitous accusation because Lloyd George, not Curzon, had pushed for accommodation with the Communists. Lord Riddell, *Intimate Diary of the Peace Conference and After*, 219.

24. George Buchanan, *My Mission to Russia*, II (London: Cassell, 1923), 260.

25. By special dispensation, Germany had been given the right to garrison as many as 17,000 troops in the Ruhr until April 1920, and the present request was really one for reinforcements.

26. *Documents on British Foreign Policy*, first series, IX, 325.

27. Donald Graeme Boadle, *Winston Churchill and the German Question in British Foreign Policy, 1918-1922* (The Hague: Martinus Nijhoff, 1973).

28. Walter A. McDougall, *France's Rhineland Diplomacy, The Last Bid for a Balance of Power* (Princeton, N.J.: Princeton University Press, 1978), 143-4.

29. *Documents on British Foreign Policy*, first series, vol. XV, 465.

30. For example, the British pointed out to the French, on May 29, 1919, that the Reparation Commission should not have "powers to dictate the domestic legislation of Germany" nor "to prescribe or enforce taxes or to dictate the character of the German budget." *Documents on British Foreign Policy*, first series, vol. XXVI, 670.

31. W. Laird Kleine-Ahlbrandt, *Twentieth Century European History* (Saint Paul: West Publishing, 1993), 176-177.

32. *Survey of International Affairs*, 1920-1923, 5-34.

33. Harold Nicolson, *Peacemaking* 1919, 207.

34. Briand to Curzon. *Documents on British Foreign Policy*, first series, XVI, 861-2.

35. *Ibid.*, 863.

36. *Ibid.*, 862.

37. *Documents on British Foreign Policy*, first series, XV, 827-8.

38. *Documents on British Foreign Policy*, first series, XIX, 6.

39. *Ministère des Affaires Étrangères*, série Y, Vol. 21 (Conférence de Cannes), Session 1, 1.

40. Harold Nicolson, Curzon: *The Last Phase 1919-1925, A Study in Post-War Diplomacy* (New York: Harcourt, Brace and Co., 1939), 195.

41. *Documents on British Foreign Policy*, first series, XVI, 827-8.

42. *Ibid.*, first series, XIX, 3.

43. At the Washington Conference in December 1921, Britain had tried to get this "poor-man's" weapon suppressed completely.

44. *Command Document* 2169, no. 38.

45. George Buchanan, *My Mission to Russia*, II, 2.

46. *Ministère des Affaires Étrangères*, série Y, Vol. 21, (Conférence de Cannes), Session 1, 3.

47. *Ibid.*, 13.

48. *Ibid.*, 6-7.

49. *Documents on British Foreign Policy*, first series, XV, 464-5; also: Ministère des Affaires Étrangères, série Y, Vol. 21 (Conférence de Cannes), 11.

50. *Ibid.*, série Y, Vol. 21 (Conférence de Cannes), Session 3, 5.

51. *Ibid.*, 6.

52. In 1922, only 13,000 people officially listed as out of work, while Britain officially counted 1.5 million, or roughly 15 percent of its work force. *European Economic Statistics*, 166, 168.

53. *Ministère des Affaires Étrangères*, série Y, Vol. 21 (Conférence de Cannes), Session 1, 1.

54. *Documents on British Foreign Policy*, first series, XV, 784.

55. *Documents on British Foreign Policy*, first series, XIX, 57.

56. Ministère des Affaires Étrangères, série Y, Vol. 21 (Conférence de Cannes), Session 1, 6-7.

57. *Ibid.*, 9-10.

58. *Ministère des Affaires Étrangères*, série Y, Vol. 21 (Conférence de Cannes), Session 10, 1.

59. Re: Léon Daudet, *Député de Paris*, 1919-1924 (Paris: B. Grasset, 1933).

60. Article 8 of the Constitutional Law of 16 July 1875 gave the president of the republic the right to negotiate and ratify treaties. Maurice Duverger, ed., *Constitutions et documents politiques* (Paris: Presses Universitaires de France, 1960), 113.

61. Édouard Bonnefous, *Histoire politique de la troisième république, L'après-guerre*, 278.

62. Lord Riddell, *Intimate Diary of the Peace Conference and After*, 7.

63. Jacques Chastenet, *Histoire de la troisième république, Jours inquiets et sanglants*, 92.

64. Joining with the nationalists in the negative votes were a group of radical anti-clericals who had opposed Briand's reestablishment of official diplomatic relations with the Vatican.

65. *Ministère des Affaires Étrangères*, série Y, Vol. 21 (Conférence de Cannes), Session 1, Session 14, 4.

66. *Ibid.*, 2.

67. *Documents on British Foreign Policy*, first series, XIX, 135.

68. Gordon Craig and Felix Gilbert, eds., *The Diplomats* 1919-1939, I (New York: Atheneum, 1963), 161.

69. Hans Mommsen, *From Weimar to Auschwitz* (Princeton, N.J.: Princeton University Press, 1991), 11-27.

CHAPTER 4

THE GRAND DESIGN

LLOYD GEORGE returned home with a partial gain. Before the Cannes conference adjourned, he had fostered the creation of an international consortium that would work on restoring the world economy. Additionally, he had arranged for another gathering to be held at Genoa, Italy, the following April.[1] At this next conference, he hoped to establish "the peace of Europe on solid foundations"[2] by having the participants agree to "abstain from all aggression against their neighbors."[3] The P.M. wanted such a pledge to eliminate the need for a special treaty of guarantee for France.

But Briand, still in office when these arrangements were under discussion, feared that any commitment to avert war could affect the authority of existing general treaties.[4] Any such scheme, which pretended to reinforce the Treaty of Versailles, would imply that the treaty alone was not strong enough. Furthermore, Briand opposed any nation, which had no obligation under the peace treaties, gaining responsibility for enforcement. He had in mind Communist Russia. How, he asked, could European economic reconstruction be discussed with the "agents of revolution," who would only seek "to jerk around (*rouler*) the bourgeoisie."[5]

Although Briand knew that France and Britain had a long way to go in resolving their differences concerning the creation of a peaceful Europe, he knew there was nothing gained in opposing Lloyd George's initiative. Even after his resignation, he told Lloyd George that he was "particularly pained" not to be able to be able to bring to "a happy conclusion" the conversations "in which we have engaged in the interests of our two countries and in the interest of the peace of Europe."[6] The wisdom of thus comforting the British, however, seemed lost on Briand's successor.

RAYMOND POINCARÉ, who took charge of the French government on 15 January,1922, came from Bar-le-Duc, that area of Lorraine that had escaped German control in 1871. He was eleven years old when the separation occurred and had never lost his sense of outrage. Lloyd George once quipped that Poincaré had the same opinion of Germany as "a Salvation Army captain about the devil." In addition to the premiership, Poincaré became foreign minister and, to increase his power further, the head of the foreign ministry's professional staff. Poincaré suspected that Philippe Berthelot was soft on Germany, and refused to retain the secretary-general.[7] Thrusting himself into this new role, Poincaré familiarized himself with the details of the foreign ministry by carefully studying the position papers of major items under discussion, memorizing dates, figures, texts of agreements, and verifying the status of negotiations.

Lloyd George knew that Poincaré was going to be much more difficult to work with than Briand, but he tried to make the best of it. On his way back to London from Cannes, he stopped off in Paris to visit with the new premier and try to convince him that the prosperity of Europe, particularly that of Britain and France, depended on German recovery and on the reintegration of Russia into European affairs. Poincaré strongly disagreed with this prescription, and he also disapproved of conducting diplomacy through international conferences. He told Lloyd George that the Anglo-French disagreement over enforcement of the Treaty of Versailles, especially on reparations and disarmament, was one of the greatest threats to a peaceful Europe. He insisted on resurrection of the Treaty of Guarantee, this time backed up with a 30-year military convention.[8] Lloyd George left the meeting depressed, but he refused to give up and arranged another meeting.

The two met again to discuss arrangements for the forthcoming conference. This time in the modest sub-prefecture at Bayonne. In their four-hour discussion, Poincaré expanded on the "obstructionist attitude of Great Britain."[9] He repeated his demands that the Germans be made to live up to their agreements, and he denounced Lloyd Georges's policy of appeasement as wrongheaded. Poincaré said that only a policy of force would make the Germans realize they had been defeated and to compel them to obey the Treaty of Versailles. He pointed out that when the French signed treaties, they became "a sacred thing," and that the British were perpetuating a "cruel misunderstanding, if they felt differently."[10] France, he insisted, needed reparations to rebuild and solve growing budgetary deficits. He declared that France would insist on Communist Russia paying the tsarist debts. Poincaré felt that reintegrating the Communist state into the European community would jeopardize France's relations with the Eastern European countries. The more the Communists stayed isolated, the better.[11]

Poincaré feared that France alone would have to enforce the Treaty of Versailles, but, knowing that only Anglo-French solidarity could make the Germans come to their senses, he wanted to avoid unilateral action. Mounting French budgetary deficits and Germany's current failure to disarm to the required levels made a unilateral military solution unwise. But the British and French could not agree upon an acceptable solution.

Lloyd George, was more interested in sparking British recovery than with promoting French security.[12] He warned Poincaré that insistence on strict enforcement of the treaty of Versailles, and on the exclusion of Russia "with its vast resources" from the "comity of nations," was disturbing the peace of the world.[13] Lloyd George was coming to the conclusion that the real threat to European peace came less from Berlin than from Paris.

The lack of progress at Bayonne convinced Poincaré that it would be unwise to attend the Genoa conference. He had no desire to negotiate with the Germans and thought he could exert more influence if he stayed away.[14] He began to set the ground rules by insisting that the conference avoid any discussion of the Treaty of Versailles, either directly or indirectly.[15] He felt that it should advise "those countries which were in a bad financial situation," as part of an effort to "reestablish exchanges in Europe." Additionally, he placed importance in examining international commerce and finance to obtain "guarantees essential to small investors."[16] Poincaré told Lloyd George that the Germans were waiting for the day when he [Poincaré] would be swept from office and replaced by someone more conciliatory. Poincaré assumed that the German leaders would refuse to fulfill their treaty obligations no matter what the circumstances.

Europäisches Variété

Die unübertrefflichen Knockabouts George und Poincaré in ihrem phänomenalen Excentric-Akt „Die Fahrt nach Genua".

European Vaudeville. *The caption reads: "Those magnificent knockabouts Lloyd George and Poincaré perform their sensational oddball number "The Trip to Genoa." The cartoon appeared in* Simplicissimus, *the German satiric weekly, on 22 March 1922, before it was known that Poincaré would not be attending the conference. The Germans assumed a higher degree of Allied unity than was warranted, not to mention the even more preposterous implictation that Lloyd George would let himself be pushed around by Poincaré.*

GERMAN PRESIDENT Friedrich Ebert believed that his country, at least for the time being, should "practice a sincere, intelligent policy avoiding confrontation at all costs, fulfilling all its duties in respect to the treaties of peace."[17] He felt that time would work to Germany's advantage and increase the possibility of revision that was based "on the most indomitable of forces: economic necessity."[18] However, other German leaders were less willing than Ebert to wait for memories and hatreds to fade.

Colonel-General Hans von Seeckt, the head of the German army, was engaged in energetic violation of the military clauses of the Versailles treaty. He reincarnated the old General Staff, forbidden by Article 160, as the *Truppenamt* (troop division) of the Defense Ministry.[19] He reinstated the war academies and staff-training institutes, forbidden by Articles 176 and 177, under the guise of special courses in military history and general culture at German universities.[20] He expanded the number of officers and non-commissioned officers, which Article 160 limited to 4,000, by conferring the responsibilities of higher ranks on those with lower "official" titles.[21] He fleshed out the Reichswehr with its own reserve army, the so-called Black Reichswehr, matching the regular formations of the army almost unit for unit.

Furthermore, he attached various military groups to the Ministry of Interior, like the *Sicherheitspolizei* (special police detachments) whose personnel was recruited from officers and non-commissioned officers of the former army having known monarchist sympathies. And he gave military training to the *Einwohnerwehr* (home guard),[22] providing these organizations with guns and ammunition, stored in secret depots throughout the country.[23] Germans under arms also included: remnants of the para-military units of the Freikorps; various labor associations and labor detachments; temporary volunteers for the Reichswehr, trained and equipped just like the regular army; border guard units of the Customs Service; and all sorts of private armies, shooting guilds, and various protection squads from organizations on the extreme right, all sworn enemies of the Weimar Republic.[24] Then there were the game keepers, foresters, railroad guards, and rural constables, who, although hardly comparable to regular army effectives, had seen service in the First World War and still possessed legal permits to carry guns.

Seeckt also circumvented the Versailles restrictions on the size and production of armaments by secretly organizing a special weaponry and mobilization division responsible for amassing enough supplies to support a million-man army. Much of the civilian production could already be converted to wartime use: the tractor industry formed the basis for the production of tanks, and civilian cargo planes were designed with the idea of conversion to military transport use. The Versailles treaty had failed to mention rocketry, whose development now received top priority. The German army also established a series of holding companies in foreign countries for the production of ships, guns, submarines, and airplanes. One of the most important of such arrangements was made with Soviet Russia.[25]

In the summer of 1921, circumstances of the Russo-Polish war encouraged renewed German-Soviet diplomatic relations. When it looked as if the Red army might capture Warsaw and sweep all the way to the German frontier, Seeckt advocated the signature of a treaty of alliance between the two countries.[26] He argued that such cooperation was the best way to reduce the Soviet threat should the Poles be defeated.[27] Seeckt found the continued existence of Poland incompatible with German survival and favored an eventual partition of the country.[28] He wrote:

> The re-establishment of the broad common frontier between Russia and Germany is a precondition for the regaining of strength of both countries.[29]

He welcomed the extension of Soviet power because he believed it could also be used as a lever in forcing the Allies to allow German rearmament as part of an overall policy of the containment of communism.[30] However, the Poles rallied and succeeded in driving the Red Army back to the east. Ironically, the Polish victory worked to Seeckt's advantage.

Following the retreat, Lenin turned to the Germans for help in reorganizing his military forces. Seeckt planned to cooperate with Lenin through a special Reichswehr unit originally established to work with the Soviet General Staff had the Red Army been victorious. Along with a promise of military assistance, however, the Germans wanted a commercial agreement between German private industry and Soviet state industry, complete with the establishment of consular services and diplomatic missions. The Soviets would be expected to refrain from agitation and propaganda.[31]

German businessmen and industrialists became convinced they could do business with the Soviets. They were particularly impressed with the reliability of Leonid Krasin, the commissar for Foreign Trade, who had worked in Berlin for the Siemens-Schukert Company before the last war—Krasin later became the managing director of the company's St. Petersburg office. German firms began to establish joint trading companies to build factories in Russia.[32] Krupp, for example, began producing tractors near Rostov; Junkers, helped with 75 million gold mark advance from the German Treasury, built aircraft at Fili, near Moscow; a joint Russian-German firm manufactured poison gas at Trotsk in the Urals; and other companies turned out artillery shells at Tula and Petrograd.[33] The Company for Development of Trade Enterprises, established by the Soviet and German War Offices, handled military needs. The Soviets gave the Germans an opportunity to manufacture forbidden weaponry, while special tank and flying schools provided for the joint training of soldiers.

Seeckt believed the Moscow connection was crucial to strengthening the Reichswehr, maintaining the "will" of the country's national defense, and advancing Germany's agenda to revise its eastern frontiers. He boasted:

> when fate again summons the German people to arms—and this day will inevitably come again—then it shall find a people of men, not weaklings, who will powerfully grasp their trusted weapon.[34]

Lenin had no reservations about doing business with such capitalists as long as it strengthened the Soviet state. For helping in rebuilding their war industries, he promised to help the Germans crush the Poles.

Although many Weimar politicians rejoiced at the prospect of a defunct Poland, they were ignorant of the details of Seeckt's activities. Of those who had a good idea what was going on, many either approved or collaborated, few objected. In resisting the rigid French policy of treaty enforcement, they felt they were performing a sacred national duty.[35] However, such clandestine activity attracted men who were by nature disciples of old regime authoritarianism, unsympathetic to the free institutions of the Weimar Republic. In the face of the German violations, the French became more defensive and intransigent. This attitude marked their performance at the Genoa conference.[36]

THE GENOA CONFERENCE opened on 10 April 1922. Delegations came from every European state, the British Dominions, and from Japan. The United States had been invited, but refused, which further limited the meeting's chance of achieving any significant results.[37] Lloyd George hoped, however, that the presence of the Germans and the Soviets might partially offset American absence. In deference to the French, he had studiously refrained from any prior discussions on reparations with German Foreign Minister Walter Rathenau, but he had preliminary discussions with the Soviets[38] He was trying to make their presence more palatable to the French by getting the communists to agree to repay the tsarist debts and to abstain from all propaganda, subversion, and aggression.[39] But they refused.

Communist dictator Vladimir Lenin welcomed the Genoa conference as a means of establishing the legitimacy of the Soviet regime, but decided against attendance. He had not been abroad since the Bolsheviks had seized power, and his declining health limited his movements. He complained of headaches and dizziness, said he had no energy, and suffered from insomnia.[40] Since the first of the year, he spent most of his time at his dacha in the village of Gorki. But he returned to Moscow at the end of March to give the keynote address at the Eleventh Congress of the Communist Party. He asserted that the Soviets were going to Genoa as merchants for the purpose of getting the best trade deal.[41] They were not going to inaugurate a policy of coexistence.[42] Lenin suspected that the western capitalist countries might be setting the Communists up for a "new form of boycott," but he believed representation at the conference was worth the chance. The importance Lloyd George attached to Russian help in promoting European economic recovery gave the Soviets a strong bargaining position.[43]

The Soviet delegates had prepared for the conference by taking special classes in diplomatic behavior; and they surprised everybody by arriving at Genoa wearing top hats and cutaway coats. Heading the delegation was Georgi Chicherin, the commissar of foreign affairs— himself trained in the graces of the old tsarist diplomatic service. Chicherin was a relief from the stereotypical wild-eyed, slogan-spouting Bolshevik to which the West had grown disgusted. He appeared a man of reason and moderation. He gave his opening speech in perfect French and then showed off by repeating it in flawless English.[44] But his affable demeanor hid a hard underside; and his speech, written with Lenin's active participation, showed the limits of Communist cooperation.

Chicherin began by saying that the Communists believed in "the primordial necessity of peace," and that they were willing to recognize that states with "different systems of property and different political and economic forms" had a right to exist. (Few statesmen whose countries were subject to Comintern subversion tactics were going to take this seriously, least of all the French and the British.) He mentioned many tangible resources the Communists could contribute to the common good of Europe:

> to deliver to cultivation millions of acres of the most fertile land in the world," and "to grant forest concessions, mining concessions for coal and minerals of an infinite richesse.[45]

He predicted, temptingly, that Soviet exports to the West in raw materials, grain, and fuel would surpass those of the prewar era.

Chicherin warned, however, that the enjoyment of all these benefits depended on capitalist willingness to liquidate the past and to write off the debts of the tsarist regime. He said that before the Soviets were ready to throw open the infinite wealth of Siberia to others, there must be an international effort to redistribute the products of industry and commerce, beginning with a redistribution of the existing gold reserves "in the same proportion as before the war."[46] And the League of Nations should become

> a real league of peoples without any domination of some nations by others, and there should be a reduction in the size of national armies without which reconstruction [would be] impossible.[47]

Chicherin, saving the most controversial for last, insisted on general disarmament.

Louis Barthou, the head of the French delegation and Minister of Justice in Poincaré's cabinet, was clearly annoyed by all these conditions, which no doubt struck him as a prime example of Soviet perfidy. He warned that, if there were any discussion of disarmament at Genoa, it would be met "not only with a reservation and a protest, but with an absolute denial, definite, categorical, final and decisive."[48] Lloyd George put it more metaphorically. He said that the conference already had too heavy a cargo and, if more tonnage were put aboard, the boat would sink.

> There is rough weather in front, and an overloaded ship does not
> get very easily through the waves.... [We should] finish this
> voyage first, and go home with all the ship can carry from here.
> We shall welcome [Chicherin] on another voyage, when we see
> what sort of a passenger he is.[49]

Chicherin protested that he was here in a spirit of cooperation and
that he would discuss disarmament no further, "if the others were
opposed."[50] But the commissar continued to insist that the issue of
tsarist debts to the West had to be settled before there could be any
general discussion on European reconstruction. Moreover, in a private
meeting he had with Lloyd George at the villa d'Albertis, the prime
minister's residence, Chicherin added that the Allies should reimburse
the Russians for the damage caused during their period of armed
intervention.

This last demand eventually produced an agreement to cancel all
war debts mutually, but this concession did not prompt the Soviets to
compensate foreigners for the private property they had confiscated.
The British and French had wanted this property restored to its former
owners, or compensated in full. Chicherin only promised he was
willing to consider "leasing" the confiscated property back to the
former owners or offering them other concessions. Lloyd George,
eager to get something, proposed the Soviets extend the owners a 99-
year lease, but Louis Barthou insisted they get full restitution. Getting
the British and French to squabble about such details delighted
Chicherin, who was not interested in having the matter solved anyway.
He had come to Genoa for more important reasons.[51]

WALTER RATHENAU waited for an opportunity to join the
discussions. He had come to Genoa with some trumps.[52] Negotiations
had been going on between Germany and Communist Russia since the
beginning of the year, resulting in the drafting of an agreement, which
the Soviets were pressuring the Germans to sign. Chicherin had
stopped in Berlin before the conference, but Rathenau had put him off,
wanting to see what negotiations with the British and French might
produce. The foreign secretary's delay was unpopular among many of
his colleagues.

Ago von Maltzan, the recently appointed head of the Eastern
Department, argued that the Russian connection would give Germany

vital political leverage in dealing with the French. Supported by Chancellor Joseph Wirth and General von Seeckt, Maltzan pushed for the immediate conclusion of the agreement. He continued his lobbying at Genoa, playing on Rathenau's fears that the Soviets might turn the tables and make a deal with the British. He even threatened to resign if there were further delays. Rathenau finally gave in. On 16 April, Easter Sunday, he met Chicherin at the nearby resort of Rapallo.

Germany and Communist Russia agreed to renounce reparations and resume formal diplomatic relations. They undertook to promote trade with the mutual application of the most favored nation principle. Germany agreed to abandon claims to private property that had been nationalized, as long as the Soviets left the claims of other states unsatisfied.[53]   The treaty had no secret military clauses—such agreements between the Reichswehr and the Red Army already existed.

The Rapallo accord eroded the Anglo-French monopoly on continental politics, and moved Europe back towards a balance of power.   It hit the Genoa conference like a bombshell.   Barthou denounced it as a deceitful violation of the Treaty of Versailles and an abuse of the resolutions under which the present conference was convoked. He claimed that the Allies had the right to void any clauses in the agreement that ran counter to existing treaties and threatened to break off negotiations with the Germans and Russians unless they disavowed it.   The French were afraid that the Rapallo agreement would undermine all their efforts to get the Germans to obey the Treaty of Versailles and pose a dangerous threat to their alliances in eastern Europe.

Lloyd George described the arrangement as "a new grouping of Powers in Europe" with global implications.[54] He agreed to a formal note of protest, but he wanted to keep the Genoa conference together at all costs because if Russia and Germany were to leave, they would "leap into each others arms," two hundred million strong. He predicted that, unless the British and French tried to prevent the crystallization of this association, "in five years time the peace treaties would be imperiled and it would be impossible to enforce them." He reminded Barthou that, even if Germany were disarmed so that "there was not a pistol in the country," it could still rearm itself from Russia because Germany had the technical skill and Russia the raw materials. The prime minister begged Barthou to avoid referring the matter to Paris as he would only get instructions from those "who were not conversant with all the circumstances and had only heard one side."[55]

Lloyd George, struggling to keep the doors open for an agreement with the Communists, suggested that punitive measures be directed only against Germany, "guilty of an act of base treachery and perfidy, which was typical of German perfidy and stupidity."[56] But, tough words aside, Lloyd George wanted no retaliation. He thought that the best way to dissuade the Germans from establishing close ties with the Soviets was by continuing to practice his policy of appeasement.

He met with Rathenau on 19 April. It was the first time they talked privately. Lloyd George was defensive and almost contrite; he apologized for any "misunderstanding" that the allied protest note may have caused, and then tried to minimize the effect of the Rapallo agreement by saying that everybody could unfortunately make a mistake now and again. Why, the Germans probably did not realize what they were doing by going behind the backs of everybody at the conference, and that for the good of everyone, the best thing for the Germans and the Russians to do was to acknowledge that they had made a mistake and withdraw the treaty so everybody could get back to business. He tried to convince Rathenau that he was on Germany's side against France. Great Britain had always stood between Germany and France, and he was working very hard to bring France around to a reasonable point of view. "The French [are] not a particularly easy people to persuade," he remarked, especially with Poincaré as head of their government. It was extremely difficult keeping them "from going into the Ruhr," he said.[57]

Lloyd George's astonishing performance showed Rathenau how frayed the Anglo-French Entente had become, and he made the most of it. He agreed that it was too bad things had turned out the way they had, but, after all, he tried several times without success to speak with Lloyd George. He thanked Lloyd George for struggling so hard for German interests, asserting that he had admired the prime minister's style ever since the conference at Cannes, which had been spoiled by the French. However, he had returned to Berlin telling himself, "Help is here, there is no need for me to despair."[58] It was getting a bit thick, but Rathenau continued pouring it on.

He said he was "disappointed" that reparations had been left off the agenda, as Germany hated being constantly asked for gold. This was most unfortunate, because, Rathenau claimed, Germany was on the brink of a great revolution, neither a Bolshevik nor a monarchist revolution, but one that would nonetheless break the country in pieces. Of course, he said, in a clear reference to France, there are those who thought it was all right that Germany be broken up and the Ruhr occupied. He knew that Lloyd George, by contrast, wanted Germany to recover, but recovery was impossible as long as Germany was being told what to do by outsiders, by those on the Conference of Ambassadors, the Reparation Commission, the Disarmament Commission, and the Supreme Council. Germany was being killed physically and morally.

Rathenau finished his scolding, but not before warning Lloyd George that, if German grievances remained unsatisfied, he would have to go home. The Germans would be "a very poor people, but they would remain honest." However, he promised to stay, if a formula could be found for restoring his country's economic life.[59]

What is your formula? the prime minister asked eagerly, searching for anything that would save his conference.

That the Allies would do what is vital for Germany, Rathenau answered vaguely.

While Lloyd George was engaged in his humiliating effort of damage control, Poincaré made a speech in his *ville natale* of Bar-le-Duc. The premier warned that he would send French troops into the Ruhr, if the Germans again defaulted in their reparations payments.[60] He said that he was willing to discuss sanctions with his allies, but he insisted that France, if need be, would go it alone. He based his authority on the Treaty of Versailles.[61] If French interests were not respected, Poincaré threatened to withdraw the French representatives and kill the conference.[62]

In fact, the conference was already dead. Discussions still continued, but there was little hope of anything beyond words. The French insisted that the Communists recognize their claims for confiscated private property and called upon the British for support.[63] Barthou struck to his instructions and obstinately refused to discuss reparations.[64] But no true European recovery was possible without resolving this critical problem.

The conference finally, and officially, ended on 19 May. Its last act was to issue a declaration in which the high contracting parties promised to refrain from any act of aggression against the territorial integrity of another and pledged, in case of violation, to resort to any organization which may be available for the discussion, consideration and adjustment by peaceful means of the dispute out of which the act of aggression arose.[65]

This was a far cry from Lloyd George's grand design and hardly adequate for the security needs of the French. Poincaré agreed to give it French endorsement only because it was so innocuous and would not, he felt, endanger the Treaty of Versailles. He still feared that to compromise any article of that treaty would prompt the Germans into claiming that all "the others have by the same token been implicitly abrogated or become a matter for discussion."[66] He had feared that the Genoa conference would only give the Germans an opportunity to thumb their noses at the West and allow the Soviets to use it for their own political advantage. Poincaré thought Lloyd George would have been better advised to follow the French lead in demanding respect for treaties, rather than persisting in a forlorn hope for a better world.[67]

The collapse of the conference was a personal defeat for Lloyd George. But some would say that he brought it on himself. He had been unable to establish significant rapport with the head of any of France's postwar governments except Briand. He had antagonized all the others: Clemenceau, Poincaré, Millerand.[68] Even Foreign Secretary Curzon found the prime minister's deep antipathy for Poincaré excessive. Lloyd George had achieved none of his goals. He had failed to satisfy the French desire for security, to attenuate the German desire for revisionism, to promote economic cooperation with the Soviet Union, and to foster European reconstruction.

Many Conservative Party leaders, upon whom Lloyd George depended to maintain the integrity of his coalition, never believed that the conference would amount to much and were not displeased or surprised when it failed. Lord Northcliffe, owner of the influential *Daily Mail*, sent a reporter down to Victoria Station to see how the crowd received Lloyd George on his return home. Northcliffe had given instructions to his editorial staff to avoid attacking Lloyd George because, "there's no need. He is going downhill fast enough without it."[69] And Curzon remarked cuttingly that the "situation was ill-adapted for the exercise of the Prime Minister's special gifts."[70]

Rathenau had ample reason to be satisfied. He would have preferred taking home an agreement with the British, but signing the Treaty of Rapallo was compensation enough, and it was now clear to many Germans that their country was again becoming a significant presence in international politics.[71] However, some discounted the importance of the Soviet connection, fearing it might give a dangerous boost to the forces of revolution.[72] Furthermore, Rathenau was generally unpopular. He was wealthy, he was Jewish, he had failed to stand up to the French. Gone were the memories of his great patriotism during the early days of World War I, when his efforts to mobilize the country's economy saved it from collapse. Rathenau's enemies denounced him, overlooking that his limited policy of fulfillment was necessary to keep the French from sending their troops into the Ruhr.

Rathenau believed that economic stability would be reestablished with the return of mutual confidence, and this could only occur when mankind was living in real peace. He sadly remarked:

> Unfortunately in many countries public opinion is not yet demobilized. The after-effects of war propaganda have not yet disappeared, and they still render the atmosphere heavy.... The world is still far from having recognized that an impoverished debtor needs to be treated kindly, and that he becomes incapable of payment if his last resource—his credit—is destroyed.[73]

On 24 June, some rightist extremists shot him to death.

The Treaty of Rapallo did not throw the Germans into the hands of the Soviets,[74] but it did expand trade.[75] Military deals, drafted before, were now finalized. The Soviets granted the German requests for bases for panzer and gas-warfare units, and they put facilities for training and the testing of weaponry at their disposal. There was special agreement for the manufacture of poison gas.[76] The deal between Junkers-Werke and the Soviet Air Ministry laid the groundwork for development of the modern German and Soviet Air Forces.[77] The German desire for revision of the Treaty of Versailles remained as strong as ever, as did the French commitment to integral enforcement. As long as this continued, there seemed little hope in laying to rest the Great War tensions. As long the national interests of the major European powers were in such opposition, the kind of international cooperation Lloyd George was trying to nurture was the stuff that dreams were made on.

Notes and Sources:

1. *Ministère des Affaires Étrangères,* série Y, volume 21 (Conférence de Cannes), session 8, 9. This body had two representatives each from Britain, France, Italy, Belgium, and Japan. Other countries could be added to the consortium later, but the initial five would get things organized and to this end contribute 10,000 pounds each. The five would conduct a preliminary investigation and report their findings to the Genoa conference.

2. *Ibid.,* Session 10, 3.

3. *Ibid.,* Session 10, 2.

4. *Ibid.,* Session 8, 5.

5. *Ibid.,* Session 5, 6.

6. *Ibid.,* Vol. 21, Annex 1.

7. Berthelot was waiting the outcome of an investigation of the charge that he had used his influence to shore up the Banque Industrielle de Chine of which his brother was managing director. Poincaré continued to perform the duties of the secretary-general until his resignation on 1 June 1924. Gordon Craig and Felix Gilbert, eds., *The Diplomats 1919-1939,* 70.

8. Lord Curzon to August St. Aulaire, the French ambassador to Britain. Auguste de Saint-Aulaire, *Confession d'un vieux diplomate,* 612-3. Curzon smugly believed Poincaré's policy was frozen and rigid, while his own was "more supple, extensive, and dynamic." *Ibid.,* 615.

9. *Documents on British Foreign Policy,* first series, XIX, 300.

10. *Ibid.,* 173.

11. Richard B. Day, *Leon Trotsky and the Politics of Economic Isolation* (New York: Cambridge University Press, 1973).

12. Re: Derek H. Aldcroft, *The Inter-War Economy: Britain, 1919-1939* (New York: Columbia University Press, 1970), and Michael G. Fry, *Lloyd George and Foreign Policy* (McGill: Queens University Press, 1977).

13. *Documents on British Foreign Policy,* first series, XIX, 171.

14. Various committees were established to handle specialized questions of commerce, transportation, and finance, but overall policy making responsibility lay in the powerful First Commission, the agency of great power control. The Germans were not represented on the First Commission.

15. *Documents on British Foreign Policy,* first series, XIX, 170.

16. *Ibid.,* 301.

17. *Ministère des Affaires Étrangères,* série Z (Europe 1918-1929), Vol. 228 (Allemagne), 17.

18. *Ibid.,* 18.

19. Walter Goerlitz, *History of the German General Staff 1657-1945* (New York: Praeger, 1959), 218.

20. *Ministère des Affaires Étrangères*, série Z, Vol. 130 (Allemagne), 198-200, 211-3, 227-242.

21. At one point the NCOs comprised almost half of those in the ranks. Junior officers frequently held the official" rank of sergeant, while those with the rank of private and corporal were, in terms of their responsibilities and training, in fact sergeants. *Ibid.*, 213-9.

22. *Ibid.*, 267-9, 341-4.

23. Francis Carsten, *The Reichswehr and Politics 1919-1933* (London: Oxford University Press, 1966), 147-52 and Benoist-Méchin, *Histoire de l'armée allemande* (Paris: Albin Michel, 1964), II, 142-159.

24. James M. Diehl, *Paramilitary Politics in Weimar Germany* (Bloomington: Indiana University Press, 1977).

25. Documents taken from a German plane, which made a forced landing in Lithuania, on 16 October 1919, revealed that the German War Ministry was angling to build a factory in Russia for the production of a new advanced type of Junkers monoplane. *Documents on British Foreign Policy*, first series, II, 44-7.

26. Edward H. Carr, *German-Soviet Relations Between the Two World Wars, 1919-1939* (Baltimore: Johns Hopkins Press, 1951) and Lionel Kochan, *Russia and the Weimar Republic* (Cambridge: Bowes and Bowes, 1954).

27. Gerald Freund, *Unholy Alliance, Russian-German Relations from the Treaty of Brest-Litovsk to the Treaty of Berlin* (New York: Harcourt, Brace and Co., 1957), 69.

28. Francis Carsten, *The Reichswehr and Politics 1919-1933*, 99.

29. *Ibid.*, 140.

30. Hans Von Seeckt, *Deutschland zwischen West und Ost* (Hamburg: Hanseatische Verlaganstalt, 1933) and *Gedanken eines Soldaten* (Berlin: Verlag für Kulturpolitik, 1929).

31. The terms of this arrangement were worked out in March and April 1921. Gerald Freund, *Unholy Alliance, Russian-German Relations from the Treaty of Brest-Litovsk to the Treaty of Berlin*, 87-8.

32. The first between the Soviet trade ministry and the Hamburg-Amerika Line handled all future cargo transport. Similar arrangements followed to handle air traffic, the import and export of iron and steel, and scrap metal.

33. Edward L. Homze, *Arming the Luftwaffe, The Reich Air Ministry and the German Aircraft Industry* (Lincoln: University of Nebraska Press, 1976), 9-10.

34. Harold J. Gordon, *The Reichswehr and the German Republic 1919-1926* (Princeton: Princeton University Press, 1957), 298.

35. Keith W. Bird, *Weimar, The German Naval Officers Corps and the Rise of National Socialism* (Amsterdam: B. R. Grüner, 1977) and Gordon Craig, *The Politics of the Prussian Army, 1640-1945* (New York: Oxford University Press, 1964).

36. *Ministère des Affaires Étrangères.* série Z, Vol. 130 (Allemagne), 311-6.

37. Re: J. Saxon Mills, *The Genoa Conference* (London: Hutchinson, 1923).

38. The conference established a special sub-committee on Russian affairs to handle questions about diplomatic recognition, war debts, indemnification for confiscated property, foreign credits, and trade.

39. Gerald Freund, *Unholy Alliance, Russian-German Relations from the Treaty of Brest-Litovsk to the Treaty of Berlin*, 8. See also: *Documents on British Foreign Policy*, first series, XIX, 24.

40. David Shub, *Lenin*, 179.

41. Vladimir Lenin, *Collected Works*, Vol. 33, 213.

42. Ivo Lapenna, "Lenin, Law and Legality" in Leonard Shapiro and Peter Reddaway, eds., *Lenin: The Man, the Theorist, the Leader* (New York: Praeger, 1967), 251.

43. Jane Degras, ed., *Soviet Documents*, I, 293.

44. Louis Fischer, *The Life of Lenin* (New York: Harper and Row, 1964), 570-3.

45. *Documents on British Foreign Policy*, first series, XIX, 349.

46. *Ibid.*, 350-1.

47. *Ibid.*, 350.

48. *Ibid.*, 352.

49. *Ibid.*, 355.

50. *Ibid.*, 353.

51. Gerald Freund, *Unholy Alliance, Russian-German Relations from the Treaty of Brest-Litovsk to the Treaty of Berlin*, 114.

52. David Felix, *Walter Rathenau and the Weimar Republic* (Baltimore: The Johns Hopkins Press: 1971), 138-42.

53. *Command Documents.* 1667, 1922, 51.

54. *Documents on British Foreign Policy*, first series, XIX, 427.

55. *Ibid.*, 428-32.

56. *Ibid.*, 445.

57. *Ibid.*, 452-4.

58. *Ibid.*, 453.

59. *Ibid.*, 456-7.

60. Anthony James Nicholls, *Weimar and the Rise of Hitler* (New York: St. Martin's Press, 1968), 81.

61. He based this authority on Annex II to Part VIII (Reparation), paragraph 18. *Documents on British Foreign Policy*, first series, XX, 40-1.

62. *The* (London) *Times*, 25 April 1922, 11.

63. *Ministère des Affaires Étrangères*, série Y, Vol. 32, 174-5.

64. *Ibid.*, 217.

65. *Documents on British Foreign Policy*, first series, XIX, 571.

66. *Ministère des Affaires Étrangères*, série Y, Vol 32 (Conférence de Cannes), 176.

67. *Ibid.*, 216.

68. For example, when Millerand decided to leave the Spa conference and return home to take part in a patriotic celebration, Lloyd George quipped that he would go home and tell the "British Parliament that the work had not been completed because M. Millerand had not been prepared to miss the applause of his fellow countrymen at a fete." Millerand did not find the joke amusing and never trusted Lloyd George again. Lord Riddell, 243.

69. Stephen Koss, *The Rise and Fall of the Political Press in Britain* (Chapel Hill: The University of North Carolina Press, 1984), II, 404-5.

70. *Documents on British Foreign Policy*, first series, XIX, x.

71. Koppel Pinson, *Modern Germany, Its History and Civilization* (New York: Macmillan, 1966), 341.

72. Viscount D'Abernon, *Versailles to Rapallo, The Diary of an Ambassador* (New York: Doubleday, Doran and Co., 1929), 315-6.

73. *Documents on British Foreign Policy*, first series, XIX, 1013-4.

74. Viscount D'Abernon, *Versailles to Rapallo, The Diary of an Ambassador*, 324.

75. Exports to Russia increased from 73 million marks in 1923 to 330 million marks four years later, and imports rose from 92 million marks to 433 million by 1927. *European Historical Statistics*, 527.

76. Xena J. Eudin and Harold H. Fisher, *Soviet Russia and the West, 1920-1927* (Stanford: Stanford University Press, 1957), 207-8.

77. The first plane produced at the Fili factory was a two-seat, low-wing monoplane, designated by the Russians as the Yu 20. This was a reconnaissance model, but became the prototype for a fighter having two fixed forward-firing machine-guns and two movable guns mounted on a ring in the second cockpit. Also produced was the H-21, a parasol-winged monoplane, mounting two forward-firing synchronized machine guns, firing forward, and a ring mounted machine gun in the rear cockpit. The plane carried a light bomb load. About a hundred of these were produced and entered service with the Soviet air force in 1924-5. Some saw action against the rebels in Turkestan. The Soviets got a heavier bomber in the Junkers R-42, capable of carrying a payload of 2,205 to 2,645 pounds. A squadron of these planes entered service in the winter of 1925 and formed the nucleus of the Soviet heavy bomber force. John W. R. Taylor, ed., *Combat Aircraft of the World* (New York: Paragon Book, 1969), 175, 576-7.

_____

SOMEBODY HAS TO PAY

FRANCE HAD COME to regard reparations as a main continuing source for funding national reconstruction. This was not the way it was supposed to be. Clemenceau had envisaged the enormous difficulty of getting the Germans to pay over an extended period and had been willing to reduce the total amount.[1] He set it between 124 billion marks and 188 billion marks—a more manageable and collectable spread that could easily be adjusted to the 100 to 140 billion mark range the Americans had proposed[2] Clemenceau hoped to mobilize as much of this as possible through the sale of bonds on the New York market. Thus France would get its money immediately, when its needs were greatest, and there would be much fewer worries over collection.

The British, with their demand of 220 billion marks, held out for the highest amount of reparations. Lloyd George felt that large indemnities would put him in a stronger position for future negotiations, but he also sincerely believed that Germany should pay dearly for the damage it had caused. His strong religious upbringing—instilled in him by his foster father and uncle Richard Lloyd, a minister of the Disciples of Christ—taught him that those who smash the lives of others should be held accountable. In such moral matters, he still remained the lad from Criccieth—the northern Welsh village of his youth, and, later, place of his burial—"who had stepped indignant out of the path of the local Tory magnate driving his four-in-hand, and revenged himself at night on the magnate's rabbits."[3] On the other hand, a desire to appear compassionate and politically wise prompted Lloyd George to avoid appearing too punitive. He wanted it both ways: a stern peace, but a kind peace: "the occasion demands it [and the] crime demands it. But its severity must be designed, not to gratify vengeance, but to vindicate justice."[4]

This sense of justice, however, did not make the British eager to help underwrite French recovery. Nor, for that matter, did it prompt the United States to do so. The Americans also rejected the French scheme to commercialize reparations debts on the New York market. They saw no reason to participate in a back-door scheme of foreign aid, nor did they welcome having American investors left holding the bag should the Germans default.[5] Moreover, both Britain and the United States proceeded rapidly to dismantle their war-time controls further removing the state from direct involvement in the recovery process.[6]

Clemenceau, Lloyd George, and Wilson failed to reach an agreement on reparations at the Paris conference, so they created a reparation commission to set Germany's final debt. This temporarily defused the issue with the public, but kept all options open. To cover up their lack of consensus, the Allies had crafted the strong, needlessly provocative, statement on Germany's moral responsibility in Article 231 and brushed aside Germany's protest against signing the treaty before exact reparations were determined.[7] The Germans also disputed their burden of war pensions and veterans' separation allowances. Pending the report of the Reparation Commission, the Allies stipulated that the Germans pay five billion dollars in gold (or an equivalent), reimburse the costs of occupation, and accord allied countries most favored nation treatment for five years without reciprocity.

The French disapproved large capital transfers; they wanted to avoid repeating the experience that had followed the Franco-Prussian war, when their own payments had created runaway inflation in Germany. The French also opposed receiving German finished goods as this could cheapen the German mark, flood world markets with German goods, and over-stimulate German, at the expense of French, industry. They estimated that the best reparations should come in direct transfers of raw materials, particularly coal. Such supplies would be insufficient to satisfy all the French claims, however, and monetary transfers therefore became inevitable.

The Germans were reluctant to pay reparations in any form; and, during the first year, they made only token outlays, such as dye-stuffs, coal, and livestock. Their foot dragging prompted the Supreme Council to charge Germany with default and order them to send representatives to Spa, Belgium, to explain the delinquency. This conference was the first time in six months that the Germans met with representatives of the allied governments following the ratification of the Treaty of Versailles and the official resumption of diplomatic relations. To forestall allied retaliation, the German delegates appeared cooperative. At the opening session on 5 July 1920, Konstantine von Fehrenbach assured the Allies,

> The German government and the people [have] always been, and [will] continue to be, motivated by a firm desire loyally to execute the treaty, and they [wish] to prove it by their actions.[8]

This same Fehrenbach had once sworn to kill himself like a Roman hero rather than approve the signing of the Treaty of Versailles.[9]

But the German government was prepared to cooperate only to hasten the restoration of full national sovereignty. Industrialist Hugo Stinnes spoke for many when he observed that the Allies were "sick beyond recovery with the disease of victory."[10] The Germans, in fact, were, determined to hand over no more raw materials, and they conveyed a bleak picture of national economic collapse and political confusion. They claimed that the value of past deliveries had already exceeded the initial payment of five billion dollars. They demanded a moratorium on the payment of reparations for at least a year and said that the current danger from insurrection prevented them from further reducing their armed forces, whose size or exact strength exceeded their capacity to estimate.[11] The tactic reinforced allied divisions.

Lloyd George argued that the Germans should be given more time before tightening the screws. He said that one should realize "that Germany had passed through two separate revolutions, one from the right, one from the left," and it was best to give "the new government a chance."[12] But Alexandre Millerand maintained that any concessions would only encourage the Germans to further procrastination and defiance. He maintained that the Germans thought that "that the treaty was too hard and did not wish to apply it and would not apply it."[13]

The Allies finally patched up their differences and demanded the delivery of two million tons of coal every month for the next six months. They also agreed to order the dissolution of the special security units and the home guard and have the Germans immediately surrender all arms and equipment in excess of the limits the treaty had specified. Germany would have until the end of the year to reduce the Reichswehr to 100,000 men.[14]

The Germans accepted the demands pertaining to the military clauses, but rejected those concerning reparations. They continued pleading insurmountable technical difficulties. Foreign Secretary Walter Simons said that the coal workers, whom nobody consulted, might refuse to work overtime. Besides, supplies of extra food were inadequate to maintain their energy.[15] Simons added that, if the coal deliveries could not be "squared with the economic situation in Germany, the miners would complain they were being asked to work under conditions of slavery and they would revolt."[16]

The exasperated French demanded that the Germans be forced to see reason. Marshal Foch advised sending troops into the Ruhr and claimed he could get the job done with seven divisions. He explained that this would be accomplished by avoiding the urban areas and occupying the rural areas to control the supplies of food. Lloyd George reluctantly agreed it was necessary to get tough—he realized the tremendous pressure the French leaders were under to make Germany pay—but he insisted that all the Allies be partners to the venture, including the United States, even if sent only one battalion. Furthermore, the operation should be handled in such a way that it "would appeal to every-fair minded man...even in Germany." Lloyd George also specified that the troops be withdrawn as soon as Germany had carried out the allied demands, and he warned that no black troops should be used as there was no use in irritating the Germans unnecessarily. He knew how the British "should have felt if we had been the beaten party and the Germans had occupied Great Britain with troops from the Cameroons."[17]

Lloyd George feared that the use of military force would be self-defeating and cost more than the amount of reparations received, and he was happy when just the threat of invasion proved sufficient to get the Germans to accept the Allies' demands. The episode, though, clearly showed that the Germans would only pay if they faced sanctions.

LLOYD GEORGE looked forward to the departure of the hard-liners from the French government to allow room for his policy of reconciliation. Even the so-called moderates, like Aristide Briand, were reluctant, however, to give the Germans the benefit of much doubt. When Lloyd George insisted that the British people had to be convinced that the use of force would "commend itself to reasonable men as fair and practicable, without offending a great people or keeping it in servitude for forty or fifty years," Briand replied that he was unsure that Germany would live up to its obligations unless forced to do so.[18]

Lloyd George was caught in the middle. He wanted to appease Germany, so Germany could recover and the British could cure their unemployment, but none of this was possible without French cooperation. The French believed that they were within their rights to extend their control to the unoccupied parts of the Rhineland, if Germany refused to honor the Reparation Commission's schedule of payments.[19] Furthermore, they felt they were within their rights to deal directly with the Rhineland industrialists.[20] The fear that such action could squeeze out British interests was added incentive for Lloyd George to allow the French leeway in prodding the Germans.

In March 1921, when the Reparation Commission held Germany in default of three billion dollars, the British prime minister agreed that French troops could occupy and seal off the Rhineland ports of Düsseldorf, Ruhrort, and Duisburg and levy a special tax on all German exports to allied countries. Germany protested to the League of Nations and appealed to the Americans to mediate. But the Americans refused to become involved in a dispute to enforce a treaty they had not ratified. Furthermore, even had they shown interest, the French and British still ran the show at the League of Nations.

The following April, the Reparation Commission made its long-awaited report on Germany's total obligation. The sum of 132 billion gold marks (33 billion dollars) was based upon an estimate of what the allied nations thought was acceptable and attenuated in part by what they thought was collectible. (The Spa conference had already set each country's "Rheingold" share with France getting 52 percent, Great Britain 22 percent, Italy 10 percent, Belgium 8 percent, and Serbia 5 percent. Romania, Japan, Portugal, and Greece divided the remaining 3 percent.) Since most of the reparations that Germany had already paid were figured as occupation costs, the country's indebtedness remained virtually unchanged.

At a conference in London, during the first week of May, the Allies decided that reparations should be paid annually in a fixed amount of two billion marks and in a variable amount that was 26 percent of the value of German exports. Germany would set aside the revenues from customs duties, monies from special tax funds, and the taxes from a 25 percent levy on exports. Germany's obligation would end only when the Reparation Commission was satisfied that the debt had been acquitted in full. This open-ended arrangement seemed like Hercules' race with the turtle—no matter how hard the Germans ran, they could never come out ahead.

The 33 billion dollar amount, however, was not chiseled in granite. Germany could acquit its obligation with three kinds of bonds: A, B, and C. The first two issues, which totaled 12.5 billion dollars, were interest-bearing and would be liquidated first over a 36-year period. The last series, which contained the rest of the debt, was a no-interest issue and would be offered for sale only after the other two had been amortized.[21] It seemed unlikely that the last series would ever be issued. So, in fact, 20.5 billion dollars of Germany's debt was virtually written off. The "London Schedule" required the Germans to pay only about seven percent of their national income in reparations, a sum believed to lay comfortably within the country's means.[22]

From the German point of view, any amount was excessive. Politicians who sincerely advocated a policy of fulfillment were as rare as French politicians who renounced reparations. The Germans worked to exploit Anglo-French disagreements; but, for the moment, it appeared Lloyd George was willing to allow France continued latitude in enforcing the Treaty of Versailles—as long as France refrained from unduly bullying or kicking Germany in the process. He also supported the London Conference schedule of reparations, which the Germans considered too harsh.

During the early days of the Weimar republic, any German politician who advocated a policy of fulfillment was in danger of physical harm. Right-wing terrorist organizations were looking for such excuses to eliminate their enemies. Matthias Erzberger, a member of the Center party and former foreign minister, was gunned down on 26 August 1921. Erzberger had headed the German armistice delegation and had reputedly favored a less confrontational foreign policy. Many Germans reacted to his death with "shameless glee".[23] Furthermore, German political parties were so much at each other's throats that it was impossible for the Reichstag to formulate a plan for stabilizing the economy, a prerequisite for paying reparations.[24]

The Socialists advocated confiscating 20 percent of the nation's private property. They proposed that business taxes be capitalized for the next forty years and that Germany's leading companies be nationalized.[25] The Socialists did not advocate a policy of fulfillment, but they wanted to insure that the working classes did not bear the brunt of reparations payments. Sir John Bradbury, the British representative on the Reparation Commission, applauded this sense of fair play. He opposed making any concessions "without making the industrialists bleed."[26]

Germany's conservative parties, however, had no special concern for the working classes. They used their opposition to reparations to score political points against their leftist opponents and to repair their own ranks, which had been tattered by the defeat and buffeted by the revolutionary forces that followed. Conservatives wanted to discard the albatross of the Hohenzollern monarchy and to consolidate their ranks through widespread denunciation of the "November criminals," a codeword for an attack against the Weimar system itself.[27] In this risky and volatile atmosphere, a realistic policy of compliance with the demands of the Allies was virtually out of the question. Small wonder that the German government authorized the deliveries of coal and paid the first monetary installment, under the London schedule of payments, only after the Allies threatened to invade the Ruhr.[28]

The Germans mobilized the necessary capital by collecting foreign currency through the sale of inflated paper marks, a practice that caused a drop in the value of the currency. For reasons already stated, a cheaper mark was not something the French desired. The Germans, however, seemed intent on taking such a step to prove how reparations were ruining their economy. The Germans might have paid from tax surpluses had they not been unwilling to tax themselves. They might also have paid through short-term loans, industrial loans, or through requisitioning a portion of the country's national wealth. The Germans, however, would have had to have created a surplus in their foreign exchange. Reaching the amount owed the Allies would mean a yearly trade surplus of 2.5 billion marks.[29] This would have led to a significant growth in German industry, which the French also opposed.

Currently, Germany had no budgetary nor trade surplus. Its exports fell below imports by 105 million marks a month.[30] In 1921, government expenditures were 298,766 billion marks and income was

149,570 billion marks.[31]   The government handled the deficit by
borrowing from itself: it took marks from the Reichsbank, reimbursing
these with promissory notes based only on an intent to repay.[32]

Der verföhnliche Briand und der verftockte Deutfche

„Seht ihn an — fpricht aus diefem Geficht der Geift der Verföhnung?!"

Conciliatory Briand and the Stubborn German. *That the Germans did not
take Briand's reputation for moderation seriously is revealed in this Wilhelm
Schulz cartoon, which appeared in* Simplicissimus *14 December 1921. Briand
shouts, "Look at him—does this face show a spirit of reconciliation?" Having
Afro-French soldiers hold down the chained German adds considerable bite to
the message.*

Meanwhile, the Germans continued to default in their reparation pay-ments. The Reparation Commission sent representatives to Berlin to find out the cause and suggest how the Germans could bring order to their finances. Finally, on 2 December 1921, the Commission ordered the Germans to take affirmative steps to meet their obligation by 15 January 1922, or face sanctions. The Germans protested that their finances were in worse shape than before. On 14 December 1921, they asked for a moratorium, but avoided mentioning what measures they were prepared to take to guarantee future payments. Constructive payment would have involved unthinkable sacrifices: a doubling of taxes and a 50 percent reduction of government expenditures. Nevertheless, they pretended they were willing to comply.[33] The Reparation Commission demanded the Germans answer three questions: How much would Germany pay? How long a delay was it necessary for Germany to pay in full? And what assurances could Germany give that it would pay at all?

The Germans avoided a direct response, but came to Paris to solicit approval for a moratorium. They said that any consideration of the substantive issues should wait pending discussion at an international conference. The Commission replied that the only questions that need trouble the Germans were the ones to which they had not responded. But the Germans again insisted that it would be useless to engage in such an exchange before the start of an international conference.[34] The Germans figured that time was on their side; the longer they delayed, the greater the division between the French and British.

THE FRENCH tried to avoid any discussion of reparations with the Germans because they felt that it would undermine allied resolve to force them to pay.[35] French determination to collect was more than psychological, but had been built into the way they had arranged their domestic finances. They had divided the state budget, like All Gaul, into three parts: a *budget ordinaire* for current expenses, a *budget extraordinaire* for expenses of an exceptional or emergency nature, and a *budget des dépenses récouverables* (budget for recoverable expenses) to pay for war pensions, interest on loans, and reconstruction costs.

The first two budgets were financed mainly from taxes and revenues, but the third budget was to be capitalized with reparation payments. In addition to reducing flexibility in foreign relations, this triple system of bookkeeping increased the difficulty of allocating funds for various projects. Monies might come from sub-divisions in all three accounts simultaneously.

The French army, for example, got funds from five main sources: (1) the ordinary budget paid for the normal maintenance of troops in metropolitan France, in North Africa, and in China; (2) the extraordinary budget covered those expenses resulting from hostilities, from the maintenance of troops in the Saar, from the costs of the Army of the Levant, and the Army of the Orient; (3) the recoverable expense budget was intended to support the French army's occupation in the Rhineland and, in the immediate years following the war, the troops in the plebiscite areas, such as Memel, Danzig, and Silesia; (4) a special security budget provided for the maintenance of domestic order in time of national emergency—that is, if the para-military gendarmerie and the *gardes républicaines*, paid out of the ordinary budget, needed assistance in maintaining domestic security; and (5) funds from the budget of the Ministry of Colonies supported the colonial forces.[36]

Despite its obvious confusion, the French viewed the system without alarm. Deficit spending and the use of financial expedients had been well-established since the founding of the Third Republic with politicians following several questionable precepts: never increase taxes; never raise money by taxes that cannot be borrowed; spend surpluses; and, let successors worry about the deficits. From 1870 until the First World War, revenues had covered expenditures in only twelve years, a little more than one-fourth of the time.[37] Borrowing had largely financed the First World War. In 1918, main tax yields covered only one-sixth of all expenditures, and this was also the case in the immediate postwar era. From 1919 to 1922, deficits usually ran around ten to twenty billion francs annually.[38]

A deep-seated fear of inflation kept the Bank of France from meeting expenses by expanding the supply of currency. From 1920 to 1923, French productivity increased by 77 percent, but the amount of money in circulation rose by only one percent.[39] This resulted in a depressed economy, but the virtual absence of unemployment (made possible by the wartime losses and the high needs of reconstruction for labor) spared France many social consequences. The French people believed that the situation would dramatically improve once the Germans came through with their share of reconstruction costs. For their leaders to assume otherwise was politically suicidal.[40]

Fiscal irresponsibility, therefore, continued. The regular budget continued to show a surplus, the reparations budget a deficit. The two together demonstrated a usual shortfall of 23 billion francs annually. Since the difference could be covered neither through borrowing nor increased taxation, the state obtained the goods and services it needed, and helped finance reconstruction by abandoning its caution and creating more money.

A policy of inflation was irresistible because of its anonymity. Whereas taxes took money away from people before they had a chance to spend it, printing money allowed spending to continue. People received the same amount of money; they just got less for it. Price increases were the policy's essence, not an unfortunate consequence. Costs had to rise if the government was to compete successfully with the private sector to get what it needed to repair the ravages of war. Since the state could "print" more new money faster than the private sector could earn it, governmental priorities could be effectively satisfied. Inflation became a permanent fixture of French life in the interwar years when the amount of money in circulation increased faster than the amount of goods and services. Since cheaper money helped promote economic expansion, the government pretended that the system worked to the national interest. But inflation spelt disaster for those on fixed incomes and for others of limited means. National bloc politicians generally blamed foreigners for the hardships.[41] At one time or another, the finger pointing might be directed at the militaristic Germans, the uncooperative British, or the money-grubbing Americans.

WAR DEBTS were closely linked to reparations: both came from the war and both caused a serious loss of purchasing power. Before American entry in the war, Britain had been the principal banker of the Allies, redeeming a large part of its overseas investment to buy armaments, principally from the United States. If Britain had been reimbursed for the money it had lent the other members of the entente, the sum would have been more than sufficient to pay back its obligations to the United States.

Britain had borrowed about six and a half billion from the United States, but had lent about eleven and a half billion to its other Allies. France had borrowed seven billion dollars from both Britain and the United States, but had re-lent about a half of that amount to other countries. About half of the British loans and about a third of the French loans had gone to the tsarist regime, whose Bolshevik successor refused repayment. On the other hand, almost all the American loans were floated directly with the British and the French. Britain regarded the debts that the Allies contracted in the common struggle subject to mutual cancellation. Lloyd George believed it was intolerable to set a price tag on the loss of life, and it was no less objectionable to treat the material assistance that one ally got from another to win the war as a business liability. Britain had spent most of its American credits in the United States, thereby contributing to the growth of American industry; and, during those years of neutrality, the Americans had gradually penetrated the world markets the British and French had abandoned.[42]

In order to balance their postwar budget, the British had reduced expenses and raised taxes, a deflationary move that caused an average annual unemployment of 10 percent (15 percent in 1921 and 1922).[43] The British government touted its policy of austerity, which demonstrated responsibility and moral superiority.[44] The same policy would have been catastrophic in France where national perfection was seen in other terms. Frenchmen were no more eager to pay taxes than were the dukes and archbishops on the eve of the Revolution, and any politician that thought otherwise was headed towards early retirement.[45]

The Americans refused to consider a connection between war debts and reparations and so demanded substantial reimbursement. The British hoped to nudge them into voluntarily canceling the war debts, thus breaking the deadlock over reparations.[46] At the beginning of 1922, the British said that they would require their debtors to pay only that amount of money necessary to pay off British creditors. They were even willing to renounce their entire share of reparations, if the whole body of inter-allied indebtedness were written off. Washington though remained obdurate and even made matters worse, increasing the difficulty of repayment by reducing foreign access to the American market when it raised tariffs beyond 30 percent ad valorem.

The Americans had come out of the war richer and more powerful than they went in. They produced forty percent of the world's industrial goods and their foreign trade had a yearly surplus of three to four billion dollars. Economically and politically, the U.S. had become the prime candidate for holder of the European balance of power. But the Americans lacked both the experience and the desire to act in that capacity. The United States remained the only country capable of providing the sort of lavish credit the Europeans needed to recover, but the Republican leaders in Washington believed that government should stay out of the foreign aid business. Prone to lecturing others on their responsibilities, they had no need to apologize when they demanded that the Europeans honor their war debts.

After all, the Americans had reluctantly joined a war started by others. Their intervention had been vital and had saved the British and French from certain defeat. Besides, the loans made to the Allies were at extremely favorable rates—about half the interest charged on the open market. The U.S. was now prepared to be generous in working out a repayment schedule. The World War Debt Funding Commission would allow the amortization spread over several generations, taking into account the debtors capacity to pay. The Americans felt that they were fair, but suspected the Europeans were looking for ways to take advantage of American generosity. They recalled that the French, for example, had once tried to charge Pershing's army rent for the use of practice trenches.

THE GERMAN AND SOVIET renunciation of reparations in the treaty of Rapallo in April 1922 made collection more difficult. Nonetheless, Poincaré continued to demand that the Germans pay what they owed. His insistence, backed by threats, prompted Berlin to agree, in July 1922, to hand over the next reparations installment of 50 million gold marks. But the Germans followed this by asking for another moratorium. Poincaré was displeased that the German treasury notes were backed only by promises, but he agreed to accept them until the end of the year.

The Germans continued to make payments-in-kind, but on a reduced basis, trying to strike a balance between how much they had to pay in order to keep the French from sending troops into the Ruhr with how much they needed in order to run their blast furnaces. Throughout 1922, they consistently failed to deliver their quotas of coal, and much of what they sent was of inferior quality. In August, the French turned back 63 percent of the deliveries with the result that, by December, almost half of the French blast furnaces were strained for fuel and had to be shut down.

The fight over reparations helped distract the German people from their domestic problems. Food shortages, unemployment, and fiscal chaos were all blamed on the French policy of enforcement.[47] German political rhetoric increased in stridency, even among the more moderate Social Democrats. At the party's congress in Görlitz in September 1922, Socialist leader Hermann Müller declared that the peace settlement was a peace of violence and that Germany was not solely responsible for having started the war.[48] He castigated the French for playing into the hands of nationalist agitators by making an alliance with Poland and by carrying out a repressive policy in the Rhineland. He specifically attacked the excesses of Moroccan troops occupation troops, which, he claimed, were terrorizing the local populations.[49]

The French denounced these socialist resolutions for playing into the hands of the nationalists and monarchists.[50] The French believed that all the agitation to revise the treaty and denounce the war guilt clause helped rehabilitate the old order and free Germany of the responsibility for having started the war.[51] Assigning blame, however, was not paying bills.

Poincaré had tried to arrange a Franco-German raw materials and marketing agreement, but the Germans insisted that the French first withdraw their troops from the Rhineland and from the Saar. He had tried to get the British to agree to a scheme to control German finances in order to keep the Germans from diverting funds away from reparation payments, but the British refused.[52] Many of his colleagues were urging him to abandon diplomacy and send troops into the Ruhr to force German compliance, but he feared that such a step would lead to the further estrangement of Great Britain, and put an enormous drain on the French treasury. He told President Millerand that he would rather resign than take such action.[53] He was boxed in.

If Poincaré wanted to safeguard his country's financial stability and keep his own position, he clearly had to do something: either get reparations, raise taxes, or obtain foreign loans—none of which seemed to promise success. France moved closer to a policy of force. Any other policy would allow Germany to default on reparations altogether and bring the entire Treaty of Versailles into disrepute. Somebody would pay for the war, the question was who. Poincaré saw nothing wrong with this being the Germans.[54] Neither did the legislature. The Chamber of Deputies refused to vote more taxes and more domestic borrowing unless "coercive measures were applied to Germany to ensure observance of her treaty obligation."[55] The cabinet agreed that the French army should invade the Ruhr if Germany be again declared in default.

In December 1922, the Germans failed to supply 23,560 cubic meters of lumber out of a required 55,000 cubic meters and 141,648 telephone poles out of a necessary 200,000. The Germans explained that a refusal of their contractors to accept inflated marks caused the shortages, and they promised rectify the situation by making future payments in gold. But Poincaré had endured too many such German assurances, and he obtained Italian and Belgian support to have the Reparation Commission declare Germany in default—the fourth time that it had done so. The threat of sanctions had accompanied each previous crisis, prompting a resolution through negotiations. The British tried to do so again.

The British called a meeting of the allied prime ministers in London, during the second week of December, and proposed that total reparations be reduced to fifty billion marks (12.5 billion dollars).[56] They again offered to cancel war debts, if the reparations the other Allies received from Germany would be used to cover their debts to the United States. But France insisted Germany meet all its obligations, otherwise France would send troops into the Ruhr, alone if need be.[57] British Prime Minister Andrew Bonar Law warned the French that using force against Germany would interfere with their recovery. A good point but one unlikely to sway Poincaré.[58] The premier's goals were political, and there was nothing contradictory about keeping Germany weak while trying to collect reparations at the same time. Poincaré would have preferred to accomplish this without sending troops into the Ruhr, but felt he had no other choice, once committed he did not look back.

Notes and Sources :

1. He first argued the French case for reparations before the Supreme Economic Council early in February 1919. This body, chaired by Étienne Clémentel, met first on 5 February 1918. It was originally called the Economic Drafting Committee, but changed to its permanent name three days later.

2. Marc Trachtenberg, *Reparation in World Politics* (New York: Columbia University Press, 1980), 63.

3. Winston Churchill, *Great Contemporaries* (New York: G.P. Putnam, 1937), 279.

4. *Hansard*, Commons, 16 April 1919.

5. Philip Mason Burnett, *Reparation at the Paris Peace Conference from the Standpoint of the American Delegation* (New York: Columbia University Press, 1940).

6. Bernard M. Baruch, *The Making of the Reparation and Economic Section of the Treaty* (New York: Harper, 1920).

7. Erich Eyck, *A History of the Weimar Republic* (Cambridge, Mass.: Harvard University Press, 1962-1863), 118.

8. *Documents on British Foreign Policy*, first series, VIII, 423.

9. Fehrenbach headed a government that came to power following the elections of 6 June 1920. The German voters had given a big boost to the rightist parties that strongly opposed a policy of fulfillment.

10. *Documents on British Foreign Policy*, first series, VIII, 52. See also: Peter Wulf, Hugo Stinnes: *Wirtschaft und Politik, 1918-1924* (Stuttgart: Klett-Cotta, 1979).

11. Colonel-General Hans von Seeckt estimated the current size of the Reichswehr at two hundred thousand men, omitting the *Sicherheitspolizei*, the *Einwohnerwehren*, and the gendarmerie. He confessed that much of Germany's military equipment was impossible to account for. This included about two million rifles, four thousand grenade launchers, 346 pieces of artillery, and a countless number of machine guns, which were either discarded, destroyed, or in the hands of "unauthorized persons". Seeckt guessed that most of the missing arms were in the private hands of opponents of the government and could only be retrieved by force. See: Claus Guske, *Das politische Denken des Generals von Seeckt: Ein Beitrag zur Diskussion des Verhältnisses Seeckt-Reichswehr-Republik* (Lübeck: Matthiesen Verlag, 1971).

12. *Documents on British Foreign Policy*, first series, VIII, 471.

13. *Ibid.*, 473.

14. *Ibid.*, 480-1.

15. The Germans had always depended heavily on food imports, but with the decline of their foreign exchange, due to the disruption of industry, the necessary credits were often lacking and general food shortages ensued.

16. *Documents on British Foreign Policy*, first series, VIII., 595.

17. *Ibid.*, 603.

18. *Documents on British Foreign Policy*, first series, vol. XV, 465.

19. Walter A. McDougall, *France's Rhineland Diplomacy, 1914-1924: the last bid for a balance of power in Europe* (Princeton, N.J.: Princeton University Press), 143-4.

20. Donald Graeme Boadle, *Winston Churchill and the German Question in British Foreign Policy, 1918-1922* (The Hague: Martinus Nijhoff, 1973).

21. Étienne Weil-Raynal, *Les réparations allemandes et la France*, vol. 1 (Paris: Nouvelles éditions latines, 1938), 640-59.

22. Étienne Mantoux, *The Carthaginian Peace or the Economic Consequences of Mr. Keynes* (London: Oxford University Press, 1946), 117-32.

23. Erich Eyck, *A History of the Weimar Republic*, 118.

24. Richard Breitman, *German Socialism and Weimar Democracy* (Chapel Hill, N.C.: University of North Carolina Press, 1981), 79-88.

25. David Felix, *Walter Rathenau and the Weimar Republic*, 31.

26. Charles S. Maier, *Recasting Bourgeois Europe* (Princeton, N. J.: Princeton University Press, 1975), 266-7.

27. Detlev J. K. Peukert, *The Weimar Republic, The Crisis of Classical Modernity* (New York: Hill and Wang: 1987), 66-77.

28. *Documents on British Foreign Policy*, first series, XV, 525.

29. *Ibid.*, 29.

30. Yearly imports 5,732 million marks, exports 4,464 million marks (est.). *European Historical Statistics*, 494.

31. *European Historical Statistics*, 700, 719.

32. David Felix, *Walter Rathenau and the Weimar Republic* (Baltimore: John Hopkins Press, 1971), 27-8.

33. *Ministère des Affaires Étrangères*, série Y, vol. 21 (Conférence de Cannes), session 11, 1.

34. *Ibid.*, 2-3.

35. *Documents on British Foreign Policy*, first series, XIX, 170.

36. *Ministère des Affaires Étrangères*, série Y, vol 504 (Internationale 1918-1940), 144-5.

37. *European Historical Statistics*, 698, 700, 710, 719.

38. 1919: 26.7 billion; 1920: 17.1 billion; 1921: 9.7 billion; 1922: 21.2 billion; 1923: 12.1 billion; 1924: 11.9 billion. *Ibid.*, 710, 719.

39. *Ibid.*, 356, 676.

40. Malcolm Anderson, *Conservative Politics in France* (London: Allen and Unwin, 1974), and Jean Touchard, *La gauche en France depuis 1900* (Paris: Seuil, 1977).

41. Michel Lescure, *Les banques, l'état et le marché immobilier en France à l'époque contemporaine, 1820-1940* (Paris: Éditions de l'École des Hautes Études en Sciences, 1982).

42. From 1914 to 1919, American exports rose from 2,532 million to 8,528 million. At the same time the excess of exports over imports climbed from 541 million to 4,457 million. *Historical Statistics of the United States* (Washington, D.C.: Department of Commerce, 1960), 537.

43. *European Historical Statistics*, 168.

44. *Ministère des Affaires Étrangères*, série Y, vol. 21 (Conférence de Cannes), session 1, 6-7.

45. See: Claude Billanger et al., eds., *Histoire générale de la presse française*, vol. 3, De 1871 à 1940 (Paris: Presses Universitaires de France, 1972).

46. See: Denise Artaud, *La question des dettes interalliés et la reconstruction de l'Europe, 1917-1929* (Paris: Librarie Honoré Champion, 1978).

47. Heinrich Bennecke, *Wirtschaftliche Depression und politischer Radikalismus* (Munich: Günter Olzog, 1970), 38.

48. *Ministère des Affaires Étrangères*, série Z, vol. 228 (Allemagne), 53.

49. *Ibid.*, 54-5.

50. Some of the major syndicates joined in a protest (12 December 1922) to the Allied Control Commission, i.e. the *Allegemeiner Deutscher Gewerkschaftsbund*, the *Deutscher Gewerkschaftsbund*, the *Gewerkschaftsbund Deutscher Arbeiter*, the *Allegemeiner Freier Angestelltenbund*, and the *Angestellten und Beamtenverbände*. Their petition said, in part: "The whole German population is convinced of the necessity of revision of the treaty of peace and of forming a bloc against the peace of violence...and the oppression coming from abroad." *Ibid.*, 144-5.

51. Memo of Pierre de Margerie, 12 Dec. 1922. *Ministère des Affaires Étrangères*, série Z, vol. 228 (Allemagne), 146-8.

52. *Documents on British Foreign Policy*, first series, XX, 68-80.

53. Steven A. Schuker, *The End of French Predominance in Europe, The Financial Crisis of 1924 and the Adoption of the Dawes Plan* (Chapel Hill: University of North Carolina Press, 1976), 21.

54. While the French government was deciding what sort of action to take against Germany, former premier Georges Clemenceau was visiting the United States. The "Tiger" was on a personal mission to "restore the relations we had in 1918." J. Hampden Jackson, *Clemenceau and Third Republic*

(New York: Collier Books, 1962), 159. Poincaré feared that Clemenceau's visit might worsen his relations with the American government and had refused to give it official sanction. Foch, Clemenceau's old adversary, remarked sarcastically, "He will cry and be sentimental like all old people." Clemenceau was then eighty-one; Foch was ten years younger. If Clemenceau shed any tears, they were tears of regret. Clemenceau made speeches in Chicago, Boston, Saint Louis, and New York. The president entertained him at the White House. In his speech on 21 November 1922 at the Metropolitan Opera House, Clemenceau said that, if he had known there would be no real reparation from Germany, "he would have insisted that Foch and Pershing go through to Berlin without pausing for an armistice." He begged the United States to become more involved in European affairs and help bring Britain and France together to combat the new danger of German militarism? Hamilton Fish Armstrong, *Peace and Counter Peace, From Wilson to Hitler* (New York: Harper, 1971) 203.

55. *Documents on British Foreign Policy*, first series, vol. XX, 317.

56. *Command Documents* 1812, 18-60.

57. *Documents on British Foreign Policy*, first series, XX, 316-7.

58. *Ibid.*, 73.

CHAPTER 6

TO GET SOME COAL

FRENCH TROOPS were on the move at daybreak and entered the Ruhr Valley before its inhabitants knew what was happening.[1] By two o'clock in the afternoon, 11 January 1923, the soldiers had occupied the center of Essen and established headquarters in the Kaiserhof Hotel. The army fanned out and in four days controlled the entire Ruhr basin. Poincaré, frustrated that France had gained so little despite four years of conferences, ultimatums, and moratoriums, was determined to keep the troops in the Ruhr until he got satisfaction.[2] He said he was just going to get some coal.[3] But he also wanted international reinforcement of French rights, new guarantees of French political and economic security, and help in solving many of the problems plaguing French industry.[4] The British immediately disassociated themselves from the French action, fearing French abuse of power more than German aggressiveness.[5]

American Secretary of State Charles Evans Hughes warned that such action would cause the United States to withdraw all its troops from Europe.[6] The Americans had been proposing to disengage themselves from the German occupation for some time, but the Ruhr invasion gave them a pretext.[7] Even though the United States had not signed the treaty of Versailles, the French dreaded an end to the American presence. U.S. participation in the occupation of Germany was added protection against German revisionism. The German government also viewed the American pull-out with apprehension. Prince Hatzfeldt, the Weimar Republic's liaison officer to the

American command, tried to get the Americans to stay, for like others he feared the French would fill the vacuum left behind.

On 24 January 1923, the stars and stripes descended over Fort Ehrenbreitstein in Coblenz for the last time, and the men of the Eighth Infantry marched down to the railway station and boarded trains for Antwerp and the voyage home. The Germans were unsuccessful in urging the disinterested British to take over the American zone.[8] So, three days after the Americans left, the French army assumed control of the American sector.

The British tried to solve the Ruhr crisis as quickly as possible. Curzon instructed Lord Kilmarnock, the British representative on the Rhineland Commission at Coblenz, to abstain from its decisions but continue to attend all meetings.[9] Curzon wanted to remain *au courant*, but he tried to avoid antagonizing Poincaré further. Despite their differences concerning Germany, Britain still needed French cooperation in negotiating a suitable revision of the Treaty of Sèvres, which had been signed with Turkey and was currently under review at a conference in Lausanne.

Curzon therefore made several conciliatory gestures: he refused to acknowledge German protests; he permitted the French to send their army into the Ruhr via the important railway center of Cologne, which was in the British zone of occupation; and he allowed French gendarmes to arrest German officials in the British zone, provided British military police accompanied them.[10] For these favors, Curzon insisted he be consulted on all matters, from running the railroads, to coal deliveries, to regulation of the activities of the police. And he made a special point of expressing his government's "great and growing anxiety" concerning the delays and losses to trade the French and Belgian control of German customs had caused.[11] Most importantly, he strongly opposed France's promotion of Rhineland separatist movements.[12]

Shortly after the occupation of the Ruhr, the Reichstag proclaimed a "national front" and insisted that there would be no negotiations until all the French and Belgian troops were gone. The Germans suspended all reparations payments, forbade their civil servants to take orders from the French, and recalled their ambassadors from Brussels and Paris. The coal syndicate in Essen, which supervised the Ruhr collieries, packed up its headquarters and archives and moved to Hamburg.[13] German passive resistance, which also spread to the areas under French occupation on the Left Bank of the Rhine, soon affected the entire industrial economy of western Germany, presenting France with a longer and more costly occupation than it had anticipated or desired. But the French refused to relax their pressure. French troops sealed off the entire area from the rest of Germany and empowered a *Mission interalliée de contrôle des usines et des mines* (Interallied control commission for factories and mines) to direct all political, legal, and economic affairs. Such control included the distribution of coal, the running of transportation, and the regulation of trade between the Rhineland and the rest of Germany.[14] The commission had the authority to confiscate German property, impose censorship, and establish martial law, which permitted firing-squad executions of convicted saboteurs. Any local official who refused to carry out its directives could be deported—a fate that nearly 150,000 bureaucrats, policemen, civil servants, industrialists, or other "trouble makers" ultimately suffered. On 25 February, the French army closed the Rhineland bridgeheads and restricted the movement of German civilians. The entire Ruhr, an area sixty miles long and 28 miles wide, was now separated from the rest of Germany. Not since the days of Napoleon had the French exercised such power over the Germans.

German passive resistance was never absolute. Though coal production declined, the mines never completely closed.[15] The directors of the Rhenish-Westphalian coal cartel, fearing a loss of revenue, rejected government offers of compensation and kept the pits open. The miners, though, refused to work directly for the French. They shoveled out the coal, brought it to the surface, but dumped it at the pit mouth for the foreign workers to haul away.[16]

In taking away the resources of the Ruhr, which supplied the rest of the country with almost three-fourths of its marketable raw materials, the invasion devastated the German economy. The French now controlled 85 percent of Germany's coal and 80 percent of its iron and steel. They expropriated raw materials and supplies, and collected taxes, customs, and excise duties. They refused to end their occupation until all resistance had ended. Poincaré believed that the Germans would honor their obligations only if he could convince them that they had indeed lost the war. He doubted the British could ever understood this simple truth. The Chamber of Deputies made a decided show of support by voting in favor of the venture, 488 to 68.

Not all Frenchmen shared Poincaré's confidence, however. These critics feared that his iron-fisted policy would drive the anti-Prussian Rhinelanders into the hands of the extreme nationalists. Édouard Herriot, leader of the Radical-Socialists, especially faulted Poincaré for isolating France from Great Britain. Socialist leader Léon Blum demanded that the League of Nations be allowed to settle the crisis.[17] These men were no lovers of the Germans, but they feared that the Ruhr invasion would make the Germans even less able to pay reparations, and they doubted whether France would even recover the costs of the occupation.[18] But such opposition had no significant support throughout the country.

Maintaining troops in the Ruhr began to get expensive—around 50 million francs a month, an amount that helped increase the budgetary deficit in 1923 by 20 percent.[19] Although this seemed in line with the deficits of previous years, the loss was especially damaging because Poincaré had led the French people to believe that the Ruhr occupation would cure, not compound, their financial problems. And the goal of exploiting the Ruhr's mineral resources to make France less dependent on imports did not materialize.

France never succeeded in decreasing its reliance on foreign supplies, especially coal, coke, and lignite— a continuing need that cut deeply into French financial reserves, shaking the value of the currency.[20] At the beginning of 1923, the franc was worth 5.1 to the dollar; at the end of the year, it was selling at 7.34 to the dollar, a 30-percent loss.[21]

The French people paid a heavy price for a fiscal system based on false hopes and expectations.[22] The government had kept taxes low, hoping that reparations would pay for the repair of the devastated regions. Because reparations were not forthcoming, this policy undermined finances and, ironically, weakened the French ability to enforce the Treaty of Versailles.[23] The invasion of the Ruhr satisfied a longing for retribution, but contributed to a growing public debt that reduced French solvency and affected the ability of the government to float loans. Moreover, even Poincaré knew that the amount of reparations that could have been collected, had the invasion achieved its purpose, were insufficient to put France's financial house in order.

The same day French troops entered the Ruhr, Poincaré introduced legislation for an across-the-board tax increase of 20 percent. He hoped the nationalist fervor produced by the Ruhr invasion would ease the bill's passage. The proposal was strongly criticized and had rough going, however. Its passage was postponed and, indeed, never brought to a vote. Poincaré had better luck in getting the Chamber to vote special credits to finance the invasion. The deputies might have been lacking in their knowledge of economics, but not literature and history. In the latter context Poincaré made his appeal. He said, in a speech before the Chamber of Deputies on 22 May:

> France has occupied the Ruhr as the Germans occupied a large part of France from 1870 to the end of 1873, in order to be paid. ...Let's have an end to these accusations and lies. We are the best friends of peace because peace would be an empty word the day when treaties can be violated with impunity before an indifferent world.[24]

He received a great ovation, the deputies voting 481 to 73 to reconfirm their earlier support. German bashing, whatever its financial liabilities, was still immensely popular.

COAL WAS an important factor in British foreign policy. The invasion of the Ruhr meant that the French could now combine their own resources with those of western Germany, Belgium and Poland, creating after the United States and Britain the third largest coal reserve in the world.[25] With a combined production of almost 200 million tons a year, this empire could squeeze the British out of continental markets.[26]

This potentiality was still distant, however. German passive resistance had caused a 30-percent drop in coal production (with the output of steel and pig iron down almost by one half).[27] Consequently, the British boosted their own output past 26 million tons, a surge of almost 10 percent.[28] The increased export revenues earned an additional 32 million pounds (145 million dollars).[29] But such good fortune was deemed temporary. German production would recover; moreover, the French could eventually establish their coal hegemony without Ruhr occupation.

Paris was working on a long-term deal with the German coal barons to get them to sell their product to France at fixed prices, below those on the free market. The French would guarantee 80 percent payment 10 days in advance with the rest transferred three days after delivery.[30] The benefits were attractive to both sides: the Germans could now sell, not give away, coal as reparations, and the French would make money reselling surplus purchases on the open market, thereby undercutting British competition.

The British coal industry was in enough trouble already. It had been in decline since 1913 when its mines had produced 292 million tons of coal. One-fourth, or 75 million tons, of this had been sold abroad.[31] During the war, average annual production dropped to 250 million tons, but the increased price per ton maintained profitability. In 1919, however, competition from continental mines began driving British coal out of overseas markets. Demand for British coal also fell because previous customers were getting German coal in reparations, and because natural gas and petroleum were replacing coal as energy sources.[32]

The British were ill-prepared to meet these challenges. They had failed to make significant advances in mechanization. In many mines, the sweaty efforts of a miner working on the coal face with pick and shovel remained the standard means of extraction. Additionally, the labor force was swollen and produced less per capita than the Germans, Dutch, and Polish. The industry suffered further from an excess of small, inefficient independent producers.[33]

The militant Miner's Federation was on the lookout for any attempt to reduce the wage-scales and add hours to the work-week. The federation believed that the best path to recovery was through nationalization. The miners begrudged the large profits that mine-owners had reaped during the war. The government tried to maintain wage-scales by pooling revenues in a fund to offset the losses of the inefficient mines. But this scheme, along with other regulations of the coal industry, was due to end on 31 March 1921.

As soon as the controls were lifted, the mine-owners demanded renegotiating the current labor contract in order to reduce wages. Some owners even posted notices at the collieries announcing what they were prepared to pay.[34] When the owners carried out their threat, the miners went on strike.[35] The government tried to minimize the damage by prohibiting the export of coal and evoking the Emergency Powers Act of 1920. This legislation called for the creation of a 75-thousand man defense force to maintain order. Its positions were filled in ten days, many with ex-servicemen, who simply needed jobs, and with other "patriotic" citizens, who saw this as their opportunity to show the miners who was boss.[36] These "soldiers" remained on duty throughout the 88-day strike, but, fortunately, never saw "action."

The government tried to get the miners back to work by agreeing to subsidize wages pending a settlement. But the miners insisted on a uniform minimum wage, with less prosperous districts being able to draw from a national pool of profits, while the owners wanted to revert to prewar wages. The Miners' Federation held out until June 1921, when they accepted a settlement that geared wages to profits, providing the government cushion any reductions with public subsidies. The politicians hoped to buy time until improvements in the mines would make them more profitable and able to support higher wages.

Tensions subsided, but the strike had cost the nation dearly. Coal production fell to its lowest level in 33 years, exhausting the balance of payments.[37] The Treasury lost 29 million pounds directly, about 111 million dollars. The strike hit those industries especially hard that depended on coal: iron production dropped from 8 million tons to 2.7 million tons and crude steel declined from 9.2 million to 3.7 million tons. Overall industrial production declined by nearly 20 percent.[38] Troubles in the coal industry added to the problem of unemployment, which, from 1920 to 1921, climbed from 2.4 percent to 14.8 percent; the following year it went to 15.2 percent. Over the next two decades, unemployment rarely dipped below 10 percent.[39]

The coal strike demonstrated the inability of the British economy to engender a serious program of industrial reform, and dramatized the decline of the British standard of living. Understandably British diplomats wanted to get the Ruhr crisis solved as soon as possible because the resulting tension threatened to increase social discord and threaten domestic violence.

THE BRITISH AMBASSADOR in Washington, Sir Auckland Geddes, reported that the Americans were sympathetic to France's enforcement of the Treaty of Versailles.[40] He explained that this toleration stemmed from a misunderstanding of the economic hardships plaguing postwar Europe but not America.

Growing prosperity in the United States made it difficult for Americans to understand how the invasion of the Ruhr could stand in the way of European recovery. Geddes also thought that the Americans might welcome a weakening of Britain's trade position.

Secretary of State Charles Evans Hughes favored ending the crisis through mediation. In a speech he gave the previous December, at the annual meeting of the American Historical Association in New Haven, he proposed that a group of financial experts, "acceptable throughout the world as the most authoritative expression obtainable," should decide Germany's obligation and the method of payment.[41] Hughes' proposal to have experts examine "Germany's capacity to pay" was his way of depoliticizing the issue by making it a technical problem. This, he hoped, would pave the way for German economic recovery, so necessary for full European recovery.[42] The American secretary of state appeared willing to have the United States serve as arbiter, if asked, thereby offering the prospect of greater American participation in European affairs.

The British were interested. Whatever their beliefs about American motives, they hoped to get Washington's help in removing foreign troops from the Ruhr, but they also wanted to induce the Americans to abandon isolationism and become more involved in European affairs.[43] The British recognized that active American participation in solving the reparations problem was in American national interest for, without such participation, Europe was headed for economic collapse with a resultant loss of world markets. Even as French troops moved into the Ruhr, the British had strengthened the American front by reaching a settlement on war debts.[44] Having removed that source of friction, they felt better able to concentrate on getting the French to accept Hughes' proposal of an "expert inquiry" into Germany's capacity to pay. Curzon insisted, though, that such mediation be coupled with the evacuation of the Ruhr, so the area could be restored to "fruitful production, rather than one of strife."[45]

The Germans were receptive and on 7 June 1923 proposed that such a conference be convoked. The French, though, objected. The French refused to consider an end to the occupation until the Germans promised to abandon their passive resistance.[46] Furthermore, Poincaré demanded "real progress" on the payment of reparations and said that only the Reparation Commission was empowered to discuss the question of indebtedness.[47] Lloyd George put his finger on the difficulty when he asked Curzon how he intended to get Poincaré to deviate from a policy that had the overwhelming support of the French parliament.[48] This pushed Curzon into ordering the publication of all the relevant correspondence between the British and French cabinets.

Englisch-französische Freundschaftsbezeugung

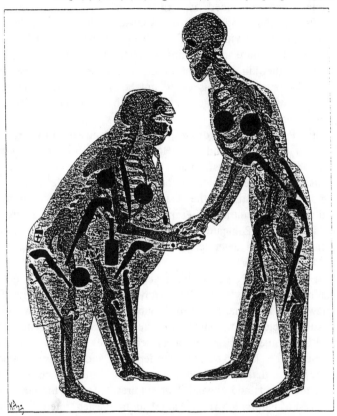

Der feierliche Moment wurde versehentlich mit einer Röntgenplatte aufgenommen.

Anglo-French Friendship Confirmed. *The caption reads, "An x-ray machine inadvertantly captures this moment of celebration." Th. Heine indulges in a bit of hyperbole in suggesting that the split over the invasion of the Ruhr led the Allies to arm secretly against each other. But that neither country was a friend of Germany can be seen in the animal-like way they are characterized: note especially the elongated coccyx bones suggesting that neither has fully evolved.* (Simplicissimus, 23 July 1923)

Poincaré answered by releasing all his own communiqués. It was difficult to see what this public relations war would accomplish; it certainly did nothing to improve Anglo-French relations. Curzon thought Poincaré was deliberately attempting to embarrass the British government and demanded an explanation.   When this was not immediately forthcoming, he, on 11 August, publicly denounced the Ruhr occupation as a violation of the Treaty of Versailles and said it was doomed to failure in collecting reparations.   He then castigated France for withholding payment of the war debts it owed Britain, declaring that such payments could not be postponed indefinitely.[49] Curzon then insisted that the crisis be solved by an expert inquiry into Germany's capacity to pay.

When Poincaré finally did respond it was to insist on the legality of the Ruhr occupation and reject the proposal for an international commission.   He said that France would renege on its war debt payments until it received satisfaction from Germany.   He denounced Curzon's characterization of the occupation of the Ruhr as "a failure." He said this only encouraged Germany to continue violating its treaty obligations.[50] Since Poincaré had taken office, the atmosphere between Paris and London had never been more poisoned.

THE DECLARATION of passive resistance sparked an upsurge in German national unity, but the Berlin government was ill-prepared for the runaway inflation that followed.[51] Subsidizing the striking workers in the Ruhr accelerated the increase in the money supply.[52] The mark declined in value and prices increased adding to the costs of reconstruction.[53]   Many business leaders and industrialists blamed France for the inflation, but took advantage of the cheap currency to liquidate their debts and expand their empires. Most of the Germans were not speculators, however, and had no vested interest in the inflation. Many were hurt, especially those people on fixed incomes, like white collar workers, bureaucrats, retired people, and teachers.[54] Work lost its value. The middle classes felt humiliated and ashamed at their increased proletarianization. The value of the mark changed so rapidly that workers were paid at noon each day, so they could rush out during the lunch period and spend their money before it devalued more.[55] Shopkeepers, in return, closed their stores at mid-day to await the new rates of exchange and open later with new price tags on their goods.

In Berlin, a loaf of bread, which cost 3,465 marks in July, now sold for 201,000,000 marks; a streetcar ride cost 150 million marks one day, and 500 million a day later. One hundred printing firms, supplied by 30 paper mills, kept their 2,000 presses in round-the-clock operation to turn out the new Reichsbank notes.[56] Yet, as bad as things were, the German government never officially renounced the Treaty of Versailles nor repudiated reparations, because it feared that this would drive the British to support the French. And the Germans needed the British to mediate a settlement.

Germany edged towards civil war. Uprisings and disturbances spread throughout the country, many of these fanned by pressure from various separatist movements. In Bavaria, separatism was associated with the rightist administration of commissioner Gustav von Kahr; in Saxony and Thuringia it was spearheaded by leftist "popular front" governments; in the Rhineland, it was sponsored by the French.

George Grosz, one of Weimar's most famous artists, thought the period was like a boiling caldron:

> We did not see those who fed the flames. However, we did feel the growing heat and watched the violent seething. There were speakers and preachers on every street corner. Sounds of hate could be heard everywhere. There was universal hatred: hatred of Jews, Junkers, capitalists, Communists, militarists, home-owners, workers, the Reichswehr, the Allied Control Commission, corporations and politicians. A real orgy of hate was brewing, and behind it all the weak Republic was scarcely discernable.[57]

POINCARÉ INSISTED that he had dispatched troops to the Ruhr only to enforce the Treaty of Versailles. He said that he wanted to coerce the Germans into developing "a will to pay" and

> to create such embarrassment in the economic and political structure of the Reich, that the execution of the treaty would be preferred to this embarrassment; to obtain what we have not obtained for the last four years, namely, the recognition by Germany of her obligations, not from the general and theoretical point of view but from the practical point of view.[58]

But he really wanted to destroy the "Germany of Bismarck," ending Prussian domination and to reconstruct the country as a confederation, such as had existed before 1866.[59] Poincaré hoped to use separatism as a bargaining counter for the payment of reparations, but also as an opportunity to gain a French position in the Rhineland denied by the Paris Peace Conference. He was at heart a revisionist. He encouraged the growth of Rhineland separatist movements and unofficially backed a "Rhine Republic," which had been established at Aachen in the Belgian zone. Ignoring British protests, he allowed French-sponsored separatist leaders to direct many of the local governments in the French zone and secretly promoted the creation of the "Autonomous Government of the Palatinate," allowing the Rhineland Commission to register its decrees.

The Franco-Belgian consortium running the Ruhr railways demanded that German workers take a special oath, pledging to work for the creation of an independent Rhenish state, as a condition for employment.[60] Poincaré tried to paint the separatist movement as a spontaneous manifestation of self-determination in keeping with the spirit of the League of Nations.[61] It was difficult, however, to get the Germans to agree.

A French firing squad executed Albert Leo Schlageter, on 26 May 1923, for blowing up a railway bridge. Schlageter was an ultra-nationalist thug whose work experience included soldering in the Freikorps army of General von der Goltz in Latvia, participating in the Kapp putsch in Berlin, and helping suppress striking miners in General Watter's force in the Ruhr. Death brought him the recognition he had never enjoyed in life. Germans demanded a statue be erected to his memory. Biographies appeared.[62] A popular play, featuring him as its main character, contained the famous line: "Whenever I hear the word culture, I release the safety of my gun."[63] Gustav Stresemann thought that in shooting Schlageter the French had committed the same monumental political blunder the Germans had in 1914, when they executed nurse Edith Cavell.[64]

Even the German Communist Party tried to use Schlageter's death to advance its revolutionary agenda.[65] In a straight-faced appeal to patriotism, it adopted the "Schlageter line" as a policy of class unification, making

> clear to the nationalist masses of the petty bourgeoisie and the
> intellectuals that the working class alone, once it wins victory, will
> be able to defend German soil, the treasures of German culture, and
> the future of the nation.[66]

Its leaders went to Moscow to plan the forthcoming revolution.[67] Karl Radek, the Comintern's leading German expert, brushing aside the dead saboteur's odious record of right-wing activity, said that this courageous soldier of the counter-revolution deserved honor by the soldiers of the revolution because he was an honest patriot and valiant adversary of French imperialism.[68] The Communists also tried to take advantage of the deep resentment the Germans felt towards the French for their use of colonial troops in the army of occupation.

FRENCH ARMY CHIEFS had insisted that the occupation of the Rhineland be shared by all those soldiers who had contributed to the defeat of Germany, including troops from the empire. Unsaid was their desire to ridicule the German sense of racial superiority. For this purpose, even small numbers of native troops would suffice.[69] Most of the *"hommes de couleur"* came from north Africa: Morocco, Algeria, and Tunisia, fewer from Madagascar, Tonkinchina, and the sub-Sahara. But German fury was primarily directed at the negro soldiers, who numbered less than 1000, assigned mainly to the garrisons at Wiesbaden and Coblenz.[70]

German magazines and newspapers routinely depicted these "Senegalese" as monkeys and wild beasts possessing huge sexually aggressive appetites. A poster showed a black soldier raping a white woman under the caption: "Mothers of the world, it this what your sons have died for?"[71] Karl Goetz, the sculptor of famous "Lusitania medal," which had lampooned the British shipowners' lust for profits at the expense of the lives of their passengers, created a new "commemorative" bronze medal, which featured an erect penis, wearing a French helmet, to which a nude woman was manacled. The inscription reads: *"Die schwarze Schande,* (The Black Disgrace)."[72] *Simplicissimus*, the satirical weekly, linked the French occupation with the "black peril".[73] Conservative newspapers, like the *Berliner Tagblatt*, the *Frankfurter Zeitung*, and the *Leipziger Neuste Nachrichten* frequently carried stories of the black "contagion" and black atrocities.[74]

In fact, most of such crimes were actually committed by north Africans. The French authorities took these assaults very seriously, the most barbarous being brought to the personal attention of Foch, Herriot, Briand, and Poincaré.[75] The French paid compensation to the victims, or their family. They also tried to reduce attacks on women—

and, at the same time, protect their soldiers from venereal disease—by establishing official military bordellos, establishments which, almost always, had the approval of the local German authorities.[76] The colonial troops had special *maisons publiques* of their own.

General Maxime Weygand, Foch's deputy at the Allied Military Control Committee at Versailles, said the presence of these brothels was "an obligatory corollary with the presence of native troops."[77] General Durand, the commander of a brigade of Spahis at Trier, insisted that his troops "uprooted in the Rhineland, in a country without resemblance to their own, under a sky which already makes them nostalgic for the beautiful sky of Africa," be guaranteed the things fundamental to their existence, "an Arab café and a prostitute." This was hardly a license for debauchery, he argued, but rather "a recognition of the inevitable and an attempt to channel it, to control it to prevent worse things from happening."[78] But not everybody agreed with the military's no-nonsense approach to sex.

From Paris, Avril de Saint-Croix, the head of the *Conseil national des femmes françaises*—National Council of French Women— condemned the practice as a moral danger and an attack against womanhood throughout the world. She demanded that the French government withdraw the black troops from Germany and suppress these *"maisons de tolérance."*[79] And Allan Lethbridge, writing in London's *Westminister Gazette*, said:

> African troops under the best control are dangerous. To put it bluntly, arouse their passions and they become animals. Again, to put it bluntly, white women arouse their passions more easily than those of their own color.[80]

The American ambassador to France also expressed disapproval of this official prostitution.

Poincaré, however, insisted that the French were not forcing German women into a life of sin. Far from it, the supply of willing prostitutes far exceeded the demand; authorities were inundated with offers of employment—*"assailliés d'offre de service."* He said that women who served in the negro establishments actually preferred *"hommes de couleur."*[81] The French government pointed out that whorehouses had been invented by others and had existed in that part of Germany before the French troops arrived. They also existed in other areas of the Rhineland where there were no French soldiers.[82] The French emphasized that the local German authorities were very cooperative. The city of Wiesbaden, for example, had created a managing director, who subjected the women to police inspection and issued wine permits.[83] The controversy, however, continued. Karl Goetz produced another metal "commemorating" the installation of French bordellos across the Rhine.[84] The Germans viewed the matter as the ultimate outrage against moral order, as well as a deliberate, persistent effort to remind them of the 1918 defeat. They believed that the French intended to humiliate them and to weaken German national pride.[85]

Lord Curzon publicly reviled the French for stationing native troops in the Rhineland and also denounced the system of military bordellos. The British government prided itself that it had not allowed similar facilities for its own soldiers and, indeed, had made brothels off-limits for its own army of occupation.[86] But the damage to Anglo-French relations far exceeded that of a disagreement over the sexual drives of the troops in the Rhineland. The French invasion of the Ruhr swept away the last remnants of obligation under the Entente Cordiale, although that change, not immediately perceptible to the British or the French, did not end attempts at reconstruction. The old rhetoric about the necessity of Anglo-French cooperation continued, but a feeling of real obligation no longer existed, and words sounded more and more like worn-out platitudes.

Notes and Sources :

1.   See: Jean-Claude Favez, *Le Reich devant l'occupation Franco-Belge de la Ruhr en 1923* (Geneva: Librarie Droz, 1969).
2.   Henri Lichtenberger, *The Ruhr Conflict* (Washington: Carnegie Endowment for International Peace, 1923), 1.
3.   The French, of course, already controlled the Saarland coal, which they had hoped would supply them coke for the near-by iron and steel industry in Lorraine. But the Saar product was unsuitable for industrial purposes, its best use being for heating houses. Consequently in 1922, the French cut back production, reducing the shifts of the miners to two a week. This made them more avid to get the hard coal of the Ruhr.
4.   Walter A. McDougall, *France's Rhineland Diplomacy, The Last Bid for a Balance of Power in Europe*, 244-9.
5.   See: Anne Orde, *Great Britain and International Security*, 1920-1926 (London: Royal Historical Society, 1978).
6.   Keith L. Nelson, *Victors Divided, America and the Allies in Germany, 1918-1923* (Berkeley: University of California Press, 1975), 246.
7.   Henry T. Allen, *My Rhineland Journal* (Boston: Houghton Mifflin, 1923), 220, 350. Many senators favored the repatriation of the American army, believing that its continued existence in Europe contravened the spirit of the Monroe Doctrine. General Peyton C. March, the former chief of staff, remarked derisively that American officers in Germany were only playing polo.
8.   *Documents on British Foreign Policy*, first series, XXI, 36.
9.   The foreign secretary sent similar instructions to Paris, to Sir John Bradbury on the Reparation Commission and to Lord Robert Crewe on the Ambassador's Conference. *Documents on British Foreign Policy*, first series, XXI, 25.
10.   *Annual Register* 1923, 5.
11.   *Documents on British Foreign Policy*, first series, XXI, 146-7.
12.   *Ibid.*, 647-8, 653-4.
13.   On 23 March 1919, the German government had organized its coal industry into twelve regional cartels under the authority of the *Reichskohlenverband* A. G., sort of a cartel of cartels, with the authority to set production quotas and minimum prices, and establish areas of distribution. This Federal Coal Council, on which the employers, workers, dealers, and states were represented, was not intended to involve a transfer of ownership. The regional cartels enjoyed the prerogatives of the old capitalist mining industry, with none more independent than the huge Rhenish-Westphalian

Coal Syndicate, which controlled the Ruhr. *Rationalization of German Industry* (New York: National Industrial Conference Board, 1931).

14. *Survey of International Affairs 1924*, 269.

15. Norman J. G. Pounds, *The Ruhr, A Study in Historical and Economic Geography* (Bloomington: Indiana University Press, 1952), 100.

16. W. F. Bruck, *Social and Economic History of Germany from Wilhelm II to Hitler, 1888-1938* (Cardiff: University Press Board, 1938), 163-4.

17. Édouard Bonnefous, *Histoire politique de la troisième république, l'apres-guerre 1919-1924* (Paris: Presses Universitaires de France, 1959), 348-9.

18. Henri Lichtenberger, *The Ruhr Conflict*, 3-4.

19. From roughly 10 billion francs to 12 billion. Édouard Bonnefous, *Histoire politique de la troisième république, l'apres-guerre 1919-1924*, 447.

20. *European Historical Statistics*, 412; *Statesman's Year Book 1925*, 889-90.

21. *Annual Register*, 1923, 78-9.

22. See: Harold G. Moulton and Cleona Lewis, *The French Debt Problem* (New York: Macmillan, 1925) and Gaëtan Pirou, *Les doctrines économiques en France depuis 1870* (Paris: Armand Colin, 1952).

23. From 1920 to 1923, direct taxes on an average never exceeded 13.5 percent of total revenues, nor went past 8 percent of total expenditures. *European Historical Statistics*, 719; Steven A. Schuker, *The End of French Predominance in Europe, The Financial Crisis of 1924 and the Adoption of the Dawes Plan*, 31-3.

24. Édouard Bonnefous, *Histoire politique de la troisième république, l'apres-guerre 1919-1924* 353-4.

25. In 1923, the French mines produced 38 million tons; Poland produced 36 million tons; Belgium produced 23 million tons. European Historical Statistics, 365, 366, 368. Although the Poles officially supported the French invasion of the Ruhr, they did so with certain misgivings. They did not want to become involved in any anti-German moves, and, to this effect, resisted French pressure to suspend their coal deliveries to upper Silesia. Piotr S. Wandycz, *France and Her Eastern Allies 1919-1925, French-Czechoslovak-Polish Relations from the Paris Peace Conference to Locarno*, 271-2.

26. **British Coal Exports to Selected Countries** (1000 tons)

	Belgium	France	Germany	Italy
1913:	2,031	12,776	8,952	9,647
1922:	3,489	13,579	8,346	6,342
1923:	6,505	18,826	14,806	7,593

Whitaker's Almanac 1923, 503.

27. **German Output**   (1000 metric tons)
              Coal   Pig iron   Crude steel
1922:   256,359,396   11,714
1923:   180,474   4,936   6,305
European Historical Statistics, 366, 395, 400. In 1922 Ruhr production was
60 million tons, in 1923 only 40 million. Norman Pounds, *The Ruhr, A Study
in Historical and Economic Geography*, 100.

28. British coal production (and exports). 1922: 249,607 (67,939);
1923: 276,001 (84,497) in thousand tons. *Statesman's Year Book 1925*, 56.

29. *Ibid.*, 56; *Annual Register 1923*, 79.

30. Henry T. Allen, *My Rhineland Journal* (Boston: Houghton Mifflin,
1923), 521.

31. *European Historical Statistics*, 364, 768, 411, 414.

32. For example, before the war the Royal Navy consumed two and a
half million tons of coal a year; now, because of conversion to oil, its
purchases fell to almost nothing. *Whitaker's Almanac 1920, 446*.

33. In 1920, the number of people employed in the coal industry was
120 thousand more than it had been in 1913 despite a decrease of 59 million
tons of coal: 1,1248 thousand as compared to 1,128 thousand. *Whitaker's
Almanac 1922*, 511.

34. Charles Loch Mowat, *Britain Between the Wars, 1918-1940*
(Chicago: University of Chicago Press, 1961), 120.

35. *Annual Register 1921*, 30-2.

36. Charles Mowat, *Britain Between the Wars, 1918-1940*, 122.

37. The output of coal dropped to 166 million tons, reducing coal
exports to 25 million tons. From the previous year foreign exchange was off
by 57 million pounds, or roughly 220 million dollars. *Whitaker's Almanac
1922*, 513, 519; *Whitaker's Almanac 1923*, 517; *Whitaker's Almanac 1921*, 76.

38. *European Historical Statistics*, 396, 401, 357.

39. *European Historical Statistics*, 168, 171.

40. *Documents on British Foreign Policy*, first series, XXI, 94.

41. Royal J. Schmidt, *Versailles and the Ruhr, Seedbed of World War
II* (The Hague: Martinus Nijhoff, 1968), 199.

42. *Documents on British Foreign Policy*, first series, XXI, 126-7.

43. The U.S. would give other countries much better deals. Belgium's
interest was set at 1.8 percent, France's at 1.6 percent, and Italy's 0.4 percent.
The Americans showed no willingness to consider lowering the rate the British
paid.

44. Stanley Baldwin, the Chancellor of the Exchequer, and Montagu
Norman, head of the Bank of England, agreed to fund the British obligation
(currently about 4.6 billion dollars) at an average interest rate of 3.3 percent,

amortized over a 61-year period. *Annual Register 1923*, 5-8; Charles Mowat, *Britain Between the Wars, 1918-1940*, 161-2.

45. *Documents on British Foreign Policy*, first series, XXI, 426-8.

46. *Documents on British Foreign Policy*, first series, XXI, 327-30.

47. *Ibid.*, 433-4

48. *Annual Register 1923*, 92.

49. *Ibid.*, 94-6.

50. *Documents on British Foreign Policy*, first series, XXI, 360-2.

51. Charles S. Maier, *Recasting Bourgeois Europe*, 356-7

52. See: Harold G. Moulton, *Germany's Capacity to Pay; A Study of the Reparation Problem* (New York: McGraw-Hill, 1923); and Frank Dunstone Graham, *Exchange, Prices and Production in Hyper-Inflation: Germany, 1920-1923* (Princeton: Princeton University Press, 1930).

53. In January 1923, the exchange rate of the mark stood at one dollar for 20 thousand marks, but this rate lasted only a few months. By July, the mark had fallen to 350 thousand to the dollar and plummeted farther. The government covered its deficits with "floating debts," that is, by increasing the supply of money as it had routinely done since the days of the First World War. See: Helmut Böhme, *An Introduction to the Social and Economic History of Germany: Politics and Economic Change in the Nineteenth and Twentieth Centuries* (Oxford: Blackwell, 1978); and James W. Angell, *The Recovery of Germany* (New Haven: Yale University Press, 1929), 17-19. During the period 1919 to 1923, the amount of money shelled out in reparations was offset by loans from abroad. Bureau of U.S. Foreign and Domestic Commerce, *German Reparations, Budget, and Foreign Trade* (Washington, D.C.: Government Printing Office, 1922).

54. See: Karsten Laursen and Jorgen Pedersen, *The German Inflation 1918-1923* (Amsterdam: North-Holland Publishing Co., 1964); and Fritz K. Ringer, ed., *The German Inflation of 1923* (New York: Oxford University Press, 1969).

55. In January, the mark was 17,972 to the dollar; in July it was 353,412; in August: 4,620,455; in September: 98,860,000; in October: 25,260,208; it reached its high by 15 November with 4,200,000,000,000 marks to the dollar. Gustav Stolper, *German Economy 1870-1940, Issues and Trends*, 151.

56. *Ibid.*, 85.

57. George Grosz, *A Little Yes and a Big No* (New York: Dial Press, 1946), 201.

58. Henri Lichtenberger, *The Ruhr Conflict*, 3.

59. *Documents on British Foreign Policy*, first series, XXI, 884.

60. Royal Schmidt, *Versailles and the Ruhr: Seedbed of World War II*, 145.

61. This did not mean, that the new state would be exempt from the obligations of the Treaty of Versailles, however.

62. Among them: Wilhelm Hügenell, Schlageter (Munich: Verlag der Deutschvölkischen Buchhandlung, 1923) and Rolf Brandt, *Albert Leo Schlageter: Leben und Sterben eines deutschen Helden* (Hamburg: Hanseatische Verlagsanstalt Aktiengesellschaft, 1926).

63. Adam Ulam, *Expansion and Coexistence* (New York: Praeger, 1974), 154. This remark was made more famous later by Hermann Göring, who supposedly remarked, "Each time I hear the word culture, I reach for my revolver."

64. Royal Schmidt, *Versailles and the Ruhr, Seedbed of World War II*, 130.

65. "One has to speak with officers very courteously and amiably, to address them by the title `Your Excellency,'" was a typical piece of advice. Ruth Fischer, *Stalin and the German Communist Party, A Study in the Origins of the State Party* (Cambridge, Mass.: Harvard University Press, 1948), 282.

66. Xena J. Eudin and Harold H. Fisher, *Soviet Russia and the West, 1920-1927* (Stanford: Stanford University Press, 1957), 171.

67. Franz Borkenau, *The Communist International* (London: Faber and Faber, 1938), 247-9.

68. Ruth Fisher, *Stalin and the German Communist Party, A Study in the Origins of the State Party*, 271-272.

69. Of the thirty infantry and five cavalry divisions, which took part in the occupation, not more than 20,000 of the soldiers were "colonial troops." The French called "*troupes noires*" or "*hommes de couleur*" any soldiers that were not European, regardless of other ethnic distinctions. Thus, in this respect, there was no difference between soldiers from Morocco, Senegal, Madagascar, and Indochina.

70. In 1924, the colonial troops in Germany consisted of the following: North-African *tirailleurs* (mostly Algerian) two battalions at Wiesbaden, Saarburg, Siegburg, Kostheim, Germersheim; one battalion at Höchst, Bensberg, Worms, Griesheim, Spire, and Bonn. There were two infantry battalions of Moroccan troops at Ludwigshafen and one at Landau. There was a battalion of Spahis (Tunisian) at both Trier and Landau. *Annuaire officiel de l'armée française* (Paris: Librarie Militaire Berger-Levrault, 1924), lxii-lxiii.

71. Jean-Pierre Auclert, *La grande guerre des crayons* (Paris: Robert Laffont, 1981), 103.

72. *Ibid.*, 94.

73. One illustration by E. Thönne entitled, "The French among themselves", has a white officer talking with a negro enlisted man. The officer says, "Why shouldn't we subjugate the Rhineland, we have Gallicanized you blacks?" To which the black replies, "But we have subjugated you, we have

Africanized you French." *Simplicissimus*, 22 March 1922, 706. Another drawing by E. Schilling, shows a squad of negro soldiers marching up a flight of stairs behind their leader who is carrying a funeral urn. The caption reads, "In the year 2020: Niggers placing the heart of the last white Frenchman in the Pantheon." *Simplicissimus*, 8 December 1920, 488.

74. One reported that blacks soldiers had cut off the hands of little children in Frankfurt. During the First World War, German propaganda portrayed Senegalese troops cutting cut off the ears of dead German soldiers to send to their tribal chiefs back home. *Revue des deux mondes*, tome soixantième, 1920, 118. Of course, the British propaganda machine was also guilty of such distortions.

75. A teen-age girl was raped in front of her mother; a twelve year old boy was sodomized and a bayonet plunged into his jaw; a drunken soldiers fired gratuitously on a group of German civilians; a sentry shot a German worker and let him bleed to death, a young man is shot while presenting his papers to a guard, etc. *"Troupes noires. Incidents causées par les soldats 1922-1929", Ministère des Affaires Étrangères*, série Z (Europe 1918-1929), Vol. 193 (Allemagne), 72-84, 86-98, 256, 333.

76. These were in Trier, Kreutznach, Düren, Bonn, Spire, Landau, Kaiserslauten, Landau, Ludwigshafen, Bingen, Höchst, Wiesbaden, Idstein, and Zweibrücken. *Ministère des Affaires Étrangères*, série Z (Europe 1918-1929), Vol. 192 (Rive gauche du Rhin), 30, 71.

77. *Ibid.*, 27.

78. *Ibid.*, 36-7.

79. *Ibid.*, 1-2.

80. *Ibid.*, 12.

81. *Ibid.*, 70.

82. *Ibid.*, 26, 41.

83. They listed three such houses in Worms, five in Mainz, seven in Düsseldorf, five in Duisberg, fourteen in Bochum, and twenty-four in Essen. Then there were the brothels in the rest of Germany in Mannheim, in Freiburg, Heidelberg, Stuttgart, Munich, Würzburg, Nürenburg, Darmstadt, Kiel, Frankfurt-am-Main, Leipzig, Hannover, Wilhelmshaven, Lübeck, and Hamburg. The French kept good records. *Ibid.*, 66.

84. *Ibid.*, 8-9.

85. On the face of the coin, a French soldier is mugging a German maiden, the blastfurnace smokestacks puffing away symbolically in the background. On the other side some blacks are terrorizing a German village. The inscription across the top says, *"Wustlinge am Rhein"* (Debauchery on the Rhine), under this is shown some women being assaulted in the town's central square, in front of a statue of the Virgin Mary. On the roof of one of the

houses is written, *"Lüsthaus fur Neger"*, (Whore House for Negroes).
Jean-Pierre Auclert, *La grande guerre des crayons*, 99.

86. Royal J. Schmidt, *Versailles and the Ruhr: Seedbed of World War II*, 137-141.

87. *Ministère des Affaires Étrangères*, série Z (Europe 1918-1929). Vol. 192 (Rive gauche du Rhin), 45..

CHAPTER 7

THE END OF PASSIVE RESISTANCE

AT THE BEGINNING OF SEPTEMBER, Prime Minister Baldwin left on his annual vacation to Aix-les-Bains, a stodgy French middle-class spa in the Haute Savoie—a spot he loved and revisited every year. While he was taking the cure, the Foreign Office finalized a proposal for ending the Ruhr crisis. It proposed that Britain sign a new security pact with France, approximating the old Treaty of Guarantee, in exchange for French evacuation. The deal was transmitted to Baldwin at Aix, who presented it to Poincaré, on 19 September 1923, on his way home through Paris. Although Poincaré should have been delighted that his venture blackmailed the British into a security treaty, he suspected a trap and avoided taking the bait.

The premier stated that such a guarantee could be made only through an agreement with all the allies, including the United States. And, in any case, no negotiations were possible until the Germans pledged to pay reparations. Poincaré claimed that the terms of the Versailles treaty precluded him from negotiating directly with the Germans, but said that "Germany might be invited to appear at a meeting after a previous agreement had been reached by the allies." He persisted in maintaining that the Ruhr invasion was "a complete success" and warned that thinking otherwise would only delay a solution to the crisis.[1] Poincaré figured that the increased political confusion and economic hardship present in Germany would soon force Berlin to end passive resistance and come to terms.[2] He was right.

Chancellor Gustav Stresemann anticipated the collapse of his government, if there were there no immediate solution, and held a series of emergency meetings with the state presidents, the deputies from the Rhineland and the Ruhr, and the leaders of workers' organizations. Few of these leaders favored giving into French demands, but, seeing the confusion and unrest the French invasion had caused—separatist activity in the Rhineland and Bavaria, runaway inflation, an increase in the threat of communism—they feared the disintegration of the moral and political integrity of the nation and were prepared to give in to Poincaré's demands.

On 26 September, President Ebert declared a state of emergency and gave the army broad powers to maintain order. Stresemann then called off passive resistance. He hoped to get British support to reach a favorable settlement.[3] London was in a good position to take the initiative.

On 5 October—at a gathering of the Dominion prime ministers, currently meeting in London—Curzon demanded that the French come up with a plan for ending the Ruhr invasion, which he called "disastrous and ruinous."[4] The British foreign secretary said that the British "would be quite ready to receive and discuss in a friendly spirit" any proposals they made.[5] With Baldwin's permission, portions of the speech were released to the press. The first positive response, however, came from the United States.

Secretary of State Hughes had President Calvin Coolidge announce that the United States was ready to work to solve the reparations problem "within the framework of a committee of experts." The Hughes initiative conformed to the Republican administration's policy of dollar diplomacy, a belief that peaceful relations among nations could be built through commerce and investment. Simply put, the Ruhr invasion had been bad for American business.

Curzon verified the genuineness of the American offer by having Henry Chilton, the British chargé in Washington, confirm it personally with Hughes. Hughes told Chilton that he had already warned the French Ambassador "that France should renounce her obstinate attitude and come into line with the other Powers."[6] But he advised Chilton to handle France with "tact and delicacy" to avoid giving the impression that there had been any collusion between Britain and the United States.[7]

Poincaré accepted the inevitability of a pull out, but he wanted to strengthen his bargaining position as much as possible beforehand. He continued his flirtation with Rhineland separatist movements in order to weaken the Weimar government further and strengthened the French position in eastern Europe. This included the extension of French military influence in that region and the resolution of a dispute between Czechoslovakia and Poland over Teschen.

Ever since the Peace Conference, both Czechoslovakia and Poland had disputed ownership of this old Austro-Hungarian duchy, located in north-eastern Moravia. The Poles insisted it belonged to them because of its large Polish population, the Czechs claimed it on the basis of the area's inclusion in the old Kingdom of Bohemia. The French had tried to resolve the dispute by arranging a plebiscite, which divided the territory into two, roughly equal, halves—a settlement which pleased neither disputant. The squabbling continued and escalated, in 1923, when the Poles also claimed Javorina, a sliver of land with a population of 450 people, which was located in Slovakia's Tatra mountains. The Poles claimed that the possession of Javorina was a matter of national honor.[8] For Poincaré, this fight could not have come at a worse time.

IN MAY, Poincaré had sent Foch to Warsaw to consolidate Franco-Polish military cooperation. The Poles received the marshal with great enthusiasm. They held parades and galas in his honor, and the government decorated him with the Order of the White Eagle, Poland's highest award. At the same time, they bombarded him with complaints about Czech intransigence.

Foch listened patiently but had little to promise by way of support for Polish territorial claims. Such matters concerned lowly politicians, not soldiers. Foch came to get the Polish general staff to agree on how to coordinate offensive operations in the event of a war with Germany. Foch would also would have liked to convince them to replace strongman Marshal Jozef Pilsudski with a "more professional" soldier.[9]

From Warsaw, Foch went to Prague. His objective was the same: to strengthen military relations. Although the French had no formal alliance with Czechoslovakia, in January 1919 the countries had signed a convention which gave France the task of reorganizing the Czechoslovak army under a French general as commander-in-chief.[10] The French had also promised to give Czechoslovakia diplomatic support—a commitment that paid off in 1923, when the Czechs honored a French request to stop coal deliveries to Germany during the period of passive resistance, even though the policy caused real economic hardship, Germany being Czechoslovakia's best customer.[11] The French wanted to turn this cooperation into a formal Franco-Czech military alliance. Czech Foreign Minister Eduard Beneš, however, had to weigh any fears he had of Germany against his desire to maintain open relations with Great Britain. He promised to think it over.[12] But Foch was insistent and pressed him to come to Paris for further discussions.

The visit took place the second week of October 1923, shortly after the Germans had abandoned passive resistance. Beneš, accompanied by Czech President Jan Masaryk, feared that any further promises they made to France might encourage Poincaré to continue his hard-line policy against Germany and involve their country in a dangerous policy of encirclement.[13] They, therefore, withstood the pressure to have them sign a military accord.[14] Beneš felt that French policy was headed in the wrong direction—that the country's best chance of security lay in strengthening German democracy, not in marshalling forces along the Rhine.[15]

Poincaré did not relate to such logic. Disappointed at the Czech refusal, he ordered withholding further military credits. At the same time, he released such aid to other eastern European countries: 400 million francs to Poland, 300 million to Yugoslavia, and 100 million to Romania. Still, although France failed to get the military alliance it wanted, it did get an agreement that obliged the Czechs to consult and coordinate their foreign policy with the French in

> all matters ... which may threaten their security or which may tend
> to subvert the situation created by the Treaties of Peace.[16]

The two countries further specified that they would settle all their disputes by international arbitration, and—in a confidential interpretive letter—they established permanent liaison between their respective general staffs. (The treaty was ratified in March 1924.)

The British feared that the extension of French military influence into eastern Europe could lead to an arms race and frustrate the building of a peaceful Europe.[17] Since there was little they could do to halt it, they had to content themselves with lecturing the French about paying off their war debts before giving military aid to their eastern allies.[18] In a sense they need not have worried. France could no more afford an expensive foreign aid program to countries in Eastern Europe than it could continue to occupy the Ruhr.

THE FRANC continued to slide. Consumer confidence and domestic spending declined. Businesses piled up unsold inventories. Foreign sellers demanded payment in pounds or dollars. The cost of living shot up by almost thirty percent; the price of basic commodities, like sugar, butter, bread, and meat increased even more.[19] Speculation in food stuffs was widespread.[20] Workers demanded the government lower tariffs on basic commodities.

The annual budget, which appeared in August 1923, almost one year overdue, allocated 13.3 billion francs for expenses, but only about one-fourth of this was to be paid from direct taxes. Loans from the United States and Great Britain were expected to cover the rest because, without monies from abroad, the government would be unable to meet its obligations.[21] Under the circumstances, however, the British and Americans were hesitant to extend more credit. The French were still reluctant to admit that their policy of force was beyond the country's economic means and suspected that these funds were being deliberately withheld to force a decline in the value of the franc.[22]

The occupation had cost France 61 million francs more than was collected in reparations.[23] It slowed down recovery, held up the repair of 3,000 factories and 152,000 houses, and delayed the cultivation of 156 thousand hectares of farmland. The Treasury fell 38 billion francs behind in war-pension payments.

Poincaré's popularity began to fade. Apart from the die-hards and revanchists, the French people got tired of hearing his stale platitudes: that France had been forced to act to protect its rights, that France had to defend the sanctity of treaties, that France had to use force to ensure respect for treaties. But as long as French troops remained in the Ruhr, there seemed little chance of improvement. Only when the Radicals withdrew from the Bloc National and formed an alliance with the Socialists—in anticipation of the 1924 national elections—did Poincaré decide it was time to bring the crisis to an end. France could not settle it alone. But Poincaré feared that a solution by the international community could cost France the initiative against

German revisionism. Nonetheless, he chose to act while he still had room to maneuver.

— Lui, c'est bien... mais Vous !
LA NOUVELLE OFFENSIVE. — *Composition d'ABEL FAIVRE.*

The New Offensive. *"Of course it's him, but (it's also) you." The French rooster, which appears on the country's metallic currency, tells Uncle Sam and John Bull that they, with the Germans, are to blame for undermining the value of the franc. Abel Faivre's cartoon thus supports the Poincare contention that the British and the Americans were waging economic warfare to get France to end its invasion of the Ruhr. Faivre was best known for his famous WWI poster "On les aura!" (We will prevail.)*

On 26 October, Poincaré informed the British that he would accept the establishment of an "advisory" committee of experts, providing it was established by the Reparation Commission and providing the experts confined their investigation to Germany's capacity to pay. Poincaré further specified that the United States be included only in an "unofficial" capacity.[24] He wanted to delay finalizing any arrangements until after the French elections the following spring, and until he had time to obtain special privileges from Rhineland industrialists.

A mining industry contract, signed on 23 November, gave France 30 to 40 percent of the Ruhr coal and coke output in exchange for the release of certain confiscated stocks of iron and steel. France concluded similar agreements for the sale and export of paper, leather, wine, textiles, and chemicals. In each case, Poincaré made sure France received more goods than were due under the London schedule of payments.

Poincaré also kept up the political pressure. When ex-Crown Prince Wilhelm of Hohenzollern left his Dutch exile and returned to Germany during the second week of November, Poincaré demanded that he be surrendered for trial under the terms of Article 288 of the Treaty of Versailles. He threatened occupation of more German territory should the Weimar government refuse. The British government immediately protested. Curzon pointed out that no German government could possibly arrest Wilhelm, as any attempt "would be frustrated by the resistance, passive and active, of his partisans among the German population."[25] The British warned that, if the French should take unilateral action, Britain would withdraw from the Conference of Ambassadors and from the Control Commission. The threat was enough to get the French to promise restraint, even though they covered this by reserving the right to do what was necessary in the future to defend their security.[26]

The British government also criticized Poincaré's constant dabbling with Rhineland separatism, warning him of the grave consequences that could result should new "sovereign states be carved out of the existing frontiers of Germany."[27] Their worry was unnecessary. German separatist leaders had little popular support and were constantly at war with themselves. Furthermore, the French were incapable of protecting them from the wrath of their own countrymen.

On 9 January 1924, the entire directorate of the Autonomous Government of the Palatinate was murdered by nationalist assassins. The killers had boated across the Rhine to separatist headquarters near Speyer, shot all five of the organization's leaders, fled the building without hindrance, and returned the way they came. The gunmen were never apprehended. The incident convinced Poincaré to withdraw his patronage—all be it unofficial—from separatism. Henceforth, he concentrated his attention and hopes on the solution of the crisis by a committee of experts.[28]

The shaky position of the franc, the budgetary disequilibrium, the need for British support, and the desire for American credits had destroyed his freedom of action. France had used its army for the last time to make Germans obey the Treaty of Versailles.

France in the Rhineland. *A French general protected by a negro sentry warns ominously, "Many more will die of starvation before I'm satisfied."* (*Karl Arnold,* Simplicissimus, *10 December 1923*)

THE WEIMAR GOVERNMENT gradually brought order to the country's politics and finances. At the end of October and the beginning of November 1923, it crushed Communist-led insurrections in Saxony and Hamburg and a rightist coup in Bavaria in which General Erich Ludendorff in the company of a political newcomer, Adolf Hitler, had tried to overthrow the local state government.

The events in Bavaria had particularly alarmed the British, who feared that a successful coup would have led to the wholesale slaughter of the French officers on the Control Commission and have prompted French intervention. The British Consul-General in Munich, R. N. Clive wrote:

> Ludendorff has lost his reason and is no longer sane. He seems to have imagined that such was the awe that he inspired that at the mere sight of him the Reichswehr and the police would fall in behind and obey his orders. Hitler, a half-educated demagogue, fired by the success of his oratory with women and young men, most of whom had not been to the war, thought he had merely to say the word and the country would flock to his standard.[29]

Clive's worries were premature.

The Weimar instituted a crackdown so effective that separatism never again became a serious threat. Chancellor Gustav Stresemann concentrated on balancing the budget and controlling the mounting inflation. On 15 November, the state bank issued a new unit of currency, the Rentenmark, which was achieved by exchanging one new mark for 4.2 trillion of the old. Germany thus had regained its prewar rate of exchange by simply wiping out a dozen zeros. The Rentenmark, however, was also "backed" by a national mortgage on landed property—that is, by government-held debt certificates on the mortgages of industrial and agricultural real estate. Although such collateral lacked the convertibility of gold, the government hoped that the German people would see the scheme as evidence of government sincerity in stabilizing the new currency, and give it their confidence. Moreover, the new bills were issued on good quality rag paper, which, unlike the flimsy inflation currency, were now printed on both sides and watermarked. More importantly, Dr. Hjalmar Schacht, the Special Commissioner for National Currency, was given power to control the money supply and rid the country of all the unofficial currencies that had appeared during the crisis.

The crisis of 1923—the occupation, the hyperinflation, the separatist movements, and the colored troop issue—showed the Germans the disadvantages of non-compliance. The French had achieved a great political victory by reminding the Germans of the depth of their defeat, creating a sense of hopelessness on which to build a policy of compliance.[30] The new German policy of realism and accommodation would, however, prove more dangerous to the French than the old, less subtle, policy of defiance and resistance, and begin a new era in France's relations with Great Britain.

One Billion Marks. *The Reichsbank put this bank note into circulation in September 1923 at the height of the German inflation. Such monetary instability, accompanying the French invasion of the Ruhr, heightened the German determination to revise the peace settlement—one way or another.*

Notes and Sources :

1. Royal Schmidt, *Versailles and the Ruhr*, 529-34.
2. Gustav Stresemann had become chancellor on 13 August 1923.
3. *Documents on British Foreign Policy*, first series, XXI, 504.
4. *Annual Register 1923*, 106-8.
5. *Ibid.*, 558.
6. *Documents on British Foreign Policy*, first series, XXI, 565.
7. *Ibid.*, 571.
8. On 12 March 1924, the Council of the League of Nations awarded the area to Czechoslovakia.
9. Piotr S. Wandycz, *France and Her Eastern Allies 1919-1925, French-Czechoslovak-Polish Relations from the Paris Peace Conference to Locarno*, 279.
10. The first commander was Maurice Pellé; he was succeeded by the current occupant General Eugène Mittlelhauser. Only in 1926, did a Czech hold the post.
11. For example, Clemenceau had helped dampen the aspirations of the Slovaks for home rule by refusing to recognize their representatives at the Peace Conference; and the French had supported the Czechs during the Bela Kun era when the Hungarians tried to reconquer Slovakia.
12. Jules Laroche, *Au Quai d'Orsay avec Briand et Poincaré*, 185-6.
13. Piotr S. Wandycz, *France and Her Eastern Allies 1919-1925, French-Czechoslovak-Polish Relations from the Paris Peace Conference to Locarno*, 298-9.
14. *Ibid.*, 186.
15. In remarks made to Walter Koch, the German minister in Prague. J. W. Bruegel, *Czechoslovakia Before Munich* (London: Cambridge University Press, 1973), 91.
16. Such cases included any attempt to bring about German-Austrian unification, or to restore the Habsburg or Hohenzollern dynasties. *League of Nations Treaty Series*, vol. XXIII (1924), no. 1-4, 164-169.
17. The British suspected the French had negotiated a secret military convention with Czechoslovakia, but they were particularly alarmed at the military convention concluded December 1923 with Poland to which the French gave a 400 million franc credit to equip its army. *Documents on British Foreign Policy*, first series, vol. XXVI, 552.
18. *Survey of International Affairs 1924*, 443-4.
19. *European Historical Statistics*, 738.
20. Édouard Bonnefous, *Histoire politique de la Troisième République, L'après-guerre*, 360.

21.   *Statesman's Year Book 1925*, 881-882.

22.   Georges Suarez, *Briand, Sa vie, son oeuvre, avec son journal et des nombreux documents inédits*, VII, 14-5.

23.   *Histoire politique de la Troisième République, L'après-guerre*, 362-3.

24.   *Documents on British Foreign Policy*, first series XXI, 595.

25.   *Ibid.*, 898.

26.   *Ibid.*, 931.

27.   ˙Walter A. McDougall, *France's Rhineland Diplomacy, The Last Bid for a Balance of Power in Europe*, 314.

28.   *Survey of International Affairs 1924*, 349-350.

29.   *Documents on British Foreign Policy*, first series, XXI, 889.

30.   Detlev J. K. Peukert, *The Weimar Republic, The Crisis of Classical Modernity* (New York: Hill and Wang, 1989), 75-77.

CHAPTER 8

GETTING THE FRENCH TO LEAVE

STANLEY BALDWIN had great antipathy for foreign affairs. He therefore believed that unemployment—Britain's "most critical problem"—was essentially a domestic problem, which could be solved by "protecting the home market." Since Baldwin felt that the Conservatives lacked a national mandate to institute protectionism, he decided to get one, and he scheduled new elections for 6 December 1923.[1]

In abandoning free trade, Baldwin was facing an uphill battle because the British people had been conditioned to believe that opening their borders to foreign goods had brought them prosperity. In fact, protectionism was unlikely to help the country's important export trade, especially the severely depressed coal and textile industries. Moreover, the imposition of tariffs on agricultural products would inevitably boost the cost of food. Such considerations prompted the British people to reject Baldwin's program, giving election victory to parties that supported free trade.

The Liberal and Labour Parties received a combined total of 92 more seats than the Conservatives. (Labour received 191 seats and the Liberals 159.) The king dutifully called on Labour to form the next government. But the Labour Party needed the support of the Liberals to remain in office.[2] Labour party leader Ramsay MacDonald recognized that there would be no chance of enacting any socialist legislation. So, unable to introduce capital gains taxes or nationalize industry, he set more general goals. MacDonald decided to demonstrate that his party, during its first time in office, could be fiscally responsible and could promote European security. Considering foreign and domestic politics to be indivisible, he assumed responsibility for both and, in addition to the prime ministry, took the portfolio of secretary for foreign affairs.

MacDonald believed he had a real chance to promote peace and harmony among nations. But, like Lloyd George, he realized that an improved standard of living for the British people, with the reduction of unemployment, depended on recovery of the export market, and that recovery of the export market depended on general European economic and fiscal health. He had great expectations of using the League of Nations to that end and hoped that collective security would lead to a reduction of armaments and the peaceful settlement of disputes through arbitration. He felt that the greatest goal of foreign policy was to prevent war.[3] MacDonald, in fact, wished to see the Geneva organization develop into an international people's tribunal, elected by the legislatures of the member states. He had been disappointed when it failed to do so, becoming instead a League of Governments.

The Foreign Office viewed MacDonald with concern. Some of the diplomats feared that MacDonald might abolish the intelligence service or dismantle the empire. Permanent Under-secretary Sir Eyre Crowe did not share their fears. He believed that MacDonald had too much common sense to go overboard and was intelligent enough to adapt to the ways of current British foreign policy. Crowe found that he and MacDonald shared many beliefs. Both wanted to heal the rupture in Anglo-French relations; both wanted to restore Germany to the European family of nations; and both opposed excessive reparations—MacDonald felt these brought too much suffering to the German working class. In addition, they both agreed on the immediate evacuation of French troops from the Ruhr, while acknowledging Britain's responsibility in helping to protect France from attack.

Shortly after assuming office, MacDonald wrote Poincaré a letter in which he assured him that he understood how the absence of a Treaty of Guarantee could "with some justification" lead France to seek "more tangible safeguards to take its place." But he said that he hoped that Poincaré would recognize how the Ruhr invasion had led to the persistent dislocation of European markets, the continued economic chaos in Germany shown so clearly by the violent fluctuations in the value of the currency and the ultimate uncertainty in the relations between France and ourselves.[4]

MacDonald said he feared France was determined "to ruin Germany and dominate the continent without consideration of our reasonable interests and future consequences to European settlement."[5] Demonstrating that there was little difference between his predecessor, Curzon, and himself on this issue, he questioned that the French government could find money for large military commitments in eastern and western Europe, but fail to pay back its loans to Britain, where taxpayers had

> to find upwards of 30,000,000 pounds [$132 million] a year as interest on loans raised in America, and...large sums to pay interest on the debt of France to us, to meet which France herself has yet neither not propounded, as far as they can see, any sacrifice equivalent to their own.[6]

MacDonald said he hoped that all issues, which undermined the mutual confidence between the two countries, could be cleared up through "frank and courageous discussion."[7]

Poincaré replied a week later, predictably denying that he was seeking to destroy Germany politically and economically. Poincaré argued that France was not stupid enough to want to reduce its German debtor to extreme poverty. Furthermore, he denied that France was seeking continental supremacy or aimed to extend its frontiers to the other side of the Rhine. He said that French foreign policy was driven by two legitimate goals: to get reparations to compensate for the war damages; and to build national security on solid foundations.[8] He insisted that France wanted only what the Treaty of Versailles had promised—no "reasonable Frenchman" had "ever dreamed of annexing any parcel of German territory or making even one German into a French citizen." He defended the size of the French army and military aid to eastern Europe as necessary for peace. He said that the Ruhr occupation was equally essential to make Germany live up to its obligations and to "crush the stubborn resistance of the German industrial tycoons."[9] Pandering to MacDonald's belief in collective security, Poincaré admitted that the League of Nations should be strengthened and its role enlarged, but, he claimed, this would have been unnecessary if the League had been given the authority France wanted it to have when it was first organized. Poincaré bemoaned Anglo-French estrangement and feared that, if it continued, their countries, and "all Europe and all humanity" would pay a heavy price.[10]

Poincaré held his ground on interallied debts, insisting that he intended to keep French troops in the Ruhr until "the express conditions of the treaty are fulfilled and our security is assured."[11] He maintained that the Reparation Commission alone could put into action any recommendations the international committee of experts made. The French wanted to maintain the power of the Supreme Council through all its various enforcement agencies, especially that of the Reparation Commission, which had the authority to determine a suitable reparations payment schedule based on Germany's economic status.

Poincaré, unlike MacDonald, interpreted the Commission's authority as executive and, in practice, as a device for interfering with German sovereignty.[12]   Moreover, the French opposed American enforcement of a treaty that the Americans had not ratified.   The British, on the other hand, welcomed American participation.

Although Poincaré's reply to MacDonald gave the impression that French policy was unlikely to change, Poincaré wanted an end to the Ruhr crisis. But, without active American participation in a committee of experts, this seemed impossible. Secretary of State Hughes made it clear that Americans would demand a major role—otherwise the "results of the enquiry...would be futile and it would not be worthwhile convening [the] commission."[13]

In December 1923, therefore, the Reparation Commission established two independent committees.[14]   One would deal with the flight of German capital abroad, the other would investigate German domestic finances.   This first was placed under Britain's Reginald McKenna; the second and most important, would be chaired by an American, retired Brigadier-general Charles G. Dawes.

IN 1918, Dawes had served in Paris on the Military Board of Allied Supply, work which had brought him into contact with many important members of the French government and armed forces. He had been decorated a commander of the Legion of Honor. He was happy now to be returning after a absence of six years, eager to recapture his former sense of exhilaration "to be with the old friends and again to be lying awake nights thinking over difficult problems."[15] He again checked into the Ritz Hotel, whose staff, he affectionately remembered, had treated him most politely and courteously.

Dawes was a director of the Federal Budget in the Harding administration and had influenced the Morgan Bank to underwrite the French franc with a $100 million loan.[16] He sympathized with French fear of an assurgent Germany and French dismay over the slow process of their recovery, but he knew that there could be no true reconstruction without the recovery of both France and Germany. From his experience in reorganizing the federal budget system, Dawes had concluded that Germany would never be able to pay reparations until its currency was stabilized and its budget balanced.[17] He was confident that his committee could make appropriate recommendations that all parties would accept.

Dawes discovered that Jean Parmentier, the French representative, was dedicated, responsible, open-minded, and unencumbered by instructions from Poincaré.[18] Their cordial relationship enabled Dawes to keep the attention of the committee focused on economics and away from politics. Dawes also received support from important Frenchmen outside the committee, having access to such men as the venerable Marshal Philippe Pétain and wartime friend General Payot, who was now the director of the Ruhr railways.[19]

Dawes feared that only prompt action could prevent Europe from slipping into another dark age, and so the work progressed rapidly. The experts submitted their evaluations to the Reparation Commission at the end of March 1924, and the Commission made few changes. The package was then released to the member states on a take-it-or-leave-it basis—there could be no amendments.[20]

The document—published on 9 April—was so full of technical data that one observer described it as the language "of a sane man who finds himself in a Madhouse and must accommodate himself to the inmates."[21] The experts had, however, fulfilled all of Dawes' basic goals: Germany must be allowed to regain its economic unity, stabilize its currency, and balance its budget. The plan established a special bank to assist Germany in building the gold reserves necessary to stabilize its currency—a bank with its own international board of directors and funded by an initial grant of 200 million dollars. The payment of reparations would be geared to an index of German prosperity and secured with specific revenues from taxes, railway bonds, transportation taxes, and industrial debentures. The plan advised that revenues from customs, tobacco, beer, alcohol, and sugar duties also be utilized. For this purpose, it required Germany to establish a special bank of issue, put industrial debentures up for sale, and modify the character of its budget.[22] If fully implemented, Germany would lose considerable freedom of action, but, in exchange, would pay less reparations than required before. Reparations would resume with an initial annual payment of 250 million dollars and, within four years, rise to a yearly sum of 625 million dollars.

The experts did not demand the evacuation of French troops from the Ruhr, claiming that this was outside their mandate. In specifying, however, that the foreign troops "must not impede the free exercise of economic activities," evacuation was clearly their intent.[23] Without evacuation, Germany could hardly regain its economic integrity and meet its obligations. The report also—importantly—stated that continued American assistance was necessary in helping Europe solve its financial and economic problems.

Certain aspects of the plan—like securing payment with state revenues, the use of an index of prosperity, and the creation of a new Reichsbank to replace the Rentenbank—had been proposed before. Allowing Germany to pay its debts in German currency, making the Allies responsible for their transfer were, however, innovations. The Allies now had a direct financial stake in the stability of the German mark. The payment of reparations was predicated now on economic practicality, not on what a country like France desired or thought it had a right to receive. The report, however, avoided fixing total German liability. As near as anyone could calculate, Germany's overall debt was about a third of what it once had been—a drop from 132 to 40 billion German gold marks, or less than 10 million dollars.[24]

Poincaré was convinced the Germans would accept the Dawes Plan in order to violate it. He thought that many of the provisions, which appeared sensible on the surface, were in fact flawed. For example, the so-called "prosperity index" was dubiously and unreliably based on the German government's assessment of factors and interpretation of statistics. Honesty of reporting, as Poincaré knew, was hardly in the German national interest. If the Germans had been able to invent "unfavorable conditions" and "technical complications" in refusing to hand over telegraph poles, what excuses might they make when it came to the transfer of capital? Furthermore, the vital problems of French security were still unsolved. That subject had been outside the mandate of the experts, but within the concerns of Poincaré. Poincaré was understandably reluctant to sacrifice a power position in the Ruhr for the dubious expectations of a Dawes Plan. He remarked that the report proved what he had maintained all along, that Germany was capable of paying reparations. He argued that the Ruhr occupation had succeeded in forcing German compliance. But he was willing to evacuate the Ruhr, providing he got an agreement on what sanctions the Allies would impose should the Germans again default.[25] And he wanted a French force to maintain control of the railways in the occupied areas.[26] The British, though, demanded evacuation without conditions. But they also wanted to make sure that France would never again use its army to enforce the Treaty of Versailles.

THROUGHOUT THE RUHR OCCUPATION, the French Treasury had tried to maintain solvency through borrowing. In January 1924, however, when the *Crédit national* loan was put up for public subscription, the Treasury failed to reach its target. Poincaré responded by proposing a twenty-percent increase in taxes (*un double décime*) and demanded special decree powers to slash government programs. He believed that he could save a billion francs by reducing the size of the civil service and by creating a special fund to reduce the expense of war pensions.[27] The Chamber of Deputies erupted in acrimonious debate, but Poincaré still commanded a majority, and his special tax was adopted by 305 votes to 219. The premier also received the power to legislate by decree for the next four months. But patriotic slogans and nationalist emotions, the rhetoric that helped hold together the Bloc National, were inadequate substitutes for a coherent fiscal policy.[28] Poincaré's supporters demanded sanctions against Germany. The well-being and security of the nation, however, could not be ensured by a mere affirmation of treaty rights.

By 8 March 1924, the franc had fallen to 29 to the dollar.[29] In order to encourage the recovery of French currency, Poincaré sought a 4 million pound advance from the Bank of England and a 100 million dollar loan from the Morgan Bank of New York . But as long as France kept its triple system of bookkeeping, any recovery would only be temporary. The normal budget stayed balanced, but the budget for recoverable expenses, which was to be financed with reparations, continued to pile up deficits. Yet the French were unwilling to alter their fiscal policies because to do so would seem like an open admission that the Treaty of Versailles was unenforceable and that money unobtained from Germany in reparations would have to be gleaned from the already economically strained French people.

Poincaré's critics accused him getting foreign credits to raise the value of the franc so he could gain votes for the next election, scheduled for 11 May. They also attacked him for raising taxes by 20 percent. The Socialist and Radical parties formed a coalition called the *Cartel des gauches*, and, taking advantage of the current electoral laws,[30] received 277 seats in the Chamber of Deputies, ten more than the Bloc National.[31] The Cartel's victory hardly repudiated Poincaré, but its leaders behaved as if they had a mandate to chart a new political direction. The Radicals could count on the support of the Socialists. But the Socialists, with their "revolutionary" domestic agenda, refused to join the government. Most of the support they gave the new government came because of agreement on foreign policy.

Édouard Herriot, the new premier and leader of the Radical party, set the tone by saying that he was "hostile to the policy of isolation and force which leads to occupations and the taking of territories as a guarantee."[32] Boiling down his policy to its essentials, he said: "What I want to get for my country is money, and I do not seek the death of Germans."[33] He also wanted to continue the efforts of disarmament by working through the League of Nations. French security, he believed, could only be achieved through cooperation with Great Britain,[34] and he was confident that he would develop a positive working relationship with British Prime Minister Ramsay MacDonald.

Herriot was less experienced in national government than Poincaré, and was especially adrift in the world of economics and finance. During the war, he had been head of the Ministry of Supply in Briand's government and, for the past dozen years, had served as mayor in his home town of Lyons. At the same time, he represented the Rhône department in the Chamber of Deputies—a dualism that was common in the Third Republic. Before becoming a politician, he had taught literature in a lycée. He had done his doctor's thesis on Madame Récamier and had published a biography on Beethoven, written, according to one critic, in a "frozen and profoundly boring" style.[35]

Herriot was willing to make concessions to avoid giving the impression that he was repeating Poincaré's mistakes, but he was no less concerned about French security. He believed that French troops should remain in the Ruhr unless there were proper assurances against further German aggression. As he explained to Prime Minister Ramsay Macdonald:

> My country has a dagger pointing at its breast, within an inch of its heart. Common efforts, sacrifices, deaths in the war, all that will have been useless if Germany can once more have recourse to violence. I think then that I should not have done my duty towards my country if I did not place Germany in a condition to do no harm.[36]

Herriot was convinced that a new international order could be built only after France had received justice—specifically the recognition of its moral and legal right to reparations. But Herriot had faith that men of good will, acting in a civilized manner, could resolve most current problems. He believed that many of his fellow countrymen shared his hope for ending the policy of confrontation and for reestablishing the Entente Cordiale with Great Britain.

HERRIOT MET MACDONALD for the first time, on 21 June, at Chequers, the official country residence of the British prime minister, located northwest of London in Buckinghamshire.[37] The 16th-century manor house did not have a telephone—calls were filtered through the switchboard at nearby Monks Risborough; a special messenger delivered only urgent messages. The villa's isolation made it ideal for measured discussion. Both men came to the meeting with high hopes, but neither expected instant results. They realized that creating a new era of peace would be a laborious process.

MacDonald was a committed internationalist and accepted that French national interest might differ significantly from British aims.[38] He began by asking what specific economic and political guarantees France wanted in exchange for removing its troops from the Ruhr. (Poincaré had insisted on a phased evacuation, which could conceivably last forty years.) Herriot replied that the French had to be assured that Germany would resume payment of reparations as was indicated by the commercialization of Germany's debts and the public sale of German railroad and industrial obligations.[39] Herriot doubted German good intentions, fearing that Germany would renege on reparations payments.

MacDonald tried to quell French fears, asserting that German default was unlikely because it would provoke American retaliation:

> You can be quite certain that the American government will not
> allow Germany to escape after the conclusion of an agreement with
> the Allies and remain indifferent before a fraudulent bankruptcy of
> Germany.[40]

An immediate conference among the Allies would be arranged, which would adopt a policy of force. "Even a Nationalist Government with von Tirpitz at its head could not escape in that case," MacDonald said.[41]

Herriot was not yet convinced. He insisted that sanctions be defined in advance, and he wanted a guarantee of permanent Rhineland demilitarization, which would be accomplished through the establishment of a reciprocal non-aggression security agreement backed by the authority of the Council of the League of Nations.[42] This agreement would outline procedures to be followed in case of danger to French national security.[43]

MacDonald insisted that he was sensitive to the perilous position of France, but refused. He said the British Foreign Office, the Dominion governments, the Committee of Imperial Defence, and the general staffs of the navy, army, and air force would likewise oppose such a scheme.[44] His government would fall, a government of reactionaries take its place, and "France would only have a false security." MacDonald promised Herriot that, once the Dawes business were settled, he would come to Paris

> and spend a couple of days talking to you on the question of debts
> and security and so on....We must assure our own well-being, but
> we will work also to resolve the great moral problems of the peace
> of the world.[45]

It was cold comfort, and Herriot replied sadly,

We must have the courage to realize that the problem of reparations is not only financial, but political and military [and Germany is to blame]. If there is a new war, France would be wiped off the map of the world....Can we not try to find a formula of guarantees against a danger of such a sort that it would render the Dawes report useless?...I cannot give up the security of France, who could not face a new war.[46]

MacDonald opposed signing a security treaty with France, but he agreed to a written declaration of Anglo-French solidarity—a significant departure from what his predecessors had been prepared to commit. This obligation would last the entire period of reparations, and MacDonald assured that he was even willing to announce it publicly.[47] Herriot felt that the French had at last gained significant ground with Britain.

Two days later in an interview he had with a journalist in Brussels, Herriot stated that Britain would now stand side by side with France and with Belgium in case of German aggression, just as it had done in 1914.[48] MacDonald immediately issued a denial, stating that Britain had made no such military commitment. Lloyd George, amused at this put-down, quipped, "Well, it seems the laundry woman's son (MacDonald) kayoed the nephew of the cook (Herriot)."[49] The French press carried his remark.

Parisian newspapers like *Le Matin*, *L'Intransigeant*, *Echo de Paris*, and *Journal des Débats*, always eager to show the British in a bad light, were willing to stretch the truth. Thus Lloyd George's remark was escalated into a British government policy to strip the Reparation Commission of its authority to declare Germany in default.[50] *Le Matin* stated that Britain even wanted to overthrow the Treaty of Versailles and deny the French their rights of enforcement.[51] This charge was so widely believed that Herriot, fearing that he might be swept from office, begged MacDonald to come to Paris to show the strength of Anglo-French cooperation.[52] MacDonald agreed to come.

The discussions were held at the Quai d'Orsay and the British Embassy on 8 and 9 July. These meetings were more than symbolic. Herriot and MacDonald made another attempt to reconcile their countries' deep-seated differences on German policy, and they continued cooperating to bring the Dawes plan into operation. Neither man had been an expert in foreign policy before coming to power, but that would have been difficult to tell from the sophistication of their conversations. Both seemed more sure of themselves than they had previously, and they deferred only occasionally to the experts who accompanied them.

Herriot knew that getting the French army out of the Ruhr, which he referred to as an "economic withdrawal," was a foregone conclusion. He continued insisting on safeguards, however. He wanted French evacuation of the Ruhr after the coming into force of the Dawes report, no modification of the Treaty of Versailles, and sanctions in case of German default.[53] Herriot stuck to Poincaré's demand that the executive authority of the Reparation Commission be increased. He feared that vital questions concerning French security would be forgotten once the reparations question was settled.[54] Herriot predicted that "if a new Bismarck appeared, there would be good reason to fear that a war-like policy would instantly make its reappearance."[55] He envisaged the "bad situation" ten years hence if France had no security pact:

> the classes of military age would have few effectives—they would be the generations born during the war—and...because the financial charges which the country would have to bear would be so heavy that it was difficult to see how it could support another war.[56]

Herriot rejected any scheme that proposed guaranteeing French security only through German disarmament and entry into the League. He wanted protection against attack through the continued demilitarization of the Rhineland—this could be guaranteed, either by the British and French alone, or in conjunction with other powers.

MacDonald failed to pick up on Herriot's suggestion about a general security arrangement; he talked, instead, about "continued moral collaboration." This sort of Wilsonian language always made the French nervous. Many British were interested in cooperation and friendship with France, but they were fearful about recreating the military alliance features of the old Entente Cordial. They wanted to establish an equilibrium between France and Germany in which Britain held the balance. MacDonald did not want the responsibility to be solely British, however. As he was to tell Herriot:

The real guarantee of peace lies in an *entente* between our two
countries. It would really be unfortunate if we could not in 1924 or
in 1925 succeed in finding a way, either through the League of
Nations or in any other way, of bringing about an entente between
us so close and complete that no country—unless its leaders were
double fools—would dare to defy two great powers like ourselves,
because as soon as one of them were provoked we should
immediately be side by side.[57]

THE NEW BROOMS.

M. HERRIOT *(to Mr. MacDONALD)*. "WE ARE ALREADY IN STEP. NOW, IF YOU WOULD
ONLY CARRY YOUR BROOM AS I DO, IT WOULD CREATE A STILL MORE EXCELLENT
IMPRESSION."

The New Brooms. *Bernard Partridge depicts the hesitancy of Ramsay
MacDonald to follow the lead of Edouard Herriot in their march towards a
new Europe.* (Punch, *July 2, 1924.*)

The French, however, felt that MacDonald's reluctance to advocate a straightforward Anglo-French alliance, signified an unwelcome desire to keep British options open. Thus MacDonald's words did not pacify the French, but heightened the unease the French already felt concerning their national security.

THE DISCUSSIONS to implement the Dawes Plan opened in London on 16 July 1924. Four separate committees divided the workload. The First Committee, under the chairmanship of Philip Snowden, Britain's chancellor of the Exchequer, handled the most important questions: how to determine the course of action for declaring Germany in default, what action should be taken in case of default, and how to stabilize the German economy.[58]

Snowden was no friend of France. This became obvious when he tried to prevent the French from seeking German reimbursement for the expenses incurred during the period of troop withdrawal.[59] Snowden argued that any recognition of the right to payment would be tantamount to accepting the legality of the occupation. Dismissing the argument that such denial would allow the Germans to benefit financially, he asked, "You mean, they get the benefit of revenue from which they have been deprived hitherto through occupation of the Ruhr?"[60] Snowden also reduced French influence by according the United States full representation on the Reparation Commission. This stung the French, who had always opposed giving the Americans responsibility for enforcing a treaty they had signed, but refused to ratify.

Furthermore, Snowden made sure that sanctions would not become automatic in case of German default. Should that occur "the interested governments acting as joint trustees for their own financial interests would confer on the nature of sanctions to be applied and on the means of their application."[61] This process would be time consuming, and, even if there were agreement, action would not be immediate. Snowden insisted that all the committee's decisions on default be appealed to a outside committee of independent experts. In case of deadlock, the matter could be taken to the International Tribunal in The Hague.[62]

French nationalists warned Herriot to make no concessions on implementing the Dawes Plan until the country's security needs were met. Minister of War General Charles Marie Édouard Nollet, current president of the Allied Military Control Commission, opposed any evacuation from the Ruhr and any relinquishing of control over the area's important railways, even if that meant violation of the Treaty of Versailles.[63]

The Germans delegates arrived on 4 August, demanding the immediate and unconditional evacuation of the Ruhr. They also wanted an impartial body, not the Reparation Commission, to decide on issues of default. The French countered by linking evacuation with German disarmament. They wanted the pullout to be phased over a year, with France retaining control over the Rhineland railroads. Complete evacuation would occur only after the Dawes plan had come into force. But Herriot could achieve none of these goals without British support.[64] Furthermore, Poincaré had already conceded the evacuation of the Ruhr, when he had accepted the Dawes plan as the basis for a settlement. And, although Marshal Foch favored a phased withdrawal, he believed that the occupation of the Ruhr was unnecessary and even undesirable for French security because it put the French army in a dangerously exposed position. Foch was more interested in maintaining a strong French presence in the rest of the Rhineland, occupied under the authority of the Treaty of Versailles.

Nonetheless, Herriot continued to insist on a prolonged French presence in the Ruhr. When logic did not serve him, he resorted to literary eloquence:

> I am in the same situation as a man going down a staircase. I am holding in my hands the precious commodity of peace. If someone gets me from behind, I fall. If I fall alone, it amounts to nothing, but if I fall I also break the precious object that I carry: peace.[65]

It was a lonely effort.

German foreign minister Gustav Stresemann had made it clear that the Reichstag would never assemble the two-thirds majority necessary to approve the Dawes plan unless the Ruhr evacuation came without conditions. MacDonald agreed. He promised Herriot that he would deal with the issue of French security, but only after the Dawes plan was in operation. Without British support, Herriot could hold out no longer, and he consented to the immediate evacuation of Dortmund, providing this remain private until final agreement.[66] He promised that the rest of the troops would leave after the Reichstag ratified the Dawes Plan.

MacDonald had achieved his aims, but allowed himself only cautious optimism.

> We have a long way to go before we reach the goal of European peace and security. The all-important thing today is that we should be sure we are on the right road.[67]

Stresemann hailed the London agreement as beginning "a new development towards co-operation of the nations."[68] The Germans, however, had consented because it was the price they had to pay to regain sovereignty over their national territory and further the process of revising the Treaty of Versailles. The Reichstag ratified the agreement on 21 August.

The Dawes Plan changed how reparations would be administered, but it did little for French security. France could no longer prevent Germany from becoming the most powerful country on the continent. Just to keep pace, France would have to increase the production of its factories and farms and put an enormous amount of the national resources into its armed forces. Even then, the French could have real protection only with strong allies. And the British were opposed to helping France increase its power.

A large crowd greeted Herriot at the Gare Saint-Lazare on his return on 18 August with cheers of "Long live Herriot!" and "Long live Peace!" Foch also approved and wrote in his memoirs that Herriot had succeeded where his predecessors had failed, "in having France's agreements accepted abroad."[69] Louis Latzarus, the influential editor of the rightist *L'Éclair*, was, however, not taken in. Of all the dangers to which France was exposed, the worst, he said, was the stupidity of Herriot, who had gotten into his head the absurd notion that he could reconcile France with the universe and erase all dissent from the face of the earth. Herriot, Latzarus said, "wanted a love fest (*embrassade*)" more than negotiations. The journalist called MacDonald "that German-lover who during the last war instigated strikes which threatened the allied security. Was this for our protection?"[70] The French were easily alarmed by a picture of the perpetually self-serving British.

ON 4 SEPTEMBER 1924, in Geneva's stuffy, austere Reformation Hall, MacDonald told the assembly of the League of Nations, that military alliances were poor guarantees of security. Security, he asserted, could only be achieved through disarmament and arbitration under the authority of the League of Nations. The speech was well received by all but—predictably—the French delegates. Georges Bonnet called it "monotonous and confused" and said the British were trying to create a pretext for French disarmament. "Germany [does] not worry them, but the strength of the French army [does]," he said ironically.[71]

In truth, MacDonald was prepared to support the League only if it conformed to British interests.[72] The previous year the League had drafted a Treaty of Mutual Assistance, which obliged the signatories to come to the aid of each other if they should become victims of aggression.[73] The French saw this treaty as reinforcement for the status quo established at the Paris Peace Conference. But the British feared that the treaty could involve them in situations outside British national interest. The British especially had no desire to be dragged into guaranteeing the precarious territorial settlements of eastern Europe, and they refused to ratify the treaty.[74]

MacDonald looked with greater favor on the so-called Geneva Protocol, which had been drafted by Czech Foreign Minister Eduard Beneš. The Protocol assigned the solution of serious disputes to the World Court, or to the Council of the League. It stated that any nation that refused arbitration and resorted to force in violation of its pledge would be branded an aggressor, with the other parties automatically coming to the aid of the victim state. The Protocol, unlike the Treaty of Mutual Assistance, put primary emphasis on the compulsory settling of disputes and imposed sanctions only after peace had been violated.[75] It also contained disarmament provisions. MacDonald hoped that the Protocol would satisfy the French longing for security. But such assumptions did not increase French confidence.

Herriot, in his next-day response to MacDonald's speech to the League assembly, demonstrated the extent of Anglo-French disagreement. Herriot pointed out that arbitration was necessary, but insufficient. "It is a means, it is not an end." What happens, he asked, if a nation refuses to arbitrate or to disarm?" Then quoting Blaise Pascal, the 17th century French philosopher/mathematician, he said,

"Right without Might is powerless. The problem is to fuse Right with Might in such a way that Right automatically has Might."[76] MacDonald's support of arbitration in the form of the Geneva Protocol also drew fire from British military chiefs and from the Dominion governments.[77] Additionally MacDonald was also facing serious opposition because of his policy toward Communist Russia.

MACDONALD PROMISED that one of his first acts as prime minister would be diplomatic recognition of the Soviet Union. But King George requested that MacDonald do nothing to compel him "to shake hands with the murderers of his relatives."[78] Many at the Foreign Office also opposed any rapprochement. MacDonald, though, thought that the time was right.

Stalin appeared to welcomed detente, abandoning the Comintern's policy of subverting western capitalist governments.[79] Even Donald Gregory, the head of the Foreign Office's Northern Department that presided over East Europe and the Soviet Union, who was a fervent anti-Bolshevik, agreed that Britain should recognize the Soviet Union providing the United States had no objections. The British wanted to encourage American involvement in European affairs. Gregory remarked that American support for British policy could be invaluable "in cleaning out the European stables."[80]

MacDonald was attracted by the advantages of getting the Communist state to join the European community. British recognition would facilitate access to the Soviet market, and more trade would eventually translate into less unemployment and a stronger British economy. Recognition would also help to weaken the Soviet Union's bonds with Germany, which would help to alleviate French fears.[81] Cooperation between the Soviet Union and Germany in the Rapallo pact had only fed French insecurity, giving France an additional excuse to occupy the Ruhr.

The belief that an agreement with the Soviets would serve to solidify security in a mercurial postwar Europe was not unique to MacDonald, indeed Lloyd George had made the same case, but MacDonald felt he was in a better position to do business with the Communists than the upper-class Tories or the bourgeois Liberals because he was the principal representative of the British working class. On 2 February 1924, he notified the Soviet Commissariat for Foreign Affairs of his intent to grant recognition, specifying that the two countries should immediately begin negotiations towards resolving the Russian debt to Great Britain.[82]   In order to spare the king the painful duty of receiving an ambassador from a regime that had murdered his first cousin, Tsar Nicholas II, the exchange of representatives would be only at the chargé d'affairs level.[83]

The Soviets promised to negotiate a settlement of the claims of tsarist bond holders, stating that the investors would receive at least half of their original investment.[84]   In exchange, the British would restore normal trade relations complete with most favored nation status and negotiations for a loan.[85]   The offer to extend credits proved to be MacDonald's undoing.   The aggressive Tories demanded a full scale parliamentary debate.[86]   The Liberals joined in and introduced a motion of censure.   MacDonald, exhausted from his efforts to solve the Ruhr crisis, petulantly, and unnecessarily, regarded this a question of confidence.   When the motion of censure passed by 359 to 198, he submitted his resignation.   Parliament was dissolved and new elections called.

Alfred Leete's **The Greedy Bolshevik** *warns that the Soviets would use an Anglo-Soviet trade pact to loot Britain. Leete was best known for his Great War recruiting poster showing Lord Kitchner demanding, "Your Country needs YOU." The Tories were fortunate in having enlisted such a popular illustrator in their campaign against Labour.*

It's Your
MONEY
He
Wants.

The electoral campaign of October 1924 was one of the dirtiest in modern British history. Conservatives warned the people that the association of the Labour Party with the Communists would destroy the institution of marriage and take children away from their parents.[87] But the final blow occurred on 25 October, four days before polling time, when *The Times* published a letter that Gregori Zinoviev, the chief of the Comintern, had supposedly sent to the British Communist Party. The communication was an attempt to gain support for an Anglo-Soviet treaty as a means of "extending and developing the propaganda of ideas of Leninism in England and the Colonies."[88] But the letter was a forgery.[89]

It made no difference. A good Red Scare was just the tonic the Tories needed to win. They increased their popular vote from 5.3 million to 7.4 million and their strength in parliament by 155 seats, giving them a majority of 413.[90] The victory sealed the fate of the Anglo-Soviet Trade Agreement. The Tories severed diplomatic relations with the U.S.S.R and either directly denounced, or took under advisement, all treaties made with the Soviet government.

Lost in all of the inflammatory rhetoric was any serious discussion of MacDonald's achievements. But elections are seldom decided on merits alone, if at all. In the brief time MacDonald had been prime minister and foreign secretary, he had presided over a policy that had brought about the end of the French regime in the Ruhr. And by keeping the reparation crisis separate from the more difficult one of French security, he had established the groundwork for the eventual reconciliation of Anglo-French differences in their policy towards Germany. He thus paved the way towards a new era of cooperation.

Notes and Sources:

1. *The Times*, October 26, 1923.

2. *Annual Register 1923*, 139-40.

3. David Marquand, *Ramsay MacDonald* (London: Jonathan Cape, 1977), 251-252.

4. The correspondence was dated 21 February 1924. *Documents on British Foreign Policy*, first series, vol. XXVI, 552.

5. *Ibid.*, 552.

6. *Ibid.*, 552. According to British calculations, the French, as of 31 March 1924) owed the British £623,279,000 (about $2 3/4 billion) in war debts. This included original capital and funded interest. *Ibid.*, 637.

7. *Ibid.*, 553.

8. *Ibid.*, 556-557.

9. *Ibid.*, 558.

10. *Ibid.*, 559.

11. *Ibid.*, 558.

12. In a wire to Robert Crew, the British ambassador. (First and second sentences out of sequence for style). *Ibid.*, 670-671.

13. *Documents on British Foreign Policy*, first series, vol. XXI, 651-2.

14. See: Royal Schmidt, *Versailles and the Ruhr*, 216-217.

15. Charles Gates Dawes, *A Journal of Reparations* (London: Macmillan, 1939), 13.

16. Royal Schmidt, *Versailles and the Ruhr*, 224-225.

17. Charles Dawes, *A Journal of Reparations*, 95-101.

18. *Ibid.*, 130.

19. Royal Schmidt, *Versailles and the Ruhr*, 226.

20. *League of Nations Treaty Series*, vol. XXX, 1924-25, no. 1-4, 72.

21. *Documents on British Foreign Policy*, first series, vol. XXVI, 630.

22. *Ministère des Affaires Étrangères*, série Y, vol. 691 (Internationale), 213-214.

23. *Command Document* 2105, *Reports of the Expert Committees appointed by the Reparation Commission* (London: His Majesty's Stationary Office, 1924).

24. That is an amount equal to "the total money value of the consumption of sugar, tobacco, beer and alcohol within Germany (measured by the prices actually paid by the consumer*)." Documents on British Foreign Policy*, first series, vol. XXVI, 632.

25. Auguste de Saint-Aulaire, *Confession d'un vieux diplomate* (Paris: Flammarion, 1953), 694.

26.   *Documents on British Foreign Policy*, first series, vol. XXVI, 658-559.

27.   Édouard Bonnefous, *Histoire politique de la troisième république, L'après-guerre 1919-1929* (Paris: Presses Universitaires de France, 1959), 403-406.

28.   Denis W. Brogan, *The Development of Modern France* (New York: Harper and Row, 1966), II, 581-589.

29.   It sold for 14.82 to the dollar on 23 April. *Les cahiers de l'histoire, La IIIème république* (Paris: Librairie Le Griffon, 1961), 101.

30.   The voters in each department voted for lists of candidates. The list that got an absolute majority of the votes was elected, winner take all. If there were no clear victors, then the seats in the Chamber of Deputies were allotted on the basis of total percentages, the number of votes divided by the number of seats. Each slate had the right to designate whom of its candidates would sit in the legislature. If there were any seats left over, they would go to the group with the most votes. Thus everything favored the best organized coalition. *Annual Register 1924*, 157.

31.   There were 29 seats occupied by the Communists and 11 by Independents. When the Cartel took power, a realignment took place, 40 centrists from the old opposition, calling themselves the Radical Left, agreeing to give the new government their support.

32.   J. Néré, *The Foreign Policy of France from 1914 to 1945* (London: Routledge and Kegan Paul, 1975), 280.

33.   *Ministère des Affaires Étrangères*, série Y, vol. 691 (Internationale), 9-10.

34.   The Radicals also agreed to get rid of Alexandre Millerand, the aggressive nationalistic president of the Republic, who, since his election four years earlier, had poked his nose into every affair of government in order to impose his rightist ideas. On 2 June, the Cartel leaders introduced motions in both the Chamber of Deputies and the Senate, stating that Millerand's continued presence at the Élysée was incompatible with the proper functioning of parliamentary government. The was followed, on 10 June, by formal motions of no confidence. The next day Millerand resigned. *Les cahiers de l'histoire*, No. 9, 104. His successor Gaston Doumergue, the first Protestant to be elected president, said that his role was to "remain above parties, so that I can be an impartial and fair judge." Georges and Janine Hémeret, *Les présidents, République française* (Paris: Socadi, 1985), 101.

35.   *Les cahiers de l'histoire*, vol. 9, 105.

36.   *Ministère des Affaires Étrangères*, série Y, Vol 691 (Internationale), 81.

37.   In fairness, MacDonald had also tried to meet with Poincaré before the elections. Some members of the Cartel de gauches criticized him for this, fearing that such a summit might gain votes for the Bloc National. *Survey of International Affairs 1924*, 362-3.

38. David Marquand, *Ramsay MacDonald*, 164-165.

39. Herriot envisaged the conversion of the reparations obligation into bonds for sale on the American market. Thus France would get its money, and if the Germans defaulted, American bondholders would be left with the bad paper. To make the latest version of this deal work, however, the Americans had to be willing to invest, that is they had to be assured that they could get a decent return plus full eventual redemption. But American bankers had told the British government that they would never risk their money as long as French troops continued occupying the Ruhr.

40. *Ministère des Affaires Étrangères*, série Y, Vol 691 (Internationale), 74.

41. *Ibid.*, 74.

42. *Ibid.*, 80.

43. Herriot's scheme was akin to the draft Treaty of Mutual Assistance, which the League of Nations had produced the previous year. This pact is discussed below. *Survey of International Affairs 1924*, 475.

44. *Ministère des Affaires Étrangères*, série Y, vol. 691 (Internationale), 81.

45. *Ibid.*, 81.

46. *Ibid.*, 81.

47. *Ministère des Affaires Étrangères*, série Y, vol. 691 (Internationale), 81.

48. Michel Soulié, *La vie politique d'Édouard Herriot* (Paris: Armand Colin, 1962), 161-163.

49. "*Eh bien, le fils de la blanchisseuse a mis knock-out le neveu de la cuisinière.*" *Ministère des Affaires Étrangères*, série Y, vol. 691 (Internationale), 98.

50. *Documents on British Foreign Policy*, first series, vol. XXVI, 669-670.

51. *Ibid.*, 744.

52. *Ibid.*, 746.

53. "*First Draft of French Proposals concerning the London Conference fixed for July 16, 1924, for the purpose of concerting the necessary arrangements for the putting into execution of the Dawes Scheme*", *Ibid.*, 759-763.

54. *Documents on British Foreign Policy*, first series, vol. XXVI, 750-753, 778.

55. *Ibid.*, 765.

56. *Ibid.*, 766.

57. *Ibid.*, 758.

58. The second committee dealt with the restoration of German fiscal and economic unity; the third considered transfers and deliveries in kind; and the fourth, a committee of jurists, studied the procedure for modifying the Dawes plan should that become necessary. *Ibid.*, 808.

59. That is those charges the Germans would have normally paid if their own officials, rather than the armies of occupation, were collecting the revenues.

60. *Ministère des Affaires Étrangères*, série Y, vol. 691 (Internationale), 216.

61. *Ibid.*, 204.

62. *Ibid.*, 204.

63. Nollet interrupted a meeting between MacDonald and Herriot in the Cabinet Room at 10 Downing Street. MacDonald excused himself to work on other business, letting the two men argue alone. They were still at it after MacDonald went to bed. Past midnight, the Number-Ten staff obligingly made them sandwiches. *Documents on British Foreign Policy*, first series, XXVI, 822.

64. *Ibid.*, 788.

65. *Ministère des Affaires Étrangères*, série Y, vol. 691 (Internationale), 178.

66. David Marquand, *Ramsay MacDonald*, 350.

67. *Ibid.*, 351.

68. *Documents on British Foreign Policy*, first series, XXVI, 857.

69. Michel Soulié, *La vie politique d'Édouard Herriot*, 180.

70. *Ministère des Affaires Étrangères*, série Y, vol. 691, 98. Latzarus obtained a copy of the minutes of the Chequers meeting probably from Herriot's enemies at the Quai d'Orsay who thought nothing of slipping friendly journalists confidential documents. The account on the meeting eventually appeared in *L'Éclair*, on 24 December 1924, (*Ibid.*, 23.) with some sections that might present Herriot in a favorable light judiciously edited out. Missing, for example, was Herriot's statement to MacDonald that what he wanted was a straightforward guarantee that could work automatically "without cracks and without possible error."

71. Georges Bonnet, *Quai d'Orsay* (Isle of Man: Times Press, 1965), 70-71.

72. Concerning the similarity of MacDonald's foreign policy with that of his predecessor, Harold Nicolson remarked, "Oh, it is simply as if Lord Curzon had gone down to [his country estate of] Kedleston for a few days." John Connell, *The `Office', The Story of the British Foreign Service 1919-1951* (New York: St. Martin's Press, 1958), 61.

73. The French insisted that for practical reasons the countries limit their influence to states located in the same part of the world. *Survey of International Affairs 1924*, 475.

74. *Ministère des Affaires Étrangères*, série Y, vol. 691 (Internationale), 81.

75. *Survey of International Affairs 1924*, 1-64.

76. *League of Nations, Official Journal, Records of the Fifth Assembly, Text of the Debates* (Geneva: League of Nations, 1924), 45-8.

77. *Ibid.*, 1925, II, 2-7.

78. David Marquand, *Ramsay MacDonald*, 304.

79. In a speech in January 1923, Stalin said: "The very existence of the Soviet state, its consolidation, and its material prosperity...are the best propaganda for the Soviet government." Xenia Eudin and Harold Fisher, *Soviet Russia and the West*, 244.

80. *Ibid.*, 328.

81. The Communists knew their markets attracted other nations. In a speech at the Second Congress of Soviets, 30 January 1924, Lev Kamenev, the deputy prime minister, said: "the world economy cannot be restored without the cooperate cooperation of the 130 million people united under the Red flag of the U.S.S.R." Xenia Eudin and Harold Fisher, *Soviet Russia and the West*, 228-233.

82. The British claimed that the Soviets owed almost a billion pounds sterling to the British citizens who invested in Tsarist bonds.

83. These diplomats would be accredited to the respective foreign ministers, not the heads of state. David Marquand, *Ramsay MacDonald*, 331.

84. *Annual Register 1924*, 104.

85. Russian expert Gregory said that unless the Soviets got money "in some form or another", the British had to "give up all idea of resuming normal relations; worse than that, it may probably be taken for granted that, should the present negotiation break down, relations will be even less satisfactory than if they had never started." *Documents on British Foreign Policy*, first series, XXV, 556, 559.

86. Lloyd George dared the government to get the treaty ratified; and, on 10 September 1924, at a party convention at Penmaenmawr, he said that the proposed loan to the Soviets was "an act of criminal recklessness" and that the money was needed to help recovery at home, not support a system of predators. *Annual Register 1924*, 97.

87. David Marquand, *Ramsay MacDonald*, 378.

88. It also called for the establishment of Communist cells in the armed forces to "to paralyze all the military preparations of the bourgeoisie, and make a start in turning the imperialist war into a class war." *Documents Illustrating* *the Hostile Activities of the Soviet Government and Third International against Great Britain. Command Document* 2874.

89. It was written by a group of anti-Bolshevik Russian émigrés in Berlin, including super-spy Sidney Reilly; but the fabrication also involved the Polish Secret Service and high ranking members of the Polish government, including Prime Minister Wladyslaw Sikorski. Reilly, who needed an event of major proportions to discredit the Soviets and to destroy the Anglo-Soviet Treaty, then delivered it to MI 5, the British Secret Service, which leaked it to the officials at the Conservative Central Office and Tory newspaper editors. Robin Lockhart, *Ace of Spies* (New York: Stein and Day, 1968), 125-9; and Lewis Chester, Stephen Fay, and Hugo Young, *The Zinoviev Letter* (Philadelphia: J. B. Lippencott, 1968), 61-3, 191-195.

90. Labour lost 40 seats, falling to 151, but managed to increase its popular votes from 4.4 million to 5.4. The Liberals were the real losers. Their strength dropped from 118 to 40 seats in Commons, and from 4.3 million to less than 3 million popular votes. The Conservatives would no doubt have won even without the Zinoviev letter, albeit with a smaller majority.

CHAPTER 9

THE BERLIN INITIATIVE

LORD CURZON looked forward to returning to the Foreign Office. But his American-born wife Grace told him not to count on reappointment. She suspected that Baldwin had Austen Chamberlain in mind. "Baldwin would never do such a thing to me," Curzon insisted.[1] After all, Chamberlain, although a veteran politician, had little experience in foreign affairs.

Grace's hunch, however, proved correct. Baldwin thought Curzon was too abrasive to carry out a policy of reestablishing friendly relations with France. Baldwin gave Chamberlain his pick between the Foreign Office or the Colonial Office.[2] Chamberlain took the Foreign Office. Baldwin offered Curzon the less significant post of Lord President of the Council.

Curzon was crushed. "I cannot believe that you would put so terrible a slur on my administration," he told Baldwin. "It would be too much to expect me to accept such a situation."[3] Baldwin tried to soothe him by discussing the fresh start he was trying to make. This would be best accomplished if the foreign secretary were a member of the House of Commons. But Curzon had heard that excuse before. The year before, the king had told Curzon that his membership in the House of Lords prevented his appointment as prime minister, and again the Marquess of Kedelston went home dejected. "I am always urged and indeed expected to do the right thing," Curzon complained to his wife.[4] He accepted the lord presidency, but his old drive was gone.[5] He died four months later following bladder surgery.

Chamberlain, the eldest son of the prominent Joseph Chamberlain, had been programmed from birth for a life of public service. Austen's political career showed he had not betrayed his father's expectations, although until his appointment to the Foreign Office, his achievement had been almost entirely confined to domestic affairs. In the 35 years Chamberlain served in Commons, he had held such posts as civil lord of the Admiralty, postmaster general, secretary of state for India, lord privy seal, and chancellor of the Exchequer. He was once considered for the post of ambassador to France—a prospective appointment that prompted the French ambassador in London Paul Cambon to remark acidly, "Ah, dear Austen. He's such a fine fellow, but not an article for export."[6]

Chamberlain might have become prime minister in 1922, but because of his association with Lloyd George the less able Bonar Law got the job instead. Colleague Leopold Amery explained that Chamberlain's weakness as a politician was due to "an exaggerated sensitiveness to the idea of being thought self-seeking or disloyal."[7] But Chamberlain also was not vindictive and had a praiseworthy lack of resentment for people more knowledgeable than himself. He welcomed and readily solicited expert opinion without feeling threatened—a quality that his half-brother Neville lacked.

Austen Chamberlain believed that British foreign policy should be built upon an entente with France. His conviction was so strong that, during his first months at the Foreign Office, some feared that he was working on some sort of Anglo-French military alliance.[8] Those who knew him well were able to trace this francophilia to attitudes he formed in his student days.

After graduating from Trinity College at Cambridge, Chamberlain had attended the *École des sciences politiques* in Paris, where he thrived on the open-minded and amiable atmosphere. His family connection gave him access to some of France's leading politicians. "M. [Alexandre] Ribot lectured me on the French Constitution, and M. [Georges] Clemenceau introduced me to the *première danseuse* of the Opera," he recalled fondly.[9] Chamberlain had also studied at the University of Berlin, but his experiences there were less pleasing. He looked on his fellow students as provincial, stuffy, and intolerant; and he found Herr Professor Heinrich von Treitschke's history lectures "narrow-minded, proud, intolerant Prussian chauvinism."[10] Although, as in Paris, he was able to gain entry into important circles, he had less pleasant memories. He remembered a dinner party with Chancellor Bismarck where he was seated between Bismarck's daughter and her dog.

Chamberlain's first important act as foreign secretary was to terminate Britain's sponsorship of the Geneva Protocol. His predecessor MacDonald had approved it despite opposition from the Chiefs of Staff and from many Tory leaders, who feared it would put the nation's fighting forces at the disposal of the League, seriously hampering Britain's freedom to deal with its world-wide commitments.[11] These opponents believed that the League of Nations could not be both an agency for conciliation and one for military action.[12] The Dominion governments were also anti-Protocol because they did not feel their vital interests included guaranteeing European frontiers.[13]

But Chamberlain's reasons for rejecting the Protocol had more to do with encouraging American participation in European economic recovery.[14] He feared that the system of sanctions contained in the Protocol could include Britain in naval and commercial blockades that would disadvantage American trade interests.[15] As he pointed out:

> We have to remember that when trade and financial interests are touched every United States government has invariably shown itself to be insistent on the pursuit of a purely national policy, without any regard to those larger interests on general principles of generous equity in the international sphere of which American orators are apt to claim almost a monopoly when only the interests of other countries are concerned.[16]

Chamberlain thought that he could best work with American Secretary of State Charles Evans Hughes by appealing to pragmatic interests. From that foundation, Chamberlain hoped to get the Americans to see that their security concerns and those of Europe were linked.[17] Chamberlain's feel for the American attitude about the Protocol proved correct.

Hughes refused to oppose the Protocol "officially" because the United States was not a signatory, nor a member of the League.[18] But he feared that, if the Protocol was instituted, it might assume the character of a concert against the United States. Nonetheless, to hedge his bets, he told Chamberlain not to discard the Protocol entirely, "for if this were done there would probably be a continuation of competitive armament in Europe which the countries concerned could not afford."[19]

Chamberlain also hoped to coax the United States into joining the League of Nations, but he carefully avoided tipping his hand.[20] For example, when the directors of the Woodrow Wilson foundation invited Viscount Robert Cecil, the under-secretary for League of Nations affairs, to Washington to accept its annual Peace Prize, Chamberlain instructed Esme Howard, the British ambassador in Washington, to make sure that the text of Cecil's acceptance speech omitted any suggestion that the United States should join the League.[21] Ambassador Howard replied that Hughes probably did not care one way or the other, and Chamberlain rescinded the order but nonetheless cautioned Cecil to keep his remarks non-committal.[22]

The death of the Geneva Protocol might have been applauded in Washington, but was aggrieved in Paris. This turn of events hardly seemed to fit in with Chamberlain's reputation of being impossibly francophilic. The French, reeling from their failure to prolong the occupation of the Ruhr, were willing to latch onto anything that might enhance national security. Premier Édouard Herriot was so eager to bring the Protocol into effect that he even broke a promise to accept it provisionally ("ad referendum to the Governments and Parliaments of the Powers represented"), and had the Chamber ratify it immediately.[23] This action gave the British no opportunity to work out any modifications or amendments. Even MacDonald, who was now out of office, felt Herriot had acted underhandedly.[24]

Chamberlain could hardly believe that the French took the Protocol so seriously considering how poor a substitute it was for a mutual defense treaty.[25] Nonetheless, he tried to soften the blow of British rejection by saying that his government was merely "reconsidering" the Protocol. At the same time, he emphasized that Britain was not going to weaken the Treaty of Versailles, nor abandon its support of the League of Nations.

Herriot seemed to take it well. On Armistice Day, 11 November 1924, he made a special point of placing a wreath in Notre Dame cathedral honoring the British war dead. Baldwin wrote that the gesture deeply touched him, thereby easing the way for a meeting between Chamberlain and Herriot in Paris during the second week of December 1924.

Chamberlain had his first opportunity to assess Herriot and was somewhat impressed.[26] Chamberlain found Herriot "much more businesslike and less verbose and declamatory" than he had expected. He was pleased with Herriot's determination to establish good relations with Great Britain, although Chamberlain believed that Herriot was totally obsessed with a fear of Germany.[27]

THE DATE FIXED for the first evacuation of foreign troops from the Rhineland (from the "Cologne Zone" occupied by the British) was 10 January 1925. The French opposed the evacuation because they believed that the Germans had failed to live up to their Versailles treaty obligations to reduce the size of their armed forces. The Germans, though, insisted that they were in full compliance. But for more than a year now, they had refused to furnish military information to the Allies to substantiate that claim. Instead, they requested that the League of Nations assume the job of supervising the disarmament provisions of the peace settlement.

During the Dawes Plan negotiations, military inspection of Germany had been virtually suspended.[28] Violations uncovered after resuming inspections in September 1924 amply supported the French argument for delaying the first evacuations.[29] Though the British had to recognize the reality of German noncompliance, they wished to avoid further postponement. On 18 December, Lord President of the Council Curzon stated painfully that the Allied Control Commission was having difficulty establishing good faith with Germany's carrying out its obligations and admitted that the evacuation might not take place as planned. Curzon's announcement alerted the German government not to count on the "scheduled" evacuation of Cologne.[30]

The German government had assumed that its conciliatory attitude in implementing the Dawes Plan would forestall sanctions. Predictably, it proclaimed that suspending the evacuation was unjustified.[31] But the Control Commission released a report that documented German failure to fulfill the disarmament obligations. The Commission, though, still held out hope that the infractions could be cleared away—possibly in two to three months—providing there was "good will on the part of the German government," and that the Allies did not become too microscopic in their interpretation of "substantial execution and effective disarmament."[32] But the subsequent discovery of a secret depot of arms at the *Berlin Industriewerke* in Karlsruhe on

23 December indicated that this evacuation might have to be considerably delayed.

On 5 January 1925, the allied governments officially announced that the any withdrawal of troops from the Cologne zone would come only after the Control Commission had made another evaluation. They explained simply that Germany had not honored the conditions laid down by Article 429 of the Versailles treaty.

The Germans continued to deny they were violating the military clauses. They said the charges against them lacked precision,[33] and they claimed that they were capable of providing detailed proof.[34] The German Foreign Office tried to get the British to promise that the Cologne evacuation would follow soon after the evacuation of the French from the Ruhr. The British refused.[35]

Two weeks later in his home town of Birmingham, Chamberlain affirmed that a priority of British policy was to renew and strengthen old ties of allied friendship and cooperation. He said that he regretted the controversy concerning the Cologne decision and was sorry the Germans were so displeased, but said he was gratified that they expressed a willingness to make good on disarmament.[36] Chamberlain then moved onto specifics.

He said he wanted the closest ties with France, but stated that France should accept a rehabilitated Germany. European harmony would be impossible without such accommodation. A policy of reconciliation, he believed, was all the more necessary in view of the "disappearance of Russia as a factor accountable in the European balance of power."[37] Although Chamberlain's theory was worthy, it was not formulated in any way to provide for French security, while turning Germany from a revisionist into a status quo power. He predicted that, if these goals were not accomplished, Britain would be

> dragged along, unwilling, impotent, protesting, in the wake of France towards a new Armageddon. For we cannot afford to see France crushed, to have Germany or an eventual Russo-German combination supreme on the Continent, not to allow any military power to dominate the Low Countries.[38]

Despite his desire to reestablish the Anglo-France Entente, he recognized that French policy could involve Britain in guaranteeing "the very unstable situation in Eastern Europe which the Peace Treaties have 'Balkanised' with a vengeance."[39]   His earlier advocacy of a formal alliance with France was now impossible because of the opposition "at home and in the Dominions."[40] Opposition to foreign entanglements was also strong in the Cabinet.[41] Chamberlain hoped the Foreign Office experts could help him to find a solution.[42]

He directed that the Foreign Office make recommendations which would fit into three categories: 1) the need for security in Europe, 2) a historical and contemporary analysis of British interests, and 3) "The Solution" dictating how Britain could commit to defend these interests without being dragged into a quarrel over "Lithuania or Latvia or Poland or Bessarabia."[43]   The British Foreign Office took up the challenge. But while its experts worked on a response, its counterparts at the German Foreign Ministry were endeavoring to produce a scheme of their own.

THE POLITICAL SITUATION in Germany remained clouded.[44] Chancellor Wilhelm Marx had resigned suddenly on 15 December 1924, and a caretaker government currently ran the country with Gustav Stresemann continuing as foreign minister.   Stresemann believed that no stable foreign policy was possible unless the rightist German National Peoples Party, whose 110 seats comprised over one-fifth of those in the Reichstag, were included in the new government. Stresemann hoped to strengthen that party's moderate elements by neutralizing the firebrands preaching open defiance of the Treaty of Versailles.[45] French refusal to carry out the first round of evacuations from the Rhineland had convinced him that accommodation with France was essential for the successful restoration of German sovereignty.

Stresemann hoped this policy of cooperation would lead to certain concessions from the Allies. He wanted to achieve the disbanding of the Allied Control Commission and witness the withdrawal of allied occupation from the Rhineland before the prescribed period of fifteen years. He also wanted to see the Saarland returned to Germany and revision of the recently concluded Dawes Plan. But his ultimate goal was the restoration of 1914 Germany—reestablishment of Germany's colonial position abroad, repossession of Eupen and Malmédy, and recovery of the "lost territories" in the East, including Danzig and the Polish corridor. He additionally worked to realize *Anschluss* (union) between Germany and Austria. In short, Stresemann's aims were substantially the same as those of the Nationalists. He merely chose different means to achieve his goals. He would support the Treaty of Versailles the better to undermine and destroy it.

Stresemann intended to take no action that might endanger the Soviet connection with its tangible military benefits. He favored continuing secret rearmament, and making maximum use of Germany's economic power.[46] He was suspicious of the British, but needed British support to curtail French enforcement of the Treaty of Versailles and prevent a recurrence of the Ruhr invasion. Stresemann held Herriot responsible for the Allied refusal to evacuate Cologne.[47] He realized, however, that the French would never relinquish their hold on the Rhineland unless they received a suitable replacement for the Anglo-American guarantee treaty.

In his recently-appointed deputy, State Secretary Karl von Schubert, Stresemann found an able and enthusiastic champion of his "reconciliation policy."[48] On 29 December 1924, Schubert had an important conversation with British ambassador Viscount D'Abernon. D'Abernon, one of the most compelling pro-Weimar envoys in the German capital, was not a career diplomat. He had been a financier, head of the Ottoman Bank in Constantinople. He had also been Curzon's classmate at Eton, and their continuing continued friendship had led to his diplomatic career. D'Abernon viewed Chamberlain's francophilia with alarm. He was strongly opposed to any sort of Anglo-French military alliance, and thought that some general multilateral non-aggression pact, devoid of any special commitment, should replace the Geneva Protocol to support the Versailles treaty.

During his encounter with Schubert, D'Abernon "quite casually" reminded him of certain proposals that Chancellor Cuno had made at the end of 1922 concerning the guarantee of French security. D'Abernon suggested that the Cuno package, made on the eve of the French invasion of the Ruhr, now be broadened into a into a nonaggression pact among the Rhineland powers.[49] The ambassador was too savvy to think he could set an independent course in British foreign policy, but he believed he could influence its direction. And, in a dispatch to the Foreign Office, he argued that France was a greater potential threat to European security than Germany:

On the one side is Germany with an army of 100,000 men, without reserve of guns and ammunition, with no up-to-date aerial equipment, and with no certain ally. On the other side is France with a peace army of 750,000 men, a considerable black reserve to draw upon in Africa; a more or less close military alliance with new states—Czechoslovakia, Poland, Jugoslavia and Roumania.[50]

D'Abernon also remarked that the financial controls present in the Dawes Plan made German rearmament less likely than before.

Over the next two weeks, Stresemann and Schubert worked out a response to D'Abernon's initiative, despite Stresemann's suspicion that Chamberlain was going to make a deal with France exchanging British support for France in Europe for French support for Britain in the Near East.[51] The German proposals involved a pledge to respect the Rhineland frontiers—but not the frontiers with Poland—and a promise that any questions left unsettled through normal diplomacy could be resolved through international arbitration. Stresemann had Schubert show these proposals to D'Abernon, on 14 January 1925, to get his reaction. Schubert insisted that all commitments be reciprocal.[52] D'Abernon, impressed, pledged to give the package his support. Stresemann then formalized the plan for presentation to the British Foreign Office.

The German initiative was received in London on 20 January. It proposed the conclusion of a Franco-German treaty of arbitration, which would protect both countries against the aggression of the other. The accord would further guarantee the "inviolability of the present territorial status of the Rhine," making any violation a matter of individual and collective international concern.[53]

Stresemann had impeccable rightist credentials—he had been one of the most outspoken annexationists in the Reichstag during World War One—but he feared that any adverse publicity could lose him the support of the Nationalists. He, therefore, had urged Chamberlain to keep the proposals confidential[54]

Chamberlain, still waiting for his own foreign policy experts to suggest a proper course of action, replied cautiously to Stresemann's initiative. He said that he "did not exclude" an agreement that would give "a mutual guarantee to the situation established by the peace treaties" providing this came "at the proper time."[55] Chamberlain defined "proper time" as following the definition of French security.[56]

Furthermore, Chamberlain suspected that Stresemann's request for confidentiality was part of a scheme to undermine British loyalty to France,[57] and he was determined to prevent this. On 30 January, he informed French Ambassador Amié de Fleuriau of the German initiative.[58] Though de Fleuriau was appreciative of the show of loyalty, he observed that the men of Baldwin's government were

> true Englishmen with a limited imagination...their intentions are vague and they do not yet have any clear ideas on any questions.[59]

In fact, Chamberlain was still unsure of his ground. He feared some sort of regional pact might jeopardize the strong position that the Conservative Party enjoyed in Britain and start the Liberal and Labour parties "on the war path."[60] He, therefore, told only his most trusted colleagues about the German initiative.

Herriot also doubted German sincerity and considered that the newly-appointed Chancellor Hans Luther might be deliberately feigning liberal tendencies to play for Socialist support.[61] Many at the Quai d'Orsay believed the initiative was a ruse to get allied troops off German soil while the Germans continued to violate the disarmament provisions of the Treaty of Versailles. They feared that the Germans were only pretending to favor the creation of a stable and peaceful Europe so they could get loans from the American bankers.[62]

But Herriot felt he had to keep one step ahead of the nationalist Right, and in a three-and-a-quarter-hour speech, in the Chamber of Deputies on 28 January, he denounced German militarism for continued to threaten French security. Herriot said that peace could only be maintained through an "effective entente" with Great Britain. He insisted that the continued occupation of the Rhineland was the necessary and "perhaps even, alas, the ultimate condition of French security."[63] He criticized the Germans for their lack of effort in creating a lasting peace and listed their violations of the Treaty of Versailles—the illegal training of substantially more soldiers than the treaty allowed, the ominous presence of para-military groups, and the secret deals for the manufacture of forbidden military equipment in factories in Sweden, Holland, Czechoslovakia, Spain, Switzerland, and especially Communist Russia. He finished by admitting that he nurtured a great hope to see the creation of a United States of Europe. The deputies gave Herriot a standing ovation.[64] From Paris, British

Ambassador Robert Crewe observed that Herriot's hard-line speech could have been written by Poincaré.[65]

In his 1924 pen-and-ink sketch, **The Generals,** *Weimar artist George Grosz confirms the pessimistic convictons of the French that the Reichwehr was commanded by arrogrant, punitive, treacherous, aggressive, and cruel Prussians.*

German Chancellor Hans Luther tried to deflect Herriot's strong words. Two days later in a speech addressed to a group of foreign journalists, Luther said that Germany was willing to cooperate in any effort to achieve a proper agreement on European security. He contended that his country had essentially completed its disarmament. "What is the importance of the discovery of some old war materials compared to such a vast undertaking of disarmament?" he asked.[66] German Ambassador Leopold von Hoesch echoed this theme in Paris. "We cannot understand why France makes such a fuss about some rusty old pieces of iron at Wittenau," he remarked, to which Herriot replied, "Only four nails were needed for the Crucifixion."[67]

Stresemann feared that his whole initiative might collapse unless he could push these "side-issues" aside. He knew that Germany had to come to terms with France and hoped to get Britain to help him make the French see reason.[68] But, now that it was evident the British would do nothing without consulting the French, he no longer had any excuse for not sending a copy of his proposal directly to Herriot.[69] In the "Paris version," however, he omitted linking the question of German disarmament to evacuation from the Cologne zone and proposed French security guaranteed within the context of an international convention in the manner of the Geneva protocol.[70] Stresemann offered to meet Herriot for direct talks, but asked the French to keep his proposal confidential, again to protect his political backside on the home front.

Herriot had similar worries about public disclosure. Aside from informing Chamberlain, French President Gaston Doumergue, and a few members of his inner circle, he told very few people. He even hesitated to inform Pierre de Margerie, the French ambassador to Germany. But de Margerie had heard rumors about the note in Berlin, and when he reported them to Paris as unreliable gossip, Herriot told him the truth.[71]

Herriot told Chamberlain that he favored all moves contributing to the peace of Europe, as long as these were taken in concert with his country's allies and in conjunction with the Treaty of Versailles. He said that France was willing to guarantee Germany against aggression, providing the security needs of France were satisfied first.[72] He said that he found the German proposals encouraging, but unacceptable in their present form. The French would refuse to accept any agreement without guarantees; to do otherwise would admit the shortcomings of the Treaty of Versailles.[73] Herriot hoped he could conclude a guarantee agreement with the British before he began direct talks with the Germans.[74]

Though Chamberlain considered the German memorandum the most hopeful sign of progress he had yet seen, he was still hung up on his suspicions that the German request for confidentiality was part of a devious effort to play the French off against the British. He instructed British diplomats to be cordial to the French diplomats.[75] To Ambassador Crewe he cabled:

What amusing people these same Germans are! First they hand a copy of their secret memorandum on a pact to D'Abernon and ask my advice about it, whilst attempting to enforce the condition that I shall say nothing to the French. I repudiated the condition, as you know, and one would have thought that they might have learned the lesson; but they next sent the same memorandum to Herriot...with the addition that they have told Herriot that he must not communicate with me. Herriot very properly responds to my confidence by giving me his confidence. But what earthly object do they think that all this tortuous duplicity would serve?[76]

Stresemann suspected that he was facing an Anglo-French conspiracy, and the greater became his apprehension the longer the Allied Control Commission delayed making its final report. Although his initiative was still officially secret, its contents in diplomatic circles were generally known. American chargé d'affaires in London, F. A. Sterling, got a copy of the memorandum simply by asking the German embassy to supply him with one.[77] Leaks of this sort prompted Stresemann to go public.

On 7 March 1925, he gave a press conference at which he explained that his main problem was to try to alleviate French fears of future German aggression. To do this, he said, it was first necessary to renounce all claims to Alsace-Lorraine, then guarantee the Rhineland. Although Germany opposed recognition of the eastern Frontiers, Stresemann insisted that any revision must accomplished peacefully. He argued that a security pact would afford Germany protection against further French adventures in the Rhineland and bring an end to military occupation before the date set by the Treaty of Versailles.

Stresemann had the support of the head of the government. Luther, who was prepared to back up the foreign secretary with the full force of the chancellor's office, agreed with Stresemann's general approach, although he disapproved of efforts to recruit the British as mediators. Luther believed that Chamberlain was so anti-German that cooperation with London was impossible.[78] But, in making it clear to the Nationalists that an attack on Stresemann was the same as an attack on himself, Luther threatened to bring down the government. He figured the Nationalists had joined his ministry because they were more interested in domestic affairs than foreign affairs: they wanted a stable currency, lower taxes, and lower tariffs. And, with the death of

President Friedrich Ebert (on 28 February), they also wanted to ensure that a staunch conservative be elected the new chief of state.[79] As Luther calculated, the Nationalists continued supporting his government.

THE REPORT on European security, upon which the British Foreign Office had been working since the middle of January, was circulated to the cabinet on 20 February. Harold Nicholson, under the direction of Eyre Crowe, had put together the final draft. It presented a pessimistic appraisal of the current situation:

> All our late enemies continue full of resentment at what they have lost; all our late Allies are fearful of losing what they have won. One-half of Europe is dangerously angry; the other half is dangerously afraid. The friction between these inflamed emotions is incessant, and acts as a septic irritant, poisoning the wounds which are yet unhealed. Fear begets provocation, armaments, secret alliances, ill-treatment of minorities; these in their turn beget a greater hatred and stimulate a desire for revenge, whereby fear is intensified, and its consequences are enhanced. The vicious circle is thus established.[80]

The report ascertained that, although a majority of Germans had little desire for a war of revenge, Germany would certainly try to recover its territory lost to Poland—Danzig, the corridor, and Silesia—when it recovered sufficient strength. But even with Germany occupied in the east, France, with its declining population, would continue to live in fear of another invasion until its frontiers with Germany were guaranteed. In the meantime, France would be "driven to expedients which in the end will only provoke the German revenge of which she stands in terror."[81]

The Foreign Office report emphasized that the old policy of "splendid isolation" was no longer economically, geographically, and, considering the advent of air power, scientifically feasible. French isolation and British neutrality would only invite Germany to occupy or dominate the Channel and North Sea ports. The safety of Great Britain and its empire and Commonwealth was, therefore, dependent on guaranteeing the security of France with a formal alliance:

It is doubtful, whether even in 1914 Germany would have risked the Great War had she known for certain that the British Empire would come to France's assistance. If she is not assured that by invading France she will inevitably incur the hostility of the British Empire, it is most unlikely she will make any such endeavor.[82]

The British had to be able to confer with France "with the authority of an Ally." Thus assured of British support, France would be able to withdraw its troops from the Rhineland and be less inclined to turn the Little Entente into an armed camp. Additionally France would be able to direct energy to stabilize finances to repay Britain the debts it owed. Then Germany, with French goodwill, could become a member of the League of Nations, leading to the re-creation of the concert of Europe. The "first hope of stability in Europe," the report concluded, "lies in a new *entente* between the British Empire and France."[83]

Chamberlain felt that he finally had a policy he could take to the cabinet for approval, and he started gathering support. The British War Office, the Admiralty, and the Air Ministry all favored a straightforward, old-fashioned Anglo-French military alliance. The British military leaders assumed that Germany would be the country's adversary in another war, and they wanted to be prepared. The army chiefs were emphatic in their belief that "renewed German aggression is the greatest danger that faces us today, and French security is our security."[84]

But the military leaders did not sit in the cabinet, where disapproval of an alliance with France still remained strong. Chancellor of the Exchequer Winston Churchill, Secretary of State for India Lord Birkenhead, and Colonial Secretary Leopold Amery all feared that an Anglo-French alliance could drive Germany to strengthen its ties with the Soviet Union. Churchill rejected the linkage of French to British security. He saw no purpose in negotiating any agreement until France had made peace with Germany.[85] Amery wanted to keep Britain entirely free from "the kind of commitment which had been involved in the staff consultations before the [First World] war."[86] The critics insisted that any security pact would have to include Germany. Against such opposition, Chamberlain could not prevail. The foreign secretary had hoped to have something positive to tell Herriot; instead he had only evil tidings.

Chamberlain met Herriot in Paris on 6 March 1925, on a stop over on way to Geneva to preside over the 33rd session of the League of Nations Council. He invited the French leader to dinner at the British embassy. Herriot came in good spirits, and all went well until Chamberlain told him the bad news. When Chamberlain said that there was no hope of concluding any bilateral security pact, Herriot blanched and began to hyperventilate, "becoming much more rhetorical." He rambled on about "the propaganda of revenge" being taught in German universities, mentioned the difficulty France had in repairing its devastated regions, and talked of the huge payments the Germans were able to make to the industrialists in the Ruhr because of the Dawes Plan loans. "I tell you I look forward with terror to [Germany] making war upon us again in ten years," he cried.[87]

Chamberlain tried to calm him down, explaining that the Labour party, the Liberal party, a large part of the Conservative party, and the British people would not support an Anglo-French pact. Chamberlain suggested that the two countries try to reach some sort of agreement along the lines of the recent German proposals. But all Herriot did was to repeat how much he distrusted the Germans. The evening had come to a bad end.

The two held another discussion at lunch the following day. Herriot had not slept well. During the night he had a rheumatic attack, and he looked as if he was still in considerable pain. Chamberlain was in despair that Herriot would insist on the indefinite occupation of the Rhineland.[88] He believed that any influence he had with Herriot was gone. Chamberlain was still brooding about his lack of success, when, later that day, he boarded the train for Geneva.

Notes and Sources:

1. Lewis Chester, Stephen Fay, and Hugo Young, *The Zinoviev Letter*, 69.

2. Keith Middlemas and John Barnes, *Baldwin, A Biography* (New York: Macmillan, 1970), 279.

3. G. M. Young, *Stanley Baldwin* (London: Rupert Hart-Davis, 1952), 88.

4. Beckhofer Roberts, *Stanley Baldwin, Man or Miracle?* (New York: Greenberg, 1937), 133.

5. Leopold Amery, *My Political Life, II*, 298.

6. Gordon A. Craig, "The British Foreign Office from Grey to Austen Chamberlain" in Craig and Gilbert, *The Diplomats I*, 42.

7. Leopold Amery, *My Political Life, II*, 304.

8. Viscount D'Abernon, *The Diary of an Ambassador, Dawes to Locarno 1924-1926* (Garden City, N. Y.: Doubleday, Doran, 1931), III, 21.

9. Sir Charles Petrie, *The Chamberlain Tradition* (New York: Frederick A. Stokes, 1938), 143.

10. *Ibid.*, 145.

11. Sir Charles Petrie, *The Life and Letters of the Right Hon. Sir Austen Chamberlain*, II (London: Cassell, 1940), 243.

12. Leopold Amery, *My Political Life, II*, 301.

13. *British Foreign Office Records*, 800/256, 301.

14. Thomas W. Lamont, the influential senior partner of Morgan's Bank and confidant of the White House, remarked to Lord Robert Cecil that the United States would not hold an endorsement of the Protocol against Britain. He said that the American people were Anglo-Saxons, who liked "to see people stick to their principles." *Ibid.*, 72-4.

15. *Ibid.*, 432-4.

16. In a dispatch to Esme Howard, the British ambassador in Washington (22 December 1924). Ibid, 74.

17. Hughes said foreign affairs resulted from "practical conceptions of national interest" that arose from "some immediate exigency" or stood out "vividly in historical perspective." John Chalmers Vinson, "Charles Evans Hughes" in Norman A. Graebner, ed., *An Uncertain Tradition: American Secretaries of State in the Twentieth Century* (New York: McGraw-Hill, 1961), 133.

18. *Foreign Relations of the United States, 1925*, I, 19.

19. *Ibid.*, 16-17.

20. Chamberlain's official association with Hughes was brief. Hughes tendered his resignation on 5 January 1925—it would take effect on 4 March.

He was sixty-three. Exhausted after twenty years of public service, he returned to private law practice to make some money for his old age. Hughes recommended that President Coolidge appoint Frank B. Kellogg as his new secretary of state. Kellogg was a former senator from Minnesota and had one-time served as ambassador to Britain. Merlo J. Pusey, *Charles Evans Hughes, II* (New York: Columbia University Press, 1963), 613.

   21. Cecil was also president of the League of Nations Union, which helped to mold British public opinion through its pronouncements and publications and by pressuring candidates at by-elections to adopt a pro-League stance. During the Twenties, its support came from many disparate sections of the electorate, from pacifists to conservatives.

   22. Cecil's speech was given on 28 December 1924. *British Foreign Office Records*, 800/256, 132, 145.

   23. *British Foreign Office Records*, 800/256, 107.

   24. MacDonald advised that something had to be put in its place "to meet the demands of France and the small nations for security." *Annual Register 1924*, 134.

   25. *British Foreign Office Records*, 800/256, 106-8.

   26. *Ibid.*, 338.

   27. *Ibid.*, 339. *"Obsédé"* was also used by Herriot to describe his own feelings. *Documents on British Foreign Policy 1919-1939*, first series, XXVII, 299.

   28. *Documents on British Foreign Policy*, first series, XXVI, 1112.

   29. It should be remembered that the 10 January 1924 date for Rhineland evacuation was well in advance of 16 August 1924 when the French were to be gone from the Ruhr.

   30. *Documents on British Foreign Policy*, first series, XXVI, 969.

   31. *Ibid.*, 1140, 1142.

   32. *Ibid.*, 1132.

   33. The demand for such precision was hardly sincere as details of the violations would only have provided ammunition to the German anti-militarist press, which attacked the government for keeping the citizenry in the dark about the state of armaments and military organization.

   34. *Ibid.*, 1139.

   35. *Documents on British Foreign Policy 1919-1939*, first series, XXVI, 1141.

   36. *Annual Register 1925*, 23.

   37. Harold Nicholson, *King George the Fifth, His Life and Reign* (New York: Doubleday, 1953), 405.

   38. *Documents on British Foreign Policy 1919-1939*, first series, XXVII, 256.

   39. *Ibid.*, 256.

40. *Ibid.*, 256.

41. Jon Jacobson, *Locarno Diplomacy, Germany and the West 1925-1929* (Princeton: Princeton University Press, 1972), 18-19.

42. His memo was dated 4 January 1925. *Documents on British Foreign Policy 1919-1939*, first series, XXVII, 255.

43. *Ibid.*, 257.

44. Viscount D'Abernon, *The Diary of an Ambassador, Dawes to Locarno 1924-1926*, III, 119.

45. Robert P. Grathwol, *Stresemann and the DNVP, Reconciliation or Revenge in German Foreign Policy 1924-1928* (Lawrence, Kansas: The Regents Press, 1980), 6.

46. Hans W. Gatzke, *Stresemann and the Rearmament of Germany* (Baltimore: The John Hopkins Press, 1954), 7-8.

47. Erich Eyck, *A History of the Weimar Republic* (Cambridge: Harvard University Press, 1962), II, 4-5.

48. Schubert's predecessor, Ago von Maltzan, would no doubt have supported Stresemann's policy of conciliation with the West, but he had been too closely involved with the Rapallo initiative. Stresemann feared that the association might impede the formulation of a security arrangement with the British and the French and sent Maltzan to Washington as ambassador. Viscount D'Abernon, *The Diary of an Ambassador, Dawes to Locarno 1924-1926*, III, 120.

49. Erich Eyck, *A History of the Weimar Republic* II, 4.

50. *Documents on British Foreign Policy 1919-1939*, first series, XXVII, 259.

51. British authority was currently under attack in Egypt and India with the Soviet Union giving aid and comfort to the local nationalists in those countries. Annelise Thimme, "Stresemann and Locarno" in Hans W. Gatzke, *European Diplomacy Between Two Wars, 1919-1939* (Chicago: Quadrangle, 1972), 81.

52. Viscount D'Abernon, *The Diary of an Ambassador, Dawes to Locarno 1924-1926*, III, 121.

53. English text of the memorandum in *Documents on British Foreign Policy 1919-1939*, first series, XXVII, 283-284   See also: Viscount D'Abernon, *The Diary of an Ambassador, Dawes to Locarno 1924-1926*, III, 276-277. See also: Charles Petrie, *The Chamberlain Tradition*, 200-201 and Harold Nicholson, *King George V*, 406-407.

54. Stresemann's note arrived in London just as the German cabinet crisis had reached its end.   A new government was installed on 22 January 1925.   It was comprised of a coalition of centrist and rightist parties, including Stresemann's own German People's Party, the Bavarian People's Party, the Catholic Zentrum, the German Democratic Party, and the

Nationalists. These parties agreed to create a "cabinet of personalities," in which they would be represented by a spokesman. The arrangement gave each party greater freedom of action than a formal political alliance would have. Hans Luther, the new chancellor, had no party affiliation. He had previously been finance minister and his success in stabilizing the mark had earned him a reputation for fiscal responsibility, something that made his present leadership acceptable to the conservatives. Robert Grathwol, *Stresemann and the DNVP, Reconciliation or Revenge in German Foreign Policy 1924-1928*, 56-61.

55. In an interview with Herr F. Sthamer, the German ambassador on 30 January 1925. *Documents on British Foreign Policy 1919-1939*, first series, XXVII, 294.

56. Viscount D'Abernon, *The Diary of an Ambassador, Dawes to Locarno 1924-1926*, III, 137-138.

57. *Ibid.*, 7. D'Abernon, saw nothing sinister about the procedure. He believed that the complaint of duplicity stemmed from a lack of understanding. "If either the Note to London or the [later] Note to Paris had been communicated to anyone outside the powers specifically addressed, the contents of these would have become a subject of public debate, and the whole work would have been undone." *Ibid.*, 141.

58. This meeting took place immediately after Chamberlain had talked to the German ambassador. *Documents on British Foreign Policy 1919-1939*, first series, XXVII, 296-297.

59. *Ministère des Affaires Étrangers*, série Y, vol. 58 (Grande-Bretagne), 2.

60. *Documents on British Foreign Policy 1919-1939*, first series, XXVII, 303.

61. *Ibid.*, 345.

62. Jules Laroche, *Au Quai D'Orsay*, 205.

63. Michel Soulié, *La vie politique d'Édouard Herriot* (Paris: Armand Colin, 1962), 207.

64. *Documents on British Foreign Policy 1919-1939*, first series, XXVII, 292.

65. *Ibid.*, 292.

66. Michel Soulié, *La vie politique d'Édouard Herriot*, 208-209.

67. Viscount D'Abernon, *The Diary of an Ambassador, Dawes to Locarno 1924-1926*, III, 134-5.

68. *Ibid.*, 142.

69. *Command Document* 2436. Miscellaneous no. 7.

70. *Documents on British Foreign Policy 1919-1939*, first series, XXVII, 298.

71. Erich Eyck, *A History of the Weimar Republic II*, 6.

72.   *Documents on British Foreign Policy 1919-1939*, first series, XXVII, 299.

73.   *Ibid.*, 206.

74.   When Jules Laroche, the Quai d'Orsay's political director, conveyed Herriot's refusal for direct talks to German Ambassador Hoesch, he could not resist questioning the sincerity of a German guarantee of the Rhine. "A guarantee of that sort given by Prussia figured in the treaties of 1839 relative to [the guaranteeing of] Belgian neutrality," he said. Jules Laroche, *Au Quai D'Orsay*, 206.

75.   Herriot gave the same instruction to French diplomats concerning the British. *Ministère des Affaires Étrangèrs*, série Y, vol. 58 (Grande-Bretagne), 6-7.

76.   *Documents on British Foreign Policy 1919-1939*, first series, XXVII, 303.

77.   *Foreign Relations of the United States, 1925*, I, 21-2.

78.   Viscount D'Abernon, *The Diary of an Ambassador, Dawes to Locarno 1924-1926*, III, 134-5.

79.   Robert Grathwol, *Stresemann and the DNVP, Reconciliation or Revenge in German Foreign Policy 1924-1928*, 70-75.

80.   *Documents on British Foreign Policy 1919-1939*, first series, XXVII, 312.

81.   *Ibid.*, 316.

82.   *Ibid.*, 317.

83.   *Ibid.*, 318.

84.   *Ibid.*, 266.

85.   Keith Middlemas and John Barnes, *Baldwin, A Biography*, 349.

86.   Leopold Amery, *My Political Life* II, 301-2.

87.   *Documents on British Foreign Policy 1919-1939*, first series, XXVII, 346; Charles Petrie, *The Life and Letters of the Right Hon. Sir Austen Chamberlain*, II, 263.

88.   *Documents on British Foreign Policy 1919-1939*, first series, XXVII, 354.

THE MODERATOR

ALTHOUGH GENEVA LACKED the excitement and high pace of great European cities, it had none of their filth and slums. Strollers could amble around town any time of the day, or night, without looking over their shoulders for possible assailants. From the quays along the unpolluted waters of the lake, there was an uninterrupted view of the Alps—providing the cloud cover obligingly disappeared. The parks and trees were splendid and even normally short-lived poplars grew to dignified, patriarchal old age. In many ways, Geneva seemed a natural ingredient to the high-hopes that had accompanied the League's birth, and, according to Deputy Secretary-General Francis Walters, to the universal optimism and dedication that infused its bureaucrats:

> All who took part in any League meeting, on whatever subject, were conscious that the success or failure of their work would necessarily contribute, in some slight degree, to the success or failure of the primary aim of the League, that is to say the maintenance of international peace.[1]

When the United States refused to ratify the Treaty of Versailles, the League fell under the domination of Britain and France, the only two Great Powers that remained members throughout the organization's life. The League, therefore, became an organization concerned primarily with the unfinished business of the peace settlement, social and economic problems becoming secondary concerns.[2]

The first secretary-general, Eric Drummond, was a lack-luster British civil servant, who felt that the League "should restrict itself as much as possible to routine and keep clear of anything that might disturb prejudices and established traditions."[3] Indeed, most of the two dozen or so disputes the League handled between 1920 and 1925 were boundary questions, like the controversy between Hungary and Czechoslovakia over ownership of the Salgótarján coal basin, the claims of Poland and Czechoslovakia for Javorzina, and a territorial dispute between Albania and Yugoslavia. The Council also handled the British and Turkish claims over the area of Mosul, and it helped resolve the controversy between Poland and Germany concerning Upper Silesia, which had been deadlocked in the Council of Ambassadors.[4] In all such cases, the litigants had willingly agreed to have the League settle their disputes, otherwise no action would have been taken. Consequently, the League did little to solve the dispute between Poland and Lithuania over Vilna, or the showdown between Italy and Greece following an attack on Italian boundary commissioners in Albania.

No problem that came before the League was as continuous, nor was a truer litmus of the organization's limitations, than disarmament. The Covenant, in Article VIII, entrusted the Council with the task of formulating disarmament proposals, but the problem became a special concern of the Assembly, which established the Temporary Mixed Commission to draft plans and present them to the Council. Disarmament, however, could only begin if international tensions were reduced, and, according to some, collective security strengthened. The Geneva Protocol was supposed to accomplish this by obliging that every signatory provide assistance to the victims of aggression.

Council meeting were held four times a year, the foreign ministers usually attending in person. The delegations established headquarters in favorite or affordable hotels located mostly near the center of town, a short distance from the Palais Wilson where many of the League's meetings were held. The British preferred the Beau Rivage on the Mont Blanc esplanade across from the point of embarkation for the lake steamers, while the French made themselves at home in the slightly more elegant Les Bergues further down the quai where the Rhône reemerges from the lake.

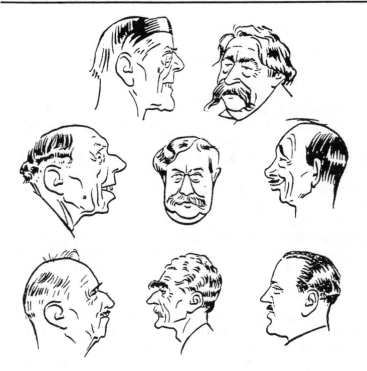

Geneva Diplomats. *Caricaturist Skwirczynski captures the League of Nations' leading personalities. Left to right, top to bottom: Austen Chamberlain (Great Britain) and Aristide Briand (France); Robert Cecil (Great Britain), Paul Painlevé (France), and Eduard Beneš (Czechoslovakia); Alessandro Scialoja (Italy), Paul Hymans (Belgium), and Aleksandr Skrzynsi (Poland).*

As foreign secretary, Chamberlain personally attended all the sessions of the Council. Indeed, his yearly presence in Geneva developed into a carefully orchestrated ritual, which began with his departure from Victoria Station where Foreign Office personnel in morning dress and a top-hatted station master saw the delegation off. At Dover, the harbormaster bowed Chamberlain and his team aboard the channel steamer. At Calais, the mayor and the local prefect welcomed them to France and escorted them to the train for Paris. Representatives from the British embassy met the party at the Gare St-Lazare and took them to the British embassy in the Rue St-Honoré where an official dinner awaited. Later that night, there was a ceremonial leave taking at the Gare de Lyon and the boarding of the sleeping car for Geneva. When the diplomats arrived at the Gare de Cornavin the next morning, they were met by the whole local diplomatic staff *en parade.* Chamberlain loved it, and the "custom" continued until 1935, when Anthony Eden ended it because he felt it was "barbaric and totally unnecessary."[5]

In March 1925, however, when Chamberlain first addressed the League, following his unsatisfactory interview with Herriot, this ceremony had yet to be developed. Chamberlain, dreading what he was about to do, was depressed over his failure to convince Herriot of British good will and get him to agree that Britain and France should approach European security along the general lines proposed by the Germans. Anglo-French relations now seemed hopelessly damaged, and Chamberlain feared that France might go off on its own, shutting out the British, perhaps working out separate agreements with Belgium, Poland, and Italy.[6] The French would continue to occupy the Rhineland indefinitely, and it

> would be patent to all the world that the days not merely of alliance but of an understanding are over, and it would be impossible to keep British and French policy in harmony in any part of the world.[7]

Moreover, Chamberlain was still unsure of his footing with his colleagues in the British cabinet, many of whom had more foreign policy experience than he. Further, Prime Minister Baldwin seemed more comfortable working crossword puzzles than giving him support and direction.

On 8 March, the day of his arrival in Geneva, Chamberlain cabled Undersecretary Eyre Crowe, imploring him to get Baldwin's agreement for negotiating a security pact with France. Chamberlain, responding to Herriot's insistence, had promised to see the premier again after the League meetings. Herriot wanted to forestall speculation that British and French relations were heading towards a breakdown. And Chamberlain, feeling that Europe was facing an indefinite, ominous future, was eager to tell Herriot something positive.

Crowe saw the prime minister on 11 March and tried to convince him that Britain express a willingness to enter some sort of pact with France—perhaps a series of separate but linked agreements, the details to be worked out later. Baldwin said he would think it over.

Later that day, Baldwin summoned those members of the cabinet he deemed hostile to a French alliance to his chambers at the House of Commons. The meeting lasted a couple of hours and, from Baldwin's perspective, was unsuccessful. Those present came to a consensus that the British government should sign no treaty with France and should decide what steps to take in case of aggression only if France had first reached an agreement with Germany.[8] Baldwin was always more comfortable preventing the mischievous policies of others than he was shaping or imposing policies of his own[9], but he knew that his stature as a leader would suffer, if he failed to champion his foreign secretary. It could be only a question of time before Chamberlain's critics turned their fire on him. Therefore, on 12 March, he wrote Chamberlain a letter of general approval:

> We have immense difficulties ahead: I only state this as a fact—we must recognize them. But we will win through.[10]

His duty done, Baldwin headed to Leeds to begin a ten-day speaking tour of the Midlands.

Not only had Chamberlain failed to receive the clear direction he desired, but he was at pains explaining to the other League delegates why Great Britain was not going to sign the League Protocol. Part of the problem lay in the difficulty Chamberlain had as a public speaker, especially when he was addressing foreigners. He lacked personal charm, seemed rather wooden, and had trouble suppressing his belief that the English were blessed with a special creation.[11] His turn-of-the-century attire—the high-wing collar and Prussian-style monocle—compounded the aura of aloofness and delighted cartoonists. "If only Austen would wear spectacles and grow a beard," lamented one of his colleagues.[12]

Concerning Britain's rejection of the Protocol, Chamberlain protected himself from criticism by assuming that he alone had the courage to express publicly what others, like the French, Czechoslovaks and Belgians, were afraid to admit: that the Protocol was a poor vehicle for guaranteeing security and would only increase the responsibility of the members of the League without contributing to their safety.[13] Chamberlain tried to soften the blow by proposing "special arrangements in order to meet special needs."[14] He felt that if

> Great Britain and the British Empire exercise in the long run the influence which is due their position and their policy, it will be because we hold but one language whether on the stage or in the coulisses [wings], because our policy and attitude, however strange or insular they may at first appear to foreign nations, are found by experience to be the true expression of our thoughts and convictions, and because it may thus in time come to be realized that what we say we mean, what we promise we perform, and that, if we are less ready than others to indulge in fine phrases and to win applause by emotional appeals, it is not because we cannot experience for ourselves or appreciate in others those elevated sentiments, but because we are less ready to raise hopes which we cannot fulfil or to give lip service to principles which we cannot put into practice.[15]

After the Council session, Chamberlain retreated to the Beau Rivage to collect his thoughts and relax. But when he arrived, he was handed a long letter from Eyre Crowe who wrote of his distress over the diffident, leaderless posture the prime minister had displayed the previous day in Commons. The prime minister had given Chamberlain little support and no direction. Chamberlain became morose after reading Crow's communication. He felt he was being put in "a false and intolerable position" and replied that if he lacked the confidence of his colleagues he was "worse than useless to his country and the world" and perhaps he should resign:

> I at any rate will not consent to hold the post if the policy of the Cabinet is to be changed every few days, if the whole effect of the conversations I have held since I left home is to be destroyed, and if my word is to be repudiated and I am to be dishonoured.[16]

Chamberlain begged Crowe to transmit these sentiments to Baldwin personally.

Crowe did so, going to Chequers to convince Baldwin of the seriousness of the situation. Baldwin, trying to avoid Chamberlain's resignation at all costs, authorized Crowe to inform the foreign secretary that henceforth he could count on the prime minister's full backing for the security-pact policy. Baldwin remarked that he did not anticipate "any serious difficulty" in obtaining the cabinet's approval. Moreover, he encouraged Chamberlain to see Herriot to hear how a week's reflection may have led [him] to look upon idea of such a pact, and if possible to get him to indicate lines on which he would be prepared to move.[17]

HERRIOT NEEDED reassurance badly. He suspected that he would be forced out, unless a viable alternative to the Protocol to contain German power were found. Herriot knew his support in the Chamber of Deputies was unstable. The Socialists supplied him with his greatest bloc of votes, but they had refused to participate directly in the ministry. His own Radicals were mostly small-town business men and lawyers whose only true bond with the Socialists was on the issue of separation of church and state. (Together, on 2 February 1924, they had managed to get a law passed to end diplomatic relations with the Vatican. The law drew the fire of the French archbishops and the conservatives who saw in it an opportunity to try to bring down the government.) Léon Blum, the leader of the Socialists, feared that the anti-clerical issue could prompt the Senate to pass a vote of no-confidence.[18] Herriot feared that any setback in foreign policy would solidify his opposition and make this certain.

At their second meeting in Paris on 16 March, Herriot told Chamberlain that his duty was to examine seriously the idea of a mutual security pact to see "whether a guarantee for French security and for peace could not be obtained." Herriot proposed that the French and British reach agreement among themselves before they negotiated anything with the Germans.[19] He also wanted Germany to enter the League of Nations[20]—only then would Germany indicate that it had accepted the post-war settlements without reserve.[21] Herriot also specified that Belgium and Holland be included in the agreement; and he wanted Czechoslovakia and Poland to be consulted. The new security arrangement must also forbid the incorporation of Austria into Germany and guarantee the Polish-German and also the Czechoslovak-German frontiers.[22] France, he said, refused to purchase its "own security at the expense of Polish safety."[23] Herriot insisted the whole settlement be based directly on the Treaty of Versailles.

Chamberlain restated British opposition to any attempt to make Britain a guarantor of eastern Europe. He thought that security for the countries of the East lay in the establishment of peace in the West. He maintained that Germany would then be able to revise its frontiers with Poland by peaceful methods in accordance with Article XIX of the

League Covenant.[24] He promised to work closely with the French in reaching a settlement.

The meeting was inconclusive, but the outline of a future agreement had started to emerge. Chamberlain had set parameters for British involvement in a European security pact, which, he hoped, would inaugurate "a new era in European pacification."[25] Chamberlain suspected that the Germans might be playing him along, but he was willing to take that chance because Germany might "dig in its toes" and rekindle "the spirit of Poincaré."[26] He also feared that the British people, despite their country's 20-mile proximity to the continent, would again turn toward isolationism. He wanted to conclude an appropriate security treaty before the parliamentary opposition took advantage of this growing anti-European mood.

ON 24 MARCH, the Commons had its first full-scale debate on foreign policy, following Chamberlain's return from Geneva. MacDonald began by attacking the government for abandoning the Geneva Protocol, which, he believed, was the best instrument for effecting disarmament.[27] Chamberlain used the occasion to make his first official statement about the German proposals, which, he described, as more promising for securing peace and disarmament. He said that Germany was now prepared

> to guarantee voluntarily what hitherto she has accepted under the compulsion of the treaty [of Versailles], that is, the status quo in the West; that she is prepared to eliminate, not merely from the West but from the East, war as an engine by which any alteration in the treaty provisions is to be obtained.[28]

And he stated that Germany promised to change its eastern frontiers only through "friendly negotiations, by diplomatic procedure, or it may be, for aught I know, by recourse to the good offices of the League of Nations."[29]

German Ambassador Friedrich Sthamer, who had been listening in the Stranger's Gallery, became furious at Chamberlain's remarks about the eastern frontiers, and he requested an immediate audience. Chamberlain made it a point of listening to a few more speeches before he left the chamber. Sthamer told Chamberlain that he had gone far beyond the position of the German government. Chamberlain, assuming that former burgermeister Sthamer was Stresemann's mouthpiece,[30] replied pointedly,

> Do you mean you reserve the right to make war in Eastern Europe in furtherance of your political aims? If so, I will go back into the House and revoke what I have said about going through with the German proposals.[31]

He advised him to send a copy of the speech to Berlin to see if the German government wished to repudiate the position he had attributed to it.[32] Because, if that were the case, and the Germans intended to use the establishment of peace in the West only to make it more possible for them to make war in the East, there was no need for any further discussion.[33]

Chamberlain returned to his office and checked with D'Abernon. The Berlin ambassador assured him that he had correctly represented the German position, that Stresemann had, indeed, renounced war as a means of rectifying Germany's eastern frontiers, but wanted this kept confidential. Chamberlain was relieved. But he never trusted Sthamer again. "I feel he is quite useless as a medium of communication with the German government."[34] He rationalized by now supposing that Sthamer's opinions lacked weight with Stresemann.[35]

Having heard what he wanted to hear, Chamberlain now began to push the French into making a positive response to the German initiative. Despite his promise to work closely with Herriot to formulate a common policy, Chamberlain did not intend to treat France as an ally, or give the impression that he was returning to prewar-style policy coordination. Chamberlain had decided to act as a "moderator" between France and Germany and to use Anglo-French friendship to help Germany take its "place as an equal with the other great nations."[36] In his role as "honest broker" between the French and the Germans, he claimed that "perhaps," he was acting "a little more honestly than [Bismarck,] the author of that famous phrase!"[37]

Herriot, already encumbered by his failed support for the Geneva Protocol, was in no hurry to begin negotiating a new security pact, because of his suspicions of German sincerity in accepting the territorial status quo established at the Paris conference. Poincaré also believed that the Germans would appear to be peaceloving in order to seize back lost territory, especially in the east.[38] The former premier even questioned the worth of a German pledge to refrain from attacking France. At speech Bar-le-Duc on 29 March, he stated that, unless the allies were willing to take a firm stand against any German revisionism, Germany "with or without the Soviet Union" might "renew the partition of Poland" and then "incorporate Austria with Germany." Then, it would

> turn against France in order to achieve a second time the evolution which brought about the loss of Alsace-Lorraine, and the foundation of the German Empire.[39]

Poincaré cautioned Herriot against sacrificing substance for shadow.[40] When he returned to Paris, he made a speech on the Senate floor, blaming the weakness of French foreign policy on Herriot's failure to bring order to the topsy-turvy state of French finances. Although Poincaré was clearly trying to deflect criticism from himself, Herriot did share the blame.

The premier had done little to control inflation. He continued making up deficits by increasing the amount of money in circulation and by continuing to rely on advances from the Bank of France. His government maintained its cash flow by dipping into the 100 million dollar loan, the so-called Morgan credits, which Poincaré had managed to coax out of the New York City bankers as operational expenses for carrying out the Dawes plan. Furthermore, Herriot had financial institutions create additional supplies of 'bank money' for reconstruction purposes and have the Treasury continue to issue short-term treasury bonds (*Bons pour la défense nationale*)—a practice that had existed during the war.[41] Herriot hoped to be saved by getting reparations from Germany, but on 10 April, the Senate brought down his government with a vote of no-confidence.

DESPITE HERRIOT'S DEPARTURE as head of the ministry—he now became president of the Chamber of Deputies—the Cartel des Gauches maintained its control of the government. Paul Painlevé, the leader of the Republican Socialists, now assumed the premiership. Painlevé had received his first cabinet post in 1915 as Minister of Public Instruction, and two years later he formed his first government, which lasted two months. Painlevé had once taught mathematics at the École Polytechnique and was a heart an academic, more committed to reflection than action. He had the ability to see all sides of a question, but had difficulty making up his mind on the best course of action. By nature he was a conciliator. He wanted to end the current religious controversy.[42] And he was inclined to follow a policy of reconciliation with Germany, providing that was done in close association with Great Britain. For this reason, he chose Aristide Briand as his foreign minister. In the previous government, Briand had handled League of Nations affairs. The choice seemed logical, but was nonetheless controversial. Briand had many enemies.

The Socialists considered him a renegade because he had deserted the party and had once suppressed a strike of railway workers with government troops. The Nationalists still blamed him for "selling out" to Lloyd George at the conference of Cannes. They thought him soft on the Germans because he had once agreed to compromise on the scheduling of reparations, conveniently forgetting that Briand had once ordered French troops to occupy the Rhineland cities of Duisberg, Ruhrort, and Düsseldorf. Chamberlain, however, called Briand's appointment "hopeful."[43]

Briand recalled Philippe Berthelot to the post of secretary general.[44] Berthelot was a tireless worker. He insisted on digesting every bit of diplomatic correspondence that passed his desk and remembered what he read. He was a master of detail, an indefatigable writer of memoranda, jealous of his prerogatives, uneasy in public and around most politicians.[45] Briand trusted him implicitly.[46] British ambassador Crewe regarded Berthelot so influential that any proposal he accepted would have the "greatest weight" with the French government.[47] Like Briand, Berthelot believed that a policy of reconciliation was superior to a policy of force. He wanted French policy to help Germany create a true democratic spirit, hostile to war. During the Ruhr crisis, he told Briand that, even should the hard-line approach succeed, it must be followed by a very generous policy, perhaps involving concessions.[48] Berthelot hoped to insure peace by the elimination of hate, as France could never find security living next to a revengeful, warlike Germany.

Briand possessed a nimble, but frequently disorganized mind. He avoided position papers, preferring to get his information through direct contact with his advisors. He would sit in his Quai d'Orsay office asking questions, listening to suggestions, puffing on his habitual cigarette, "watching the blue spirals of smoke climb towards the ceiling."[49] He seldom wrote things down and often would come to meetings unprepared. After assembling his information from the discussions of others, he could make a presentation that appeared as if he had put in long hours of study. He was said to have developed this technique at the college of Saint-Nazaire where he learned Latin and Greek by strolling along banks of the Loire in conversation with his teacher, Father Genty.[50]

Briand believed that any new agreement with Germany must strengthen the Treaty of Versailles. He specified that any German attempt to remilitarize the Rhineland be considered an act of war. But the best guarantee of the status quo lay really in the strength of the French army.[51]

> Are not our French officers capable, after the proofs they gave in the war after the defeat of Germany and the condition into which she has been thrown, of organizing an army which can put the country in safety.[52]

He wanted a specific arrangement to guarantee Poland and France's western frontiers, and to strengthen collaboration with Great Britain. The best way to guarantee French safety was an Anglo-French treaty with military clauses.

Berthelot agreed but wanted to make sure that an Anglo-French treaty would not be "a pact of vassalage," giving Britain veto power over French action. Berthelot doubted that Britain could be induced into coercive action against Germany. "It's unacceptable." he said, "that the unwillingness to act on the part of one of the contracting parties is sufficient to paralyze the action of the others." Therefore, the best sort of arrangement was "an affirmation of reciprocal good will, each party in fact keeping its freedom."[53]

Briand acknowledged that an agreement with Germany was essential to prevent the solidification of the alliance with the Soviet Union.[54] He continued to insist, though, that it be preceded by an agreement with Britain.[55] Briand was still unsure in what form this should be cast, and, until he had a better notion, he was in no hurry to respond to the German initiative. Another reason for delay was the uncertainty surrounding the German presidential elections.

SIXTY-SIX CANDIDATES presented themselves for the first round of balloting in the German presidential elections on 29 March 1925. The leading contenders were ex-chancellor Wilhelm Marx of the Center party, Dr. Otto Braun, the choice of the Socialists, and Dr. Karl Jarres, the nominee of the Nationalists. Jarres received the most votes with almost 11.5 million, but this was short of the absolute majority necessary for election. In the second ballot, scheduled for 26 April, only a relative majority was needed to win. Two coalitions formed. The moderates, the so-called Weimar coalition, selected Marx to be their spear-carrier; the Nationalists dumped Jarres in favor of the 77-year old Paul von Hindenburg, who won and took office on 12 May.

Monarchists hoped that the marshal's victory would pave the way for the return of the Hohenzollerns.[56] But most Germans had no desire to bring back the kaisers; they even rejected a proposal to ditch the red-gold-black colors of the republican flag in favor of the old imperial red, white and black. Hindenburg's victory, therefore, brought no dramatic change, especially in the conduct of foreign policy.

Stresemann grew increasingly impatient at not receiving an answer to his February note, and he suspected that Britain and France were conspiring against him. If "the problem [of security] were settled without Germany, it would be settled against Germany."[57] He feared that more delay might allow his critics to convince the German people that he had made concessions and received nothing in return.[58]

The same day that Hindenburg assumed office, the French gave the British Foreign Office a copy of their reply to the German initiative. The draft reiterated most of the demands that Herriot had made to Chamberlain two months earlier, including German entry into the League of Nations and protection of the integrity of the Treaty of Versailles. It also insisted that the "Rhineland Pact" signatories enter into treaties of arbitration with states that desired them.

Chamberlain liked "the spirit" of the French note.[59] He insisted, however, that any new obligations the British assumed be limited to guaranteeing the frontier between Germany and France and Germany and Belgium. Under no circumstances would the British guarantee the Polish-German frontier.[60] Chamberlain clarified this in a revised draft, which avoided suggesting how France might otherwise protect the eastern settlement.[61]

Briand decided to accept the British reservations, insisting that France "would spare no efforts" to strengthen its association with Great Britain to keep the German wolf at the door.[62] Briand suggested that Chamberlain meet him in Geneva during the first part of June, and discuss these matters with him privately "outside the limelight of the press."[63]

The two had their one-on-one on the afternoon of 7 June 1925 when they loaded themselves into a touring car and drove up the lake in the direction of Ouchy where they stopped for tea. They got along so well that Briand remarked that, if the German government carried out its disarmament obligations in such a spirit, there would be no difficulty in concluding a mutual security pact, solving the problem of the evacuation of the Rhineland, and reaching an agreement over the eastern frontiers. They covered a range of other subjects: revisionism in the Balkans, the export of arms to Morocco, the activities of the Bolsheviks, and the settlement of war debts. They also chatted about Sir Walter Scott novels, Lord Byron poems, and the philosophy of Jean-Jacques Rousseau and Voltaire.

Chamberlain was captivated by Briand's sense of moderation and his sense of realism. Briand knew that France could hardly enforce the Treaty of Versailles by itself and might have to settle for something less than desirable. Unfortunate, but things were like that.

When the two called for the bill, they discovered that neither had brought any local currency. The waitress adamantly refused to accept anything but Swiss francs, and it was some time before the owner could be located and alternative payment in British pounds accepted. Not until half past seven did they get back to Geneva.

ON 16 JUNE, the French forwarded their reply to Berlin, proposing negotiations for a mutual security pact with a comprehensive arbitration treaty to handle future disputes. Briand and Chamberlain had agreed that such a treaty

> must apply to all disputes and must leave no scope for coercive action except when undertaken in accordance with treaty stipulations in force between parties...or by guarantees to be given by parties, or any of them, to an arbitration treaty.[64]

Briand wanted Germany to sign specific agreements with Poland and Czechoslovakia, giving France the right to take independent action in case Germany threatened the security of those countries.[65] (Briand, though, did not intend to guarantee the integrity of Poland forever. He thought that the peace settlement had given the Poles more German territory than they deserved, and that they eventually would have to agree to give some of it back.)[66] Briand further stipulated that the mutual security pact not modify the Paris peace settlement and that Germany agree to enter the League of Nations.

Stresemann picked the French note apart, refusing to recognize the inviolability of the eastern frontiers and objecting to the arbitration treaty with Poland. He also wanted to avoid any implication that Germany had renounced its claim to Eupen and Malmédy, if it guaranteed the Rhineland frontier. Stresemann considered those territories lost to Belgium still to be part of the Reich, and he hoped to get them back. Finally, he affirmed that Germany would enter the League of Nations, only if its special geographical position and current military circumstances were considered. Stresemann felt that the French reply, which he knew was British-French joint effort, was a caricature of the original German offer. Nonetheless, he accepted it as a starting point for negotiations.[67]

In the German foreign office, the French response became known as the "Lorelei note" after the famous poem by Heinrich Heine.[68] But where Heine wrote, "*Ich weiss nicht was soll es bedeuten dass ich so traurig bin.*" (I cannot understand why I should be so sad), the critics recited: "*Ich weiss nicht was soll es beduten dass ich so skeptisch bin.*" (I cannot understand why I should be so skeptical.) Some nationalists tried to form an alliance with the Socialists to get Stresemann removed from office.[69] Extremists even refused to surrender German claim to Alsace-Lorraine. Hans von Seeckt insisted that, when the time was right, all Germany's lost territories should be forcefully reincorporated into the Reich.[70] Seeckt believed that armies, not diplomats, determined frontiers.

Stresemann managed to hold off his detractors with help from Chancellor Luther. Stresemann believed that a policy of accommodation served the national interest better than truculent appeals to the memory of Bismarck and Friedrich der Grosse, and he hoped the German people would agree. His position was strengthened, when the French and Belgians agreed to withdraw their troops from the sanction-towns of Düsseldorf, Duisburg, and Ruhrort, and eventually from the rest of the Ruhr.[71] The evacuation of the Ruhr would begin on 15 July and be completed by 15 August, the date specified by the London Conference.[72] But these concessions did nothing to get Stresemann to abandon his reservations. Chamberlain began to lose patience and complain that Stresemann was putting him in an embarrassing position:

> I have staked much on the good faith of the German offer. I am now forced to ask myself whether I am being used as the dupe in a negotiation in which the German proposals were only put forward with the hope of creating dissention in the councils of the allies or to enhance the price which Germany might obtain from Russia in return for breaking them off.[73]

The foreign secretary feared that, if Stresemann delayed much longer, the French might again decide to dig in their heels and the moment for conciliation could pass. Chamberlain applauded Briand's reply as a great act of peace, but felt that, if Germany were going to continue to put up roadblocks, "all the world will see that Germany does not mean peace and will have to frame its policy in consequence."[74] He, nonetheless, decided to press ahead.

On 11-12 August, he met with Briand in London to work on a treaty of mutual guarantee, which would form the basis for negotiations with Germany. But they first had to iron out their own differences. The British were reluctant to formulate sanctions that would join them with France in a policy of force against Germany. They refused to sign any military alliance and insisted on having wide latitude in interpreting any obligations.

The French, on the other hand, demanded specificity. They wanted to know how the British would respond if the Germans threatened another country's frontiers or sent troops into the demilitarized zone. They suggested clear procedures in case of "violations" or "manifest violations."[75] The French insisted that a German violation of the demilitarized zone would bring automatic British military intervention. Briand, however, realized the risks of pushing his interpretations too far. And he tried to avoid giving the Germans the impression that the proposed treaty of guarantee was a "cut and dried scheme" presented on a-take-it-or-leave-it basis.[76] He felt that the greatest chance of success lay in a truly mutual agreement, "not another treaty imposed by the allies upon Germany."[77]

Chamberlain suggested that the German jurists be invited to sit down with the British and French jurists on a basis of equality "to enable Stresemann to know in advance the general character of the propositions we shall make, and to enable him to consult...with his colleagues in Berlin before he sees us."[78] But Stresemann considered that a committee of experts might tie his hands and lead him to make too many concessions.[79] And he was still haunted by an Anglo-French cabal. Nonetheless, he agreed to participate.[80]

On 1 September, the German jurists joined their British, French, Belgian, and Italian counterparts at the British Foreign Office for a three days of meetings.[81] Sir Cecil Hurst and Henri Fromageot had prepared a justification for the deliberations:

> The provisions of the present treaty do not affect the rights and obligations of the High Contracting Parties under the Treaty of Versailles or under arrangements supplementary thereto..., nor yet the rights of any one of the High Contracting Parties to take action...in fulfillment of a guarantee given by it to the observance of the arbitration conventions concluded this day between Germany and Poland and between Germany and Czechoslovakia, if the party which violates such a convention resorts to force.[82]

The words reflected French concerns, but the jurists conducted their deliberations in a spirit of good will and common sense.

IT WAS NO SECRET that Stresemann was set on revising the Treaty of Versailles. At present, conciliation seemed the only realistic, but Stresemann still longed for a mighty, hegemonic fatherland. He remained a closet royalist actively interested in a restoration of the Hohenzollern monarchy. He regretted that his two sons had not joined an ancien régime students fighting corps so they could get their faces slashed with the appropriate aristocratic dueling scars.[83]

On 7 September 1925, he presented his wish-list to the former crown prince Wilhelm, telling him that he intended to use the forthcoming negotiations as an occasion for driving a wedge between the British and French in order to create new opportunities for German power in eastern Europe.[84] He indicated that his goals went beyond the immediate aims of ending allied occupation and solving the problem of reparations: Stresemann wanted recovery of the Polish Corridor and Danzig and "correction" of the frontier in Upper Silesia. He wanted union with Austria, despite his recognition that bringing so many Catholics into the Reich might bring untold problems. Stresemann stated that the Germans had to get through finesse what they could not achieve through strength. He left the letter unsigned.

The letter begged many questions. Did Stresemann use the word "finesse" (*finassiere*) to mean "duplicity" or "deceit", or was he using it as a bridge term, a game currently all the rage, trying to take a trick with a queen when you lacked the king? Was Stresemann's vaunted advocacy of peaceful revisionism a sham? Was he just posturing for the German right?

Whatever his motives, Stresemann saw that a policy of force was presently out of the question. Certainly no German nationalist, of which he was one of the strongest, would be squeamish about forcing Poland back to its ethnic frontiers should the opportunity arise.[85] His general views on this and the other subjects were generally known and seeing them in a letter to the former crown prince would hardly have shocked either Briand or Chamberlain. Stresemann relied on furthering his ends by an adroit use of Germany's economic strength. He knew he had to convince the Allies, especially the British, that his revisionism was not aimed at destroying the balance of power.

To strengthen his hand in negotiating with Briand and Chamberlain, Stresemann resorted to threats and blackmail. He said he would refuse to participate in the forthcoming conference until all foreign troops were withdrawn from the Cologne zone. He demanded that the question of war guilt be settled, pretending that he was a force for reason and common sense against xenophobia.[86] The Nationalists, he claimed, wanted to load him down with so many "demands and reservations that his commission would collapse," and he would be then dispatched "to the wasteland."[87]

Chamberlain complained that the German government was "a nagging old woman" who "must have the last word."[88] He refused to budge; and Stresemann, not wanting to push it too far, abandoned the preconditions. But there would be other occasions when Stresemann would demand eleventh-hour concessions. And other occasions when Chamberlain would compare German demands to those of a nagging old woman.

Stresemann was pleased he had so boldly stated the German position. In a contemporary cartoon, Stresemann is proclaiming: "We have no more territorial claims." To which a pacifist replies, "I knew it." Stresemann then adds: "The borders of 1914 are perfectly adequate for us."[89] Stresemann liked the drawing so much that he put a copy of it in his personal files.

COMMISSAR FOR FOREIGN AFFAIRS Georgi Chicherin was convinced that the Soviet Union would be invited to take part in the forthcoming talks on European security, and he had assured the Party Executive:

> German politicians will always recognize the need of securing their rear in the East...[that] in the final analysis Germany will not break with us, will not abandon that policy of friendly relations with us which has already lasted some years.[90]

Chicherin believed that Great Britain was the communist state's most dangerous enemy, especially because of its association with the United States, the world's chief creditor nation. He believed that the Tory government was trying to surround the U.S.S.R. with anti-communist states. He blamed Britain for not inviting him to the conference.

He feared that Britain would make alliances with both Germany and France against the Soviet Union. Britain would promise Germany help in revising its frontiers with Poland, and promise France support against Germany.[91] Left alone, France would pursue a policy of rapprochement with Moscow. But Germany might have to be bought off with a commercial treaty and an extension of the Treaty of Rapallo. Chicherin also wanted to conclude a treaty of friendship to lessen the danger of Poland being used as "the advance guard" of a military offensive against the Soviet Union.[92]

On 30 September, Chicherin came to Berlin to try to disrupt the forthcoming negotiations. He came uninvited, but Stresemann saw him anyway in two lengthy meetings, the first lasting well past midnight. Chicherin explained that he was just passing through, on his way to he-did-not-know-where in central Europe for medical treatment.[93] Chicherin was suffering from rheumatism and diabetes, made worse by heavy drink.

Chicherin denounced the League of Nations as a coalition of the victors and warned Stresemann that German entry and participation in a security pact was contrary "to the whole spirit of the Rapallo treaty" and would make Germany part of the British anti-Soviet front. He warned that Ambassador D'Abernon would become the dictator of Berlin, and the German army "the landsknechte of Great Britain."[94] He said the mutual security Germany and the Soviet Union would be jeopardized, and he tried to frighten Stresemann with the prospect of a Soviet treaty with Poland.

Stresemann found the Soviet position absurd, particularly Chicherin's threat to conclude an alliance with Poland. He believed that the interests of these countries were too divergent to produce anything concrete. The Soviets, for example, were still demanding the revision of the Treaty of Riga, which had given huge chunks of White Russia to Poland. Stresemann also discounted any Soviet association with France. He told Chicherin that he must decide which horse he meant to ride.

> If there was a Franco-Polish understanding with Germany, it was obvious that the Western Pact could not have as its basis or object an attack on Germany. If on the other hand, an agreement between France and Germany was to be taken as indicating a danger to Russia, it was obvious that there would be no such Franco-Russian rapprochement.[95]

Stresemann, however, gave final approval to the conclusion of a Soviet-German commercial treaty.[96]

Stresemann was careful to assure the British government that this agreement had resulted from negotiations that had been in progress for the past two years, that it should not be construed as evidence that Germany was being drawn into the Soviet orbit. Stresemann feared a repetition of the repercussions following the signature of the Treaty of Rapallo.[97] Stresemann believed that the strengthening of the Soviet connection could work to his advantage in negotiating with the British and French, but he wanted to avoid the suspicion that he was playing a double game.[98]

Notes and Sources:

1. Francis P. Walters, *A History of the League of Nations*, I (London: Oxford University Press, 1952), 296.

2. *Ibid.*, 72-4

3. Robert Dell, *The Geneva Racket 1920-1939* (London: Robert Hale, 1941), 329.

4. The Treaty of Lausanne specified that, if the two parties failed to reach an agreement within nine months, the Mosul question would be referred to the League of Nations, .

5. Earl of Avon, *The Memoires of Anthony Eden, Facing the Dictators* (Boston: Houghton Mifflin, 1962), 9.

6.*Documents on British Foreign Policy 1919-1939*, first series, vol. XXVII, 354.

7. *Ibid.*, 355.

8. Keith Middlemas and John Barnes, *Baldwin, A Biography*, 353-4.

9. Leopold Amery, *My Political Life*, II, 299.

10. Keith Middlemas & John Barnes, *Baldwin, A Biography*, 354.

11. Gordon Craig and Felix Gilbert, eds., *The Diplomats 1919-1939*, I, 42-43.

12. Leopold Amery, *My Political Life*, II, 303.

13. Charles Petrie, *The Life and Letters of the Right Hon. Sir Austen Chamberlain*, II, 285.

14. *International Conciliation, European Security* (New York: Carnegie Endowment for International Peace, 1925), no. 212, 254-255.15

15. *Documents on British Foreign Policy*, first series, vol. XVII, 768-769.

16. *Ibid.*, 264.

17. Keith Middlemas and John Barnes, *Baldwin, A Biography*, 355.

18. *Documents on British Foreign Policy 1991-1939*, first series, vol. XXVII, 396. The government's attempt to republicanize the schools of Alsace-Lorraine, which had been confessional under the German administration, also backfired as vigorous local protest forced the government to abandon the policy.

19. *Documents on British Foreign Policy 1919-1939*, first series, vol. XXVII, 389.

20. *Documents on British Foreign Policy 1919-1939*, first series, vol. XXVII, 389; Viscount D'Abernon, *The Diary of an Ambassador, Dawes to Locarno 1924-1926*,III, 149.

21. Jules Laroche, *Au Quai d'Orsay avec Briand et Poincaré*, 207.

22. Michel Souilé, *La vie politique d'Édouard Herriot*, 210-211.

23. *Documents on British Foreign Policy 1919-1939*, first series, vol. XXVII, 388.

24. *Ibid.*, 389-390.

25. Viscount D'Abernon, *The Diary of an Ambassador, Dawes to Locarno 1924-1926*, III, 156.

26. *Documents on British Foreign Policy 1919-1939*, first series, vol. XXVII, 400.

27. Chamberlain got the impression that MacDonald would support any alternative as long as it had the same intent. Sir Charles Petrie, *The Life and Letters of the Right Hon. Sir Austen Chamberlain*, II, 272. Lloyd George, however, called the Protocol "a booby-trap...baited with arbitration." *Annual Register 1925*, 32.

28. *Survey of International Affairs*, 1925, II, 28-29.

29. *Ibid.*, 29.

30. See: Hajo Holborn, "Diplomats and Diplomacy in the Early Weimar Republic" in Gordon Craig and Felix Gilbert, eds., *The Diplomats 1919-1939* I, 151-152.

31. Charles Petrie, *The Life and Letters of the Right Hon. Sir Austen Chamberlain*, II, 270-271.

32. *Documents on British Foreign Policy 1919-1939*, first series, vol. XXVII, 422.

33. *Ibid.*, 422.

34. *Ibid.*, 437.

35. Charles Petrie, *The Life and Letters of the Right Hon. Sir Austen Chamberlain*, II, 272.

36. *Documents on British Foreign Policy 1919-1939*, first series, vol. XXVII, 405.

37. Charles Petrie, *The Life and Letters of the Right Hon. Sir Austen Chamberlain*, II, 274-275.

38. So did the Poles. To emphasize how implausible was "peaceful' revision of the eastern frontiers, Polish Minister of Foreign Affairs Count Aleksander Skrzynski stated that "no democracy could voluntarily surrender a single yard of its territory, and that to raise the question of frontiers now would be playing with fire." *Ibid.*, 425.

39. *Ibid.*, 428-229.

40. Some critics went beyond Poincaré's interpretation and warned that, if France were to go to war against Germany to defend Poland, thereby crossing the demilitarized zone, the new security pact could prompt Great Britain to go to war against France.

41. Thus it created a special joint stock company, the *Crédit national*, capitalized with appropriations from the public treasury and with special bond issues, to indemnify private war losses, and similarly sponsored the

Agricultural Credit Fund, the Maritime Credit Bank, the Credit for Artisans, the National Bank for Foreign Trade, and the *Banques populaires* for small businesses.

42. When he presented his cabinet to the parliament, he promised that France would continue to maintain its ambassador at the Vatican because that was demanded by "the exigencies of national politics and the delicate conditions of the politics of the world." *Les cahiers de l'histoire, La troisième république,* 110.

43. *Documents on British Foreign Policy 1919-1939,* first series, vol. XXVII, 456.

44. Berthelot had been accused of using his influence to try to save the beleaguered *Banque industriel de Chine.* The first step his of rehabilitation had been taken in December 1924, when Herriot revoked his suspension and had all the incriminating records destroyed in Berthelot's presence.

45. Richard D. Challener, "The French Foreign Office: The Era of Philippe Berthelot" in Gordon Craig and Felix Gilbert, eds., *The Diplomats 1919-1939,* I, 71-73.

46. Joseph Paul-Boncour, *Entre deux guerres, souvenirs sur la troisième république,* II (Paris: Plon, 1945), 161.

47. *Documents on British Foreign Policy 1919-1939,* first series, vol. XXVII, 557.

48. Challener in Gordon Craig and Felix Gilbert, eds., *The Diplomats 1919-1939,* I, 78.

49. *Ibid.,* 146.

50. André Beauguitte, *Le Chemin de Cocherel* (Paris: Alphonse Lemerre, 1960), 143-144.

51. Defined as disturbing the peace in Articles 42, 43, and 44. *Survey of International Affairs 1925,* 31.

52. *Documents on British Foreign Policy 1919-1939,* first series, vol. XXVII, 459.

53. Georges Suarez, *Briand, sa vie, son oeuvre, avec son journal et des nombres documents inédits* (Paris: Plon, 1952), VI, 83-84.

54. It was then rumored that a Russo-German military alliance was about to be signed.

55. Briand supposedly had a personal reason for wanting to making France a partner in a European security pact: his desire to take revenge "on Millerand who had him recalled from Cannes and forced him to resign, [and] on his old enemy Clemenceau who had played with the idea of impeaching him for his pacifism in 1917." Georges Bonnet, *Quai d'Orsay,* 79.

56. Hindenburg got 48.3 percent of the vote. Marx got 45.4 percent, the communist candidate Ernst Thälmann essentially the rest. The Weimar constitution made taking a religious oath optional, but the president had to swear to defend and protect the Weimar constitution. *Annual Register 1925*, 166.

57.   Georges Suarez, *Briand, sa vie, son oeuvre, avec son journal et des nombres documents inédits*, VI, 89.

58.   *Documents on British Foreign Policy 1919-1939*, first series, vol. XXVII, 476.

59.   Charles Petrie, *The Life and Letters of the Right Hon. Sir Austen Chamberlain*, II, 276.

60.   *Documents on British Foreign Policy 1919-1939*, first series, vol. XXVII, 535.

61.   *Command Document* 2435, 18.

62.   *Documents on British Foreign Policy 1919-1939*, first series, vol. XXVII, 559.

63.   *Ibid.*, 560.

64.   *Ibid.*, 590.

65.   *Command Document*, 2435, 28.

66.   *Documents on British Foreign Policy 1919-1939*, first series, vol. XXVII, 586.

67.   *Ibid.*, 651.

68.   Viscount D'Abernon, *The Diary of an Ambassador, Dawes to Locarno 1924-1926*, III, 174.

69.   Erich Eyck, *A History of the Weimar Republic*, II, 16-17.

70.   Robert Grathwol, *Stresemann and the DNVP, Reconciliation or Revenge in German Foreign Policy 1924-1928*, 86.

71.   Viscount D'Abernon, *The Diary of an Ambassador, Dawes to Locarno 1924-1926*, III, 175, 182.

72.   *Documents on British Foreign Policy 1919-1939*, first series, vol. XXVII, 1042, 1054.

73.   *Documents on British Foreign Policy 1919-1939*, first series, vol. XXVII, 652.

74.   Charles Petrie, *The Life and Letters of the Right Hon. Sir Austen Chamberlain*, II, 280; Viscount D'Abernon, *The Diary of an Ambassador, Dawes to Locarno 1924-1926*, III, 180.

75.   A "violation" had to be brought to the Council of the League for "a finding." If the Council decided the allegation had merit it would notify the other signatories who then would assist the power "against whom the act complained of is directed." This process took time. In a "manifest violation" the signatories would decide what action to take among themselves. This took less time.   Immediate action by one of the powers was, however, only authorized if their were an actual outbreak of hostilities or an assembly of armed forces in the demilitarized zone. *Documents on British Foreign Policy 1919-1939*, first series, vol. XXVII, 728.

76. *Ibid.*, 731.

77. Charles Petrie, *The Life and Letters of the Right Hon. Sir Austen Chamberlain*, II, 282.

78. *Ibid.*, 282.

79. Erich Eyck, *A History of the Weimar Republic*, II, 20.

80. Mixed signals still came from Berlin. The German Ministry of the Interior, apparently acting on its own, decided to publish a book on the Separatist movement in the Rhineland in which the French had played a prominent part two years before; and it signaled its intent to come out with a White Book detailing outrages committed by the French Army of Occupation. At the same time, some German politicians demanded that the entrance of Germany into the League of Nations entitled it to share in the colonial mandates on the same footing of the other such countries. *Documents on British Foreign Policy 1919-1939*, first series, vol. XXVII, 746-747.

81. The principals were Cecil Hurst from Great Britain, Henri Fromageot from France, Friedrich Gaus from Germany, M. Rolin from Belgium, and Massimo Pilotti from Italy.

82. *British Foreign Office Records*, 840-1, File 3. No. 10. Briand had reassured Czech foreign minister Edvard Benes and Polish foreign minister Count Aleksander Skrzynski that no accord would be signed for the Rhineland unless adequate protections were given at the same time for both their countries. Jules Laroche, *Au Quai d'Orsay avec Briand et Poincaré*, 212-213.

83. Viscount D'Abernon, *The Diary of an Ambassador, Dawes to Locarno 1924-1926*, III, 228.

84. Gustav Stresemann, *Vermächtnis: der Nachlass in drei Bänden*, II (Berlin: Ullstein, 1932), 553.

85. Erich Eyck, *A History of the Weimar Republic*, II, 26-30.

86. *Survey of International Affairs*, 1925, II, 47-48.

87. Erich Eyck, *A History of the Weimar Republic*, II, 22.

88. Charles Petrie, *The Life and Letters of the Right Hon. Sir Austen Chamberlain*, II, 286.

89. Hans Gatzke, ed., *European Diplomacy between Two Wars* (Chicago: Quadrangle, 1972), 114.

90. *Soviet Documents on Foreign Policy*, II, 17.

91. *Ibid.*, II, 57-8.

92. *Ibid.*, 37. While there, Chicherin claimed that friendship between Poland and Russia was steadily increasing and would lead to the inauguration of a new era, which would result in "close and deep economic ties." He said that this new policy was part of a general policy of friendship for all the peoples of Eastern Europe, "based on our recognition of the principle of all nations to self-determination," but insisted, this would not in any way "infringe upon the interests of the Polish state." *Ibid.*, 56.

93.   *Ibid.*, 55.

94.   *oviet Documents on Foreign Policy*, II, 55.

95.   *British Foreign Office Documents*, FO. 840/1, file 5. no. 1.

96.   This agreement enabled the Russians to obtain an immediate credit of 100 million marks, one-fourth of this coming from German industry, the rest from the Deutsche Bank and the Reichskredit Gesellschaft.   Although the Soviets were disappointed that these monies were only short-term loans, Chicherin triumphantly called the deal the "first breach in the credit blockade against the USSR." *Soviet Documents on Foreign Policy*, II, 60.   With these funds, the Soviets would be able to purchase capital equipment without having to dip into their meager foreign exchange reserves.   The Germans also benefitted.   The money would be spent for the purchase of German goods, and would be repaid in New York in American currency.   In this way, the Germans could now meet their reparation payments without being compelled to purchase dollars on the world market.   *Documents on British Foreign Policy*, first series, vol. XXV, 703.

97.   *Documents on British Foreign Policy*, first series, vol. XXVII, 817-818.

98.   Erich Eyck, *A History of the Weimar Republic*, II, 24.

_____

THE MEETING AT LAKE MAGGIORE

THE SCENERY WAS SPLENDID: snow-covered mountains, manicured parks and gardens, pastel-colored houses, a clear blue lake. William Wordsworth remembered Locarno with affection:

> But let us hence; for fair Locarno smiles
> Embowered in walnut slopes and citron isles.[1]

Austen Chamberlain, comfortably installed in the Grand Palace Hotel, found the city a most heavenly spot and declared, "If we cannot make peace here then peace in the world must be impossible."[2]

The British foreign secretary was still stewing over the difficulties of dealing with the Germans. At the meeting of the jurists in London, from 1 to 4 September, they had tried to keep the French from guaranteeing the Polish arbitration treaty even though they knew the French would not conclude an agreement without such a provision.[3] The Germans had claimed it would look as if they had recognized the Franco-Polish military alliance. Furthermore, the Germans seemed unwilling to give any written assurance that they had renounced war as a means of revising the eastern frontiers.[4]

Chamberlain had insisted that German attendance at a security conference be made without prior conditions. Any reservations could be cleared up in ensuing discussions. Chamberlain also had a bad first impression of the German delegates. He found them "bald and ugly and unhealthy looking, with rolls of fat at the back of their necks."[5] Stresemann looked like a typical Junker.[6]

The British came to Locarno with different expectations than the French and the Germans. Chamberlain hoped that his position of makeweight between the others would help him insure that British soldiers would never again fight on the continent of Europe. He believed that the achievement of full reconciliation between the French and German would allow the British to regain freedom of action.

Briand, on the other hand, wanted to tighten his country's association with Britain and strengthen the Treaty of Versailles. Additionally, he wanted to avoid making concessions to Germany on disarmament and to maintain French control of the occupied territories. He was committed to preserving the frontiers of Poland and Czechoslovakia, and intended to make Germany participate in upholding the status quo by insisting that any agreement be girded by German membership in the League of Nations.

Stresemann, however, wanted to avoid guaranteeing the eastern frontiers, drive a wedge between the British and the French, and get foreign troops off German soil as soon as possible. He did not believe he could get an agreement that modified the Treaty of Versailles, but he hoped to be able to end the German position of inferiority. He wanted to settle grievances with the French over the Rhineland, but curtail the French ability to ever again abridge or threaten German sovereignty.   Chancellor Luther doubted the Nationalists, whose support was necessary for ratification by the prescribed two-thirds vote, would accept a treaty that did not include the evacuation of foreign troops from Cologne. Luther argued that "a pact endorsed by German Nationals had far greater value as a means of pacification than any instrument carried by the Left against German National's opposition."[7]

The Germans wanted to put an end to French pressure to get them to disarm, and they wanted to isolate Poland. Stresemann even desired to avoid all mention of the Polish frontiers because this could imply recognition.[8] He wanted to undermine the French connection with the other countries of eastern Europe, while achieving special privileges. The Germans were not opposed to entering the League of Nations, provided they could enjoy all its privileges, as well as responsibilities, including the right to exercise trusteeship over colonial peoples.[9]

CHAMBERLAIN OPENED the Locarno Conference on 5 October in the large, drab meeting rooms of the Palais de Justice with a gushy welcoming speech. He rhapsodized about the beautiful country of

Genève et Locarno.

Switzerland with its smiling and majestic valleys, which would "assure success to our labours."[10] And he said he was determined to eliminate once and for all the division of Europe into rival camps. He emphasized, however, that British security did not include guaranteeing the territorial arrangements in eastern Europe.

Luther spoke next and began to enumerate German grievances. But suddenly Briand changed the mood. Putting his hand on the chancellor's shoulder, he protested, "Please stop, you'll have us all in tears."[11] The remark made Stresemann laugh, and the tension eased.

The jousting began when Chamberlain nominated Briand as the conference's permanent chairman. Briand declined, explaining that he "would be embarrassed by the restrictions of the chair" and proposed Chamberlain instead.[12] Chancellor Luther objected.[13] He maintained that nominating Chamberlain as permanent chairman would have "an unfortunate effect on German public opinion."[14] By this he probably meant that he, as head of a government, would have to take second place to a foreign secretary—an inappropriate breach of diplomatic protocol. Stresemann pretended the matter was inconsequential but naturally supported Luther.[15] The conference, therefore, adopted the round table system, with everybody and nobody being chairman; and the furniture was arranged accordingly.

At the plenary sessions, the tables were positioned in the shape of a rectilinear horseshoe. For the executive sessions, they formed a huge square, which to maintain equality had no designated head, nor foot. No true round table had been found and the square was formed by sawing a larger rectangular table in two.[16] Chamberlain felt slighted by not having being designated permanent chairman, while Briand viewed the whole flap as typical of the strange mentality of the Germans.[17]

Briand rejected the preparation of an "official" transcript. Each country would keep its own record which would periodically be compared with the others to insure standardization.[18] It was also agreed that any statements released to the press had to have joint approval.[19]

Stresemann spent most of the first meeting sparring with Briand over what circumstances could lead to the security pact's termination. The experts had suggested that it remain in force until the Council of the League, acting on a petition from at least two of the signatories, decided that the Geneva organization was strong enough to guarantee peace. But Stresemann claimed that such an arrangement would only ensure Germany's isolation:

> it would be easy for an allied power to find another power willing to act with it, while the German government...could not so easily find another power.[20]

Briand, annoyed by Stresemann's suspicions, refused to debate an issue that he thought had already been decided and replied:

> Public opinion will hardly be reassured, if the edifice we are building is so fragile that it is sufficient for one or two or even three contracting parties to get rid of it, that will make this something completely different.[21]

Briand denied that he wanted to trap Germany in a hostile alliance.[22] Failing to get any satisfaction from Chamberlain, Stresemann let the matter drop.

Locarno's most crucial issue was guaranteeing the frontiers between Germany and Poland. Failure to reach agreement on this issue would most likely destroy the conference. Stresemann decided the best approach was to have Chancellor Luther sound out Chamberlain privately.

This meeting took place the following morning (6 October) in Chamberlain's suite at the Grand Palace Hotel. Coming right to the point, Luther said that no German government could ever accept any Polish-German treaty of arbitration, guaranteed by France. Surprised, Chamberlain replied that he considered the obligation more a protection for Germany than an opportunity for France, and explained that such a guarantee would really "limit the obligations of France and Poland to one another as laid down by the existing alliance." It would even exclude many cases where Poland might call for the assistance of France.[23] Luther hastily conceded the point to avoid further argument and left.

That afternoon at the executive meeting, Stresemann took on Briand. He accused France of having a conflict of interest in agreeing to guarantee a security pact while maintaining special alliances with Poland and Czechoslovakia.[24] But Briand met the objection head on. He made it clear that French priorities were with its allies, emphasizing that, if it came to a choice between the treaties of alliance and the Locarno pact, France would refuse to sign the Locarno pact.[25] Briand then questioned Stresemann's motives. Was the foreign secretary trying to find a formula to appease the German electorate or was he making a fundamental objection? Briand pretended not to understand Germany's concern, because the Eastern Guarantee was akin to the arbitration treaty that Germany said it was willing to sign concerning the western frontiers.

> If there was to be a similar treaty for the Polish and Czechoslovak frontiers, ruling out resort to war, what difficulty could result from the fact that there was a special agreement in the spirit of the Covenant between one nation and another?[26]

Briand put the Germans in the uncomfortable position of, either agreeing with him, or admitting that they were insincere about using peaceful means to revise the Treaty of Versailles. Briand emphasized that these treaties were not signed to harm other powers, especially since Germany had already promised to rule out war in revising its frontiers.[27] Moving on, Briand insisted that Germany enter the League of Nations "because it is only within the framework of the League that their two peoples could cooperate."[28] Even if the present German government was unlikely to revise the eastern frontiers by war, the future was unpredictable. One day there "might be some public outcry; and, when public opinion became heated, it was impossible to say what might happen." Briand doubted the League Covenant afforded France adequate protection. It was natural to protect oneself "against certain eventualities, however, even if one does not believe that they will come to pass; [and] a little extra guarantee was not to be neglected if conceived in the spirit of the League of Nations."[29]

When Stresemann continued to denounce special guarantees to Poland and Czechoslovakia for showing "a distrust of the competence of the League of Nations and the strength of the Covenant," Chamberlain tried to set his minds at ease.[30] He insisted that Britain could never be a party to an agreement that guaranteed the eastern frontiers and said that in a dispute involving the "western" frontiers the British would support the Germans, if they were attacked by France, as much as they would support the French, if they were attacked by the Germans.[31] He underlined this commitment by claiming that Britain would put all its forces at the disposal of the League of Nations.[32] This implied refusal to support the French alliance system helped save the conference.

Stresemann had avoided renouncing war "as a means of ultimately changing their eastern frontiers."[33] Revisionism would depend on political circumstances that made force unlikely at the present time.[34] The "Eastern Question" was, therefore, resolved without further delay, and the Germans shifted their attention to their entry into the League of Nations. They hoped to use the issue of membership to achieve the complete evacuation of foreign troops from the Rhineland and end allied insistence on German disarmament. This time the Germans decided to meet privately and separately with *both* Chamberlain and Briand.

THE MORNING of October eighth, Stresemann went to see Chamberlain at the Grand Hotel to tell him that Germany could not fulfill its obligations under Article 16, which prescribed sanctions against an aggressor.[35] He said that disarmament had left his country without power to defend itself and that such weakness affected the country's ability to participate in any League-initiated military action and make it impossible to permit foreign troops to cross German soil. Stresemann insisted that Germany would also have difficulty participating in any economic sanctions because these could be regarded as an act of war and invite an attack Germany would be powerless to oppose.

Chamberlain avoided the question of German disarmament and kept the discussion focused on the League of Nations. First, he said, that he did not see how an exception could be made, since "the Covenant does not permit that each member of the League decide separately whether it shall take part in that action."[36] But then, he admitted that, "it would be for Germany herself to say to what extent she could comply with the recommendations of the Council", which Germany as a member would have a direct hand in formulating.

At the same time, Luther and Briand were discussing identical subjects at a country inn in the a small fishing village of Ascona, five miles south of Locarno. Luther had refused to meet Briand at his hotel, also the Grand, because he feared German nationalists would accuse him of paying court to the French.[37] Luther also blamed Germany's inability to fulfill any League obligations on its lack of arms. And he pushed for recognition of Germany's right for territorial revision.

Briand countered that such questions could be discussed after Germany became a member of the League, and were not conditions for membership. He then said:

> You are a German and I am a Frenchman. But I can be French and
> a good European. And you can be a German and a good European.
> Two good Europeans must be able to understand each other.[38]

This remark seemed to inaugurate a new beginning in Franco-German cooperation, or so it appeared later, but, at the time, Briand's intention was more narrowly focused. It was his round about way of telling Luther that he could expect no concessions for German membership in the League.

Later that day, when Article XVI was discussed at the Palais de Justice, Stresemann had refined his demands and claimed that he was asking "only for special treatment during a transitory period," to last until general disarmament was accomplished.[39] Stresemann reminded Briand and Chamberlain of the risks: that Germany might get into a war with the Soviet Union, if it had to participate in an economic boycott of Russia.[40]

> In case of a Russo-German war the Russian fleet could bring
> German territory under its guns and advance Bolshevism to the
> Elbe. In such a situation Germany would find itself without
> allies.[41]

And Luther insisted that the conference had to find a formula to "safeguard Germany from moral isolation."[42] By this he meant that German obligations under the Covenant could only be effective if there were complete and universal disarmament.[43] Until then, "Germany felt the necessity of provisions which would shelter her from bearing the general dangers of the League of Nations."[44]

Stresemann attacked the British and French for having carried the principle of German disarmament too far and for having created "the situation in which they are seeking help from Germany, which that country is not in a position to provide."[45] This was Stresemann's way of demanding parity with the great powers.

Briand held his ground. League membership was intended to dampen, not reward, Germany's passion for revisionism. Germany would, therefore, get no concessions for entry. To Stresemann, and Luther, he stressed the benefits of membership, namely that Germany was "coming into an organization for mutual security, she would be among the directors of the society."[46] There was no such thing as "a sort of equality"; a nation could not have the benefits of an organization and make exceptions to the rules. Briand said that, if Germany came into the League of Nations under special circumstances, Germany's "voice will lose much of its force."[47]

To help resolve the dispute over German entrance into the League, Briand arranged that tomorrow's session take place on board the *Fiore d'arancio* (Orange Blossom), a wedding-party launch, during a cruise around Lake Maggiore Chamberlain was delighted: "Then we are celebrating a marriage," he quipped. "It's a real departure for Cythera."[48] Chamberlain was counting on Stresemann and Briand with their classical educations to catch his witticism about the Greek isle where a fully-grown Aphrodite emerged from the sea. Then in front of photographers, the normally-reserved foreign secretary threw out his arms and, in one huge gesture, embraced both Briand and Stresemann.

Briand's *coup de théâtre* paid off. Chamberlain was almost ecstatic.

Briand, Stresemann, and Luther...discuss with the most discretion and good humor their various difficulties. Each goes out of his way to show that he realizes those of the other two; each is obviously genuinely desirous of helping the other out so far as he can consistent with his own national interests. In short, there is a complete absence of bitterness and backbiting.[49]

But skimming the crisp, blue, as yet unpolluted, waters of the lake, probably had less effect than being cooped up on a small boat for five hours. The results, though, were undeniable. From the discussions, emerged an acceptable interpretation of Article XVI in which each pledged:

loyally and effectively to work together to make the Covenant respected and to oppose every act of aggression, in so far as this is not out of proportion with its military situation and which is in conformity with its geographical position.[50]

Bottom line: Germany would enter the League without conditions.

The "*texte du bateau*" (boat accord) was put in final form later that evening. The irrepressible Chamberlain said that he could not tell whether he was standing on his head or on his heels. He cabled to William Tyrrell, the permanent under-secretary of the Foreign Office, in London:

What would you have said, if on the platform at Victoria [station], I had told you that in a week's time I should be joining in a pleasure party in a launch on the lake with the Chancellor and Foreign Minister of the Reich as the guests of the Foreign Minister of France?[51]

Chamberlain was now sure he would get his security agreement and that it would be ratified—no parliament would want to "draw upon its country the universal condemnation that would follow upon rejection of the agreement."[52] Chamberlain boasted (to Stresemann's deputy, von Schubert) that his own careful nurturing of the French connection had created the Locarno Conference:

I had always felt that it was only on the solid foundation of loyal friendship between France and England that a reconciliation with Germany could be affected.[53]

THE NEGOTIATIONS were held with the greatest effort to ensure privacy, the sessions took place behind closed doors. Chamberlain disliked reporters, calling them "those ravening wolves," and he determined to give them a "complete lack of real news."[54] Shortly after his arrival, he held an "official briefing" in which he instructed the journalists to characterize the forthcoming talks as a case of the "dead past burying its dead" and not as some sort of contest in which one power triumphed over another. In subsequent lectures, Chamberlain glossed over differences and minimized disputes. He described the discussions concerning Germany's entry into the League, as "conducted with uniform courtesy and good-will with the arguments pro and con expressed in the "most conciliatory as well as the most able manner;" he insisted that he was "profoundly impressed by the high level of the discussion."[55] Consequently, reporters took him less and less seriously and often built their stories around impressions, gossip, rumors, leaks, and breaches of confidentiality.

Popolo d'Italia (The People of Italy), for example, reported remarks that Émile Vandervelde, the Belgian delegate, had made during an executive session concerning his country's treaty with France. According to the Fascist daily, Vandervelde had insisted on the inviolability of his country's independence and had requested that the wording in the Franco-Belgian treaty be changed--from "the frontiers between France and Belgium and the frontiers of Germany" to "the frontiers between France and Germany and the frontiers between Belgium and Germany."[56] The article claimed that Belgium was changing its foreign policy and bringing an end to its alliance with France.[57] Vandervelde blamed Vittorio Scialoja, the head of the Italian delegation, for the breach of security. But Scialoja smoothly denied everything; he promised to make an investigation.[58]

October ninth, the *Neue Zürcher Zeitung* (The New Zurich Times) reported the main arguments of the previous day's meeting, complete with direct quotes from Chamberlain, Briand, Vandervelde, and Stresemann. Chamberlain was furious and complained to Stresemann that this latest breach placed him in a position of some difficulty by the inaccuracy of the account attributed to me, and by a report which purports on your authority to give a resumé of arguments employed at the conference.[59]

The German foreign minister accused the Swiss paper for having distorted his remarks and making up the dialogue. He assured Chamberlain that any leak did not come from him.[60] Chamberlain suspected the real blabbermouths were the Italians. They were leaking as much information as they could "without creating too great a stir". If a fuss occurred, "they just denied having done so and no one could or would refute their denial."[61]

No one knew better than Stresemann the importance of manipulating the press, but he had no control over the activities of the foreign press.[62] Nonetheless, he told Chamberlain that he intended to get his minister at Berne to protest to the Swiss Telegraph Agency and force the *Neue Zürcher Zeitung* to print a retraction.[63]

Incidents like these to the contrary, there generally was little off-the-record news and no good scandals. Many of the delegates had brought along their wives, and the women reinforced the atmosphere of polite provincial gentility. Chamberlain extolled the grace and charm of his wife Ivy, who, he bragged, had captured everybody's' heart and even helped make the agreement possible. He wrote to William Tyrrell, the permanent under-secretary of the foreign office,

I shall demand that her expenses be paid not for the sake of the payment itself, but because it is the only outward sign that I can give of the help that she gave us.[64]

Considering that the British government's refusal to shoulder travel expenses for the foreign secretary's parliamentary private secretary, the suggestion to have a spouse put on the payroll was rather bold.[65]

The boat excursion received the most media attention, some of the event was even filmed and promoted an image of the conference as civilized and genteel, the delegates affable and professional. But the celluloid footage could tell nothing about the thrust of the discussions or the intentions and efforts of the diplomats. Stresemann worried about his public persona.[66] He feared that the German people might view him as someone having a good time on a cruise, rather that as a dedicated statesman working hard for the interests of the nation. Concerning the jaunt on the *Orange Blossom*, he admitted:

> I have never been so tired and done up as I was on that occasion. And the discussions were so acrimonious that I wished the minutes of them could have been published afterwards.[67]

Although constantly stymied in their attempts to get hard copy, the reporters seemed to take it with good grace. At the end of the conference, the Press Association of the League gave a luncheon to honor the 200 delegates. The guests sat at two long tables and were served a dinner consisting of "*oeufs froids de toute sécurité*" (complete security chilled eggs), "*salade d'arbitrage*" (arbitration salad), and "*vacherin en désarmament*" (disarmament meringue). The menu cards were shaped like angels holding a chalice in both hands and were adorned with caricatures of the chief delegates. After the dinner, the journalists made a mad scramble to get the diplomats to autograph the angels' wings.[68] Now they had something tangible to take home.

AS LONG AS the negotiations continued, Chicherin hung around Berlin, still smarting from the rebuff given him by the German Foreign Ministry. Disgruntled, he concluded that the Soviet Union "must now seek her salvation through other channels."[69] This meant making new friends and whatever economic concessions were necessary to get a rapprochement with Poland and France, including a settlement of the tsarist debts. British ambassador D'Abernon observed that Chicherin must be as frustrated as "an operatic artist who knows that his best audience is to be found in Paris."[70]

Stresemann continued to reassure Chamberlain that the Germans had nothing up their sleeves. He termed Chicherin's mission a total failure and downplayed Germany's Moscow connection, saying that Prussian conservatives were its main support.

> They had evolved a formula which was summed up in the phrase that Soviet Russia was the Russia of Frederick William—the same centralization, the same stern discipline, and stark authority—and they had found in this comparison a new point of sympathy between them.[71]

Stresemann insisted that the recent commercial agreement with the Soviets affected, in no way, the attitude of the Germans towards the Locarno conference.

Briand persisted in trying to shake Germany's association with the Soviets. He questioned the Communists' peaceful intentions and asked Stresemann if Germany was "going to cross her arms and assist in the disappearance of Western civilization?"[72]   Briand dismissed Chicherin's threat to conclude alliances with Germany and Poland. (He had also heard rumors that the Soviets were going to sign treaties with Italy, Turkey, and China.) Briand claimed he was delighted that Poland would get on good terms with the Soviets,

> if Poland had nothing to fear from Russia, it might help dispel from the minds of the Germans their nightmare of a French army marching across Germany to the relief of Poland.[73]

But he warned Pierre de Margerie, the French ambassador in Berlin, to be on his guard against any attempt by Chicherin to divide Britain and France.[74]

Chicherin cornered de Margerie at a luncheon party on 10 October, and immediately began to attack Chamberlain for "endeavoring to organize a crusade against the Soviet [Union]." Chicherin said that it was incredible that the French failed to realize that British animosity was directed against France as well as the Soviet Union.

> Was it not due to England that the occupation of the Ruhr failed and that France had to capitulate and come down to a very inferior solution for her of a pact of security?[75]

De Margerie told Chicherin he was "totally misinformed, and that there was not a word of truth in these allegations." Chicherin pretended to be offended, abruptly turned his back on de Margerie, and left.[76]

Two days later, having recovered from his diplomatic anger, Chicherin again sought out the French ambassador. He denied he was out to ruin the Locarno negotiations and pretended that he was prepared to accept the ambassador's assurance that Britain had no evil designs against the Soviet Union. He said that he could approve Germany's entry into the League, as long as it was "possible to reconcile the maintenance of Soviet principles with the obligations of that society."[77]   And he said he was not trying to establish a Russo-German alliance, indeed, he hoped to come to Paris soon to come to an understanding directly with Briand.

Chicherin doubted that he could succeed in detaching France from its association with Britain. He considered an Anglo-French combination to be the inevitable result of French economic dependency.

> There is practically no corner of the earth where English and French interests do not diverge. But in the first place France is subject to financial pressure. World financial power is in England's hands. If England ceases to discount France treasury bonds, that would mean bankruptcy for the French Government. Moreover, the Treaty of Versailles bound them together. So long as the Versailles treaty exists you cannot get away from it. Therefore French attempts to pursue an independent policy are frequently shortlived. Its policy changes and vacillates; attempts are made to set it free, but in the end the pressure is put on, and frequently, indeed always, France goes with the Entente Powers.[78]

Chicherin spent his remaining days in Berlin trying to foster better relations with the states of the Middle East and Asia, where, he thought, the essential struggle between the Soviet Union and Britain would occur. He said he hoped that the non-European peoples would view the Soviet Union as their natural protector against western imperialism. Chicherin left the German capital on 18 October to take the cure at Wiesbaden.

IN ADDITION to its charming landscapes and comfortable hotels, Locarno was convenient as the site for the conference because its proximity to Italy was expected to facilitate the participation of Mussolini.[79]   The Duce had even solicited an invitation, and Chamberlain had personally requested his presence.[80]   Briand was also anxious to do everything possible to encourage active Italian participation, hoping for additional support in guaranteeing the Rhine frontier and reaffirming the inviolability of the peace treaties.[81]

Mussolini, though, saw little benefit in guaranteeing the Rhine frontier. He feared that the lessening of tension between France and

Germany could remove a cover for Italy's forward policy in the Balkans, and give German nationalists an opportunity to shift their attention to the cause of the 200,000 Germans in the South Tyrol, where an intensive campaign of Italianization was currently under way.[82] The much weaker Austrian state had already supported the cause of the South Tyrolese. Mussolini also worried that the German's might try to annex Austria thereby establishing a common border with Italy. Mussolini saw in the Locarno conference an opportunity to forestall Anschluss by having France and Great Britain guarantee Italy's frontiers.[83]

The French, however, would hardly accept any arrangement that did not include a guarantee of their frontiers with Germany. Any protection of Italy would have to include an Italian commitment to protect the integrity of the Paris Peace treaties.[84] While not eager to do so, Mussolini admitted such a security pact was plausible providing it include protection of the Brenner frontier and prohibit German annexation of Austria. He also said that he was even willing to consider some sort of bilateral agreement with France.[85]

Furthermore, Mussolini wanted France to fulfill its obligations under the 1915 Treaty of London, which had promised that Italy would be compensated with African territory in exchange for joining the war against Germany.[86] Many of the professionals at the Italian Foreign Office, however, opposed such crass horse-trading because it could only weaken the real benefits that Italy would get from participation in a general European security pact. They feared Italian exclusion from the great power councils of Europe. The argument paid off, and Mussolini dropped his demand for linkage.

The duce had wanted the security conference to be held in Italy where he would have become its chairman and have been able to control the news media.[87] He was annoyed at the coverage in the British press.[88] He assumed that any unflattering remark in the French newspapers had been planted by the French government.[89] His sensitivity to criticism determined his decision to avoid active participation in the Locarno conference and send Vittorio Scialoja, a former foreign minister, as his "official observer." He also wanted to remain in Rome for the meetings of the Fascist Grand Council.[90] He promised, however, to come for part of the conference, if it seemed that his personal presence would be useful.[91] He wanted to see how things developed before he showed his hand.[92]

Briand had grown tired of Mussolini's attempts to hustle concessions. "The beauty of the view from [my hotel] terrace...more than compensates for the absence of the Prime Minister of Italy," he said sarcastically.[93]   Nonetheless, Briand promised that France was prepared to review the questions of Tunis, Tangiers, and the African colonial mandates, providing Italy was willing to help guarantee the European status quo. Mussolini assumed this meant that France was now willing to pay up on its debts under the Treaty of London.[94]

With the Locarno agreement was almost complete, Mussolini announced his intention to attend. He arrived in town in a speedboat loaded with Blackshirts and, shortly after landing, gave a press conference. Many reporters refused to attend in protest against the suppression of freedom of expression in Italy. Mussolini blamed the boycott on the French, although more British journalists stayed away than did French.[95]

Mussolini received a friendlier reception from Chamberlain. The foreign secretary believed that Mussolini, by his attendance, was paying him a personal compliment.[96] Chamberlain was captivated by the duce's charm, by his tenderness and loneliness of heart.[97] He also found him friendly and cooperative, and suggested that they meet periodically to discuss their common concerns, "if anyone of us thought that a dangerous situation was arising, or that united action might have a salutary effect." Chamberlain told him that he hoped that the Balkan powers might one day have a Locarno pact of their own—the last thing that Mussolini wanted to hear.[98]

Mussolini participated only in the conference's final session, but he claimed that his presence had been critical for success.[99] He praised the delegates for laying the basis for a new Europe and, going farther, said that he was convinced that, if the formulas inscribed in the acts of Locarno became a living reality, a new era must open in the history of the world.[100]

But such grand rhetoric could not quell the duce's fear the Germans might annex Austria and encourage separatism in South Tyrol. Even so, Mussolini seemed blind to the dangers of German revisionism elsewhere and, therefore, failed to recognize that a firm commitment to maintaining the European equilibrium in association with France, the chief defender of the status quo, could best reinforce his country's security.

Notes and Sources:

1. *The Complete Poetical Works of William Wordsworth* (Boston: Houghton Mifflin, 1904), 12.
2. *British Foreign Office Documents* 840/1, file 1. no. 3.
3. *Documents on British Foreign Policy*, first series, vol. XVII, 761.
4. *Ibid.*, 764.
5. *British Foreign Office Documents*: FO. 840/1, file 1. no. 3.
6. Charles Petrie, ed., *The Life and Letters of the Right Hon. Sir Austen Chamberlain*, II, 286.
7. *British Foreign Office Documents*: FO. 840/1, file 2. no. 3.
8. *Ibid.*, file 2. no. 3.
9. The question of German membership had first become a serious prospect the year before, during the formulation of the Geneva Protocol. Then, the German government asked specific questions about the conditions of entry: Would Germany be considered "sufficiently advanced to have colonial mandates?" Would recognition of international treaty obligations "be considered as a new recognition on Germany's part of moral responsibility for the war?" And, considering that Germany was already disarmed, what sort of special exemptions might be created freeing Germany from participation in League sanctions? (*Ibid.*, file 5. no. 4.) Germany had been assured that it could expect a permanent seat on the Council, but nothing more.
10. *Ibid.*, file 2. no. 4.
11. Georges Suarez, *Briand, Sa vie, son oeuvre, avec son journal et des nombreux documents inédits*, VI, 116-7.
12. *British Foreign Office Documents*: FO. 840/1, file 1. no. 3.
13. *Documents on British Foreign Policy*, first series, vol. XVII, 822.
14. *British Foreign Office Documents*: FO. 840/1, file 1. no. 3.
15. *Gustav Stresemann: His Diaries, Letters, and Papers*, II, 172.
16. Charles Petrie, ed., *The Life and Letters of the Right Hon. Sir Austen Chamberlain*, II, 286, 289.
17. *Documents on British Foreign Policy*, first series, vol. XVII, 822.
18. *Ministère des Affaires Étrangères*, série Y (Internationale 1918-1940), vol. 28, 3.
19. *Ibid.*, 4.
20. *British Foreign Office Documents*: FO. 840/1, file 2. no. 11.
21. *Ministère des Affaires Étrangères*, série Y (Internationale 1918-1940), vol. 28, 9. In the matter of expiration: at least two states would give notice and the League Council would decide only after three

months. If the Council agreed, a year would pass before its decision became final, enough time for states to make alternative arrangements.

22. *Ibid.*, 11.

23. *British Foreign Office Documents*: FO. 840/1, file 3. no. 7.

24. *Ministère des Affaires Étrangères*, série Y (Internationale 1918-1940), vol. 28, 15.

25. *Ibid.*, 16-17.

26. *British Foreign Office Documents*: FO. 840/1, file 3. no. 8.

27. *Ministère des Affaires Étrangères*, série Y (Internationale 1918-1940), vol. 28, 17-18.

28. *Ibid.*, 18.

29. *Ibid.*, 21-22.

30. *British Foreign Office Documents*: FO. 840/1, file 3. no. 8.

31. Stresemann's account of the meeting in *Gustav Stresemann: His Diaries, Letters, and Papers*, II, 173-6.

32. *Ministère des Affaires Étrangères*, série Y (Internationale 1918-1940), vol. 28, 23-24.

33. Chamberlain to William Tyrrell, 14 October 1925, *British Foreign Office Documents*: FO. 840/1, file 8. no. 13.

34. Cf. Earl of Avon, *The Memoirs of Anthony Eden, Facing the Dictators* (Boston: Houghton Mifflin, 1962), 10.

35. Including severing "all trade or financial relations", contributing "to the armed forces to be used to protect the covenants of the League", providing mutual support to minimize loss and inconvenience, and affording "passage through their territory to the forces of any Members which are cooperating to protect the covenants of the League."

36. *British Foreign Office Documents*: FO. 840/1, file 5. no. 2.

37. *Gustav Stresemann: His Diaries, Letters, and Papers*, II, 175.

38. Georges Suarez, *Briand, Sa vie, son oeuvre, avec son journal et des nombreux documents inédits*, VI, 120.

39. *British Foreign Office Documents*: FO. 840/1, file 5. no. 5.

40. *Ministère des Affaires Étrangères*, série Y (Internationale 1918-1940), vol. 28, 41.

41. *Ibid.*, 41.

42. *British Foreign Office Documents*: FO. 840/1, file 5. no. 5.

43. The goal of relaxing enforcement of the military clauses of the Treaty of Versailles was modest compared to the demands of an ultra-nationalist diplomat like Konstantine von Neurath, the ambassador to Rome, who demanded that German entrance into the League be made conditional upon the revision of the entire Versailles treaty. John L. Heineman, *Hitler's First Foreign Minister, Konstantine Freiherr* *von Neurath, Diplomat and Statesman* (Berkeley: University of California Press, 1979), 29.

44. *British Foreign Office Documents:* FO. 840/1, file 5. no. 5.

45. *Gustav Stresemann: His Diaries, Letters, and Papers,* II, 177.

46. *British Foreign Office Documents:* FO. 840/1, file 5. no. 5.

47. *Ministère des Affaires Étrangères,* série Y, (Internationale 1918-1940), vol. 28, 42-45.

48. *British Foreign Office Documents:* FO. 840/1, file 7. no. 9.

49. *Ibid.,* file 5. no. 11.

50. *Ibid.,* file 7. no. 15.

51. *Ibid.,* file 7. no. 9.

52. *Ibid.,* file 7. no. 9.

53. 13 October 1925. *Ibid.,* file 8. No 5.

54. *Ibid.,* file 5. no. 25.

55. *British Foreign Office Documents:* FO. 840/1, file 6. no. 14.

56. *Ministère des Affaires Étrangères,* série Y (Internationale 1918-1940), vol. 28, 5-6.

57. *Ibid.,* 28, 14.

58. *Ibid.,* 14.

59. *British Foreign Office Documents:* FO. 840/1, file 5. no. 7.

60. *Ibid.,* file. 6. no. 2.

61. *Ibid.,* file 7. No 6.

62. Hans Gatzke, *European Diplomacy,* 75.

63. *British Foreign Office Documents:* FO. 840/1, file 6. no. 2.

64. Charles Petrie, ed., *The Life and Letters of the Right Hon. Sir Austen Chamberlain,* II, 288.

65. Earl of Avon, *The Memoirs of Anthony Eden, Facing the Dictators,* 8.

66. *Ibid.,* II, 216.

67. *Gustav Stresemann: His Diaries, Letters, and Papers,* II, 216.

68. *Ibid.,* II, 185.

69. *British Foreign Office Documents:* FO. 840/1, file 7, no. 2.

70. Viscount D'Abernon, *The Diary of an Ambassador,* III, 198.

71. *British Foreign Office Documents:* FO. 840/1, file 5, no. 1.

72. *Ministère des Affaires Étrangères,* série Y, vol. 28 (Italie), 46.

73. *British Foreign Office Documents:* FO. 840/1, file 1. no. 3.

74. *Documents on British Foreign Policy,* first series, XXV, 704.

75. *British Foreign Office Documents:* FO. 840/1, file 9. no. 4.

76. *Documents on British Foreign Policy,* first series, XXV, 704.

77. *Ibid.,* 704-5.

78. *Soviet Documents on Foreign Policy,* II, 16.

79. Jules Laroche, *Au Quai d'Orsay avec Briand et Poincaré,* 212.

80. *Ministère des Affaires Étrangères*, série Z, vol. 96 (Italie), 115.

81. *Documents on British Foreign Policy*, first series, XXVII, 750.

82. The Italian language had been made compulsory in all elementary schools, people were forced to adopt more Italian sounding names, and even change their architecture: the bell towers of the German churches being torn down and replaced by free standing *campanile* in the Italian style.

83. Denis Mack Smith, *Mussolini*, 96.

84. *Ministère des Affaires Étrangères*, série Z, vol. 96 (Italie), 119-20.

85. *Ibid.*, 121-2.

86. C. J. Lowe and F. Marzari, *Italian Foreign Policy 1870- 1940* (London: Routledge and Kegan Paul, 1975), 205.

87. He had created a special department, headed by Under-secretary of State Dino Grandi, in the foreign affairs ministry to strong-arm foreign journalists. The newspapermen were forbidden, among other things, to send cables abroad that the fascist censors had disapproved. Denis Mack Smith, *Mussolini*, 92.

88. *British Foreign Office Documents*: FO. 840/1, file 1. no. 4.

89. *Ministère des Affaires Étrangères*, série Z, vol. 96 (Italie), 31.

90. The Council was making important changes in the Italian constitution, like the 7 October decree that abolished the democratically-run provincial councils, turning over their civil authority to the Fascist prefects. This enabled Mussolini to govern without the consent of parliament. *Annual Register*, 1925, 160 and "Decree on the Powers of the Head of the Government" (December 24, 1925) in Charles E. Delzell, ed., *Mediterranean Fascism* (New York: Harper and Row, 1970), 62-4..

91. *British Foreign Office Documents*: FO. 840/1, file 1. no. 4.

92. *Ministère des Affaires Étrangères*, série Z, vol. 96 (Italie), 117-8.

93. *British Foreign Office Documents*: FO. 840/1, file 1. no. 3.

94. Cedric Lowe and F. Marzari, *Italian Foreign Policy 1970-1940*, 206.

95. *Survey of International Affairs*, 1927, 138.

96. He told some British reporters to avoid writing about Mussolini's attendance as if it were a spur-of-the-moment decision, as "this would be resented by them, would be offensive to them, and does not correspond with the facts." *British Foreign Office Documents*: FO. 840/1, file 6. no. 19.

97. Charles Petrie, ed., *The Life and Letters of the Right Hon. Sir Austen Chamberlain*, II, 295.

98. Mussolini replied evasively that the Balkan countries had first to make up their minds whether to tell anyone who tried to disturb the status quo that "he would not be permitted to do so, or whether the situation might be in some cases so unfavourable or intolerable from one or the other parties that some change ought to be introduced." Chamberlain, in a rare removal of his rose-colored glasses, read this to mean that the Duce had designs on Albania. *British Foreign Office Documents*: FO. 840/1, file 9. no. 5.

99. Denis Mack Smith, *Mussolini*, 97.

100. *Ministère des Affaires Étrangères*, série Y, vol. 28 (Tchécoslovaquie), 117.

CHAPTER 12

A MARRIAGE OF CONVENIENCE

STRESEMANN FEARED that the Locarno conference had given Germany very little. He believed that the Anglo-French Entente had strengthened, that Germany's connection with the Soviet Union had weakened, and that the guarantee extended to France's eastern treaties had given France an additional excuse to interfere in German-Polish relations. Moreover, French troops remained in Cologne for no purpose than "to display the colors of their regiments." Stresemann despaired his failure to gain recognition of Germany's right to have a military force "proportional to the other powers," fearing that his conciliatory spirit gave him only a collection of general, practically worthless, promises.[1]

Determined not to go home empty-handed, he demanded that the *protocol de clôture* (the final document) promise the reduction of occupation troops, the withdrawal of black soldiers, and the release of prisoners still held for offenses committed in protest against the invasion of the Ruhr. He further stipulated that limits placed on the number of German policemen in the Rhineland be lifted and there be an early plebiscite in the Saarland.[2] Chancellor Luther also pressed for a date for evacuation of the Cologne-zone without which he "would not be able to get German public opinion to understand the work the German Delegation had done at Locarno."[3] Stresemann claimed that Briand almost fell "off the sofa" when he read the list of German demands.[4]

Stresemann continued. He even attacked the Rhineland Control Commission's refusal to allow German police officials to bear the title of "*Hauptmann*" (Captain), insisting that they be called "*Inspektor*" instead. Stresemann explained that in Germany the title of "Inspektor" was of low social rank, one unlikely to impress the young ladies who preferred going out with a Hauptmann.[5]

Briand reminded the Germans that the main purpose of the Locarno conference was not to list grievances, but to make a new departure in European relations. He promise to urge the French military representative on the Control Commission to achieve "an early settlement of the outstanding points," but only after the security pact had been signed.[6] As to the issue of what to call German policemen, he said that as far as he was concerned "they can call the men generals if they like." Briand tried to steer the discussion back to more significant matters. He explained that the Locarno pact would lead to a mitigation of the conditions of occupation and promised to stake his political career on it. He pointed out, however, that task would be easier, if the Germans would "try to do something to control their Right [wing], and their excited elements."[7] Briand also said that he would like to set a date for the Cologne evacuation, but in doing so he would exceed his mandate, and "would be disavowed."[8]

Stresemann brought up another new issue when he asked if German entrance into the League would be an admission that Article 213 of the Treaty of Versailles (the one related to the investigation of German armaments) was binding on Germany. Briand asked if Stresemann were making the resolution of this matter a condition for entry and said that, if so, "it was the destruction of all that we had done at Locarno." Chamberlain warned that trying to deal with every possible contingency could wreck everything. "If [the Germans] sought to clear the whole path, we should never reach a settlement." Chamberlain refused to believe that the Germans' eleventh-hour demands would really prevent the conclusion of an agreement. Indeed, satisfied that they had put their reservations on record, Luther and Stresemann dropped their objections Chamberlain could now looked forward to a triumphal return home and a proper place in history. He euphorically cabled the Foreign Office: "Cock-a-doodle-doo!"[9]

ON 16 OCTOBER 1925, the delegates, seated at their accustomed places in the Palais de Justice conference room, watched three photographers scurrying around taking their pictures. Although he had little to do with the negotiations, Mussolini showed up for inclusion.

The picture-taking over, Chamberlain gave the delegates' wives, who had been invited as witnesses, a tour of the conference rooms. Then, Chamberlain's wife Ivy proposed that everybody have tea in a nearby restaurant.[10] The assembly headed for the doors.

Outside, a crowd of people waited to greet the peacemakers. When they emerged, they were greeted by shouts of praise in German, English, Italian, and French. Lady Hurst, the wife of the British legal advisor Sir Cecil Hurst, was so moved that she felt she was walking in a wedding procession.

Stresemann, though, found it hard get in a festive mood. He still brooded about his lack of success and, later, sought out Chamberlain at the Grand Hotel to reiterate his and Luther's concerns privately, warning him that the Reichstag would refuse to ratify the agreement, unless the League of Nation's relationship with German disarmament were clarified. The conversation dragged on past the dinner hour. Chamberlain later complained: "Stresemann is like a nagging old woman who must always have the last word."[11] Chamberlain suspected that Stresemann was like an actor over-playing his part. The performance showed him "once again how difficult it is to help a German or make him understand any argument but a bludgeon."[12]

The conversation may have caused Chamberlain to miss his evening meal, but it did not prevent approval of the final draft, which, originally scheduled for 6:30 p.m., was signed two hours later because the experts needed more time to get it in shape.[13] Stresemann, unlike Chamberlain and Briand, lacked full powers to sign, and the final instrument could only be initialled.[14] Afterwards there were toasts. Stresemann drank to the peaceful cooperation of states, saying he was confident that the political effect of the treaties will be to Germany's advantage "in relieving the conditions of our political life." But, he added that such success was only possible if Locarno were regarded as "the beginning of confident cooperation among nations," implying that Locarno must serve as the basis of future concessions to Germany.[15]

Briand, at the top of his game, hailed the Locarno treaties as beginning an era of sincere collaboration between nations. He said he was confident that France, despite its differences with Germany, would apply the Locarno treaty in "a true spirit of appeasement" and prove that the two nations could work together to realize the same ideal of "a Europe fulfilling her destiny while remaining faithful to its past of civilization and nobility."[16]

Die Kriegsschuld in Locarno

„Jedem das Seine: uns das schlechte Gewissen — dir die Schuld!"

War Guilt at Locarno. *Briand to a shackled Stresemann: "To each his own. We [French] have the bad conscience, you [Germans] get the blame." Chamberlain looks on approvingly while other Locarno delegates chortle in the distance. Wilhelm Schulz in* Simplicissimus *(19 October 1925) expresses Stresemann's fear that Briand had got the better of him.*

Chamberlain was full of admiration. "Briand spoke the true heart of chivalrous France," he said. "In his words, shone the spirit of a Bayard, *sans peur et sans reproche* [fearless and blameless], of all that is best and noblest in her people and her history."[17]   Briand returned the compliment. *"Ah, sans lui, je ne l'aurais jamais tenté"* (Without [your husband] I would never have tried to do it), he tearfully told Chamberlain's wife, Ivy.[18]   Harold Nicolson was more cynical. He viewed the occasion as one played out "amid scenes of almost orgiac gush."[19]

Fifteen-hundred people enthusiastically cheered when the conference room windows were thrown opened. The treaty, like a precious relic from the Holy Land or the new-born son of a king, was held aloft for them to see. Celebrations and rejoicing lasted throughout the night. It was Chamberlain's sixty-second birthday, an experience, he believed, that no man in his lifetime could hope to repeat: "I felt myself a little child again in spirit," he said.[20]

The following day the delegates left for home and the details of what they had accomplished were made public.[21]

THE SIGNATORIES—Germany, Belgium, France, Great Britain, and Italy—had recognized the inviolability of the German-Belgian and German-French frontiers. They guaranteed the demilitarization of the Rhineland, already established by the Treaty of Versailles, and pledged to commit no aggression against each other and arbitrate all disputes. If one party committed a "flagrant violation," the others promised to come immediately to the aid of the country against which the violation had been directed. This would occur

> as soon as the said Power has been able to satisfy itself that this violation constitutes an unprovoked act of aggression and that by reason either of the crossing of the frontier or of the outbreak of hostilities or of the assembly of armed forces in the demilitarized zone immediate action is necessary.[22]

The specification of the "crossing of the frontiers" was an amplification of the original draft, which had only mentioned "the assembly of armed forces."[23]

Germany signed arbitration conventions with France and Belgium. Stresemann accepted the loss of Alsace-Lorraine, but balked at doing the same for Eupen and Malmédy, the land the Versailles Treaty awarded to Belgium. He had even tried to have all mention of the Belgian boundaries omitted from the final instrument. The French, however, were quite emphatic that *all* the western frontiers be included. Accordingly, the treaty specified that the signatories "collectively and severally" guaranteed

> the territorial status quo resulting from the frontiers between Germany and Belgium and between Germany and France, and the

inviolability of the said frontiers as fixed by or in pursuance of the
Treaty of Peace signed at Versailles on June 28, 1919.[24]

The Belgians insisted that the three states be specifically named to
reinforce their separate identities.[25]

The obligations seemed clear: Germany had accepted the clauses
of the Treaty of Versailles that pertained to the western frontiers in
their entirety. This, at any rate, was the interpretation of the British and
the French. But Friedrich Gaus, the Wilhelmstrasse's legal adviser,
claimed that Germany had pledged only to foreswear revision "by
force." He based this opinion on the phrase "in the manner provided in
the following articles", which, he said, contained only a promise to
refrain from mounting an attack and a commitment to settle differences
through peaceful means.[26] Thus the Germans believed that Locarno
had authorized revisionism of the western frontiers, as long as that was
done peacefully through diplomacy. No other power accepted this
cunning interpretation, but none protested it openly.

Briand told Stresemann privately that he disapproved, but he
hesitated to turn it into a major issue because he wanted to avoid giving
the German nationalists ammunition to prevent the Reichstag from
ratifying the treaty. Stresemann could, therefore, pretend, or hope, that
some sort of a settlement could be worked out with Belgium for
reincorporating Eupen and Malmédy into the Reich perhaps through an
offer of money. France was sure to object, but France had financial
difficulties and might likewise be bought off: by the capitalization of
Dawes Plan bonds, for example. The Germans knew how desperate
France was for hard currency. Its financial weakness had already put it
at the mercy of Britain and the United States. Furthermore, the reliance
of France on reparations would put Germany in a decided position of
strength.

Eupen and Malmédy would add little to German power—together
these territories had only about 1000 square kilometers of land and
64,000 inhabitants. But their reacquisition would establish a precedent
for revisionism of the Polish frontiers, which Locarno failed to have
Germany recognize as permanent. This omission acknowledged that
they were subject to change, even though Germany promised that
revision would be accomplished peacefully and had signed treaties to
that effect with Poland and Czechoslovakia.[27] Stresemann, though, had
insisted that these agreements omit any reference to the main security

treaty to avoid even implicit recognition of the Polish, and also the Czechoslovak, frontiers.[28] He had not expressly articulated revision of the German-Czechoslovak frontier, but had maintained Germany's right to act for the three million Sudetenland Germans, who lived in the mountainous region of northwest Bohemia, compromising about 23 percent of Czechoslovakia's population.[29]

The Czechs, like the Poles, had not been party to the Locarno negotiations. Eduard Beneš, the Czech foreign minister, had arrived at Locarno, on 7 October, but was not allowed to sit with the conference delegates until the agreement had been concluded. The Polish representative, Aleksandr Skrzynski, was also allowed to attend only at that time. Neither Beneš nor Skrzynski were encouraged to make comments.[30] Their counterproposals were not discussed.[31] Beneš, for example, could only emphasize the importance of having all disputes settled by peaceful means.[32] Stresemann thought that even this brief and innocuous comment was excessive, although he was overjoyed that he could treat the allies of France with such disdain.

In guaranteeing Czechoslovakia, France went beyond its previous commitment, which provided only for policy coordination if Czech security were threatened. Now, if Germany were to commit an unprovoked act of aggression, France promised to provide "immediate aid and assistance."[33] Unlike the treaty France had with Poland, however, the new obligation contained no specific military provisions. This was as much a Czech desire as French. Benes, alarmed at the French invasion of the Ruhr, decided to rely on the collective security of the League of Nations for protection. He also wanted to avoid making any agreement that could weaken the Little Entente—Romania and Yugoslavia had no desire for a military alliance with France. Benes apparently believed that the Germans were sincere about their promise to seek revision by peaceful means, and he hailed the treaties of arbitration as a moral force for national defense. He further reasoned that the Rhineland pact would promote the consolidation of eastern Europe, making conflicts there less likely. He hoped that the pact of guarantee would ease the way for better relations with the U.S.S.R. for European security could never be really achieved without Soviet cooperation.[34]

Lord D'Abernon believed that the Czechs welcomed the Locarno pact because it relieved them of the responsibility of having to chose between French and Germany "with whom they have long conterminous frontiers, and who buys 30 per cent. of their exports."[35] Benes, he said, was in favor of creating a central European industrial force that would be independent of Germany's economic power, a goal that reinforced the desire of the Little Entente powers to avoid the danger of becoming satellites of the great powers.[36]

France also reinforced its commitments to Poland, promising to provide "immediate aid and assistance" in case of unprovoked aggression.[37] This assistance would be forthcoming, however, only after Poland invoked Article 16 of the League Covenant. Such an appeal might delay action, but the French felt they had gone as far at they dared to protect Polish security. Briand did not intend to subordinate French interests to the demands of Poland, which he once described as "the rheumatism of Europe."[38]

The Locarno accords could not change geo-politics, much less Polish attitudes.[39] Poland remained squeezed between two revisionist neighbors, which were cool to peaceful coexistence. The Polish contradictory and provocative foreign policy, however, often made the situation worse. Poland tried to form an anti-Communist bloc with states that had little skill in cooperating with one another.[40] It poisoned relations with two of its closest neighbors: Lithuania and Czechoslovakia.[41] It refused to sign a non-aggression pact with the Soviets, while failing to reach an accord with Germany.[42] Foreign Minister Skrzynski even pretended that Poland would refuse to sign an agreement that would involve recognition of the existing frontiers and told Stresemann so at Locarno. Stresemann was surprised and delighted. But Chamberlain was dumbfounded. "You have, therefore, the Pole laying down a condition to the German which the German had intended to impose on the Pole," he said.[43]

The Poles hoped the British would give them support, at least diplomatically, and they solicited Chamberlain's help in getting them a permanent seat on the League of Nations Council as given to the Germans.[44] Chamberlain was not encouraging, advising Skrzynski that Poland's real safety lay in its ability to get along with its neighbors, including the Soviet Union, and to "create an atmosphere of trust and confidence between herself and Germany."[45] Chamberlain, though, had little hope such a settlement could be purged of unrest and dissatisfaction.

The British left the Poles to their own devices. Chamberlain specified that his country was unwilling "to assume any responsibility outside the terms of the Covenant of the League for the territorial settlement between Poland and Germany."[46] The British were no more willing to guarantee the frontiers of eastern Europe now than they had been six years earlier. Their position was unambiguous. Small wonder that the Poles left Locarno still feeling insecure. They had hoped the accords would increase their security, not facilitate the revision of treaties.[47] To avoid guaranteeing the eastern frontiers was, according to Skrzynski, like

> having a house which contained beautiful tapestries and taking precautions for them alone, abandoning all the objects accumulated in the neighboring rooms to the danger of fire.[48]

Skrzynski knew that, once Germany was free from pressure in the Rhineland, it would be more inclined to push its power on the Vistula.[49]

CHAMBERLAIN CONSIDERED the *mariage de convenance* on the shores of Lake Maggiore to be the line of demarcation between the years of war and the years of peace. He hailed the Locarno settlement as his greatest achievement, and he never tired talking about it.[50] He had achieved his goal: "restoring such relations of mutual confidence as might enable [Britain] to exercise a moderating influence on [French] policy, and prevent a renewal of the folly of the Ruhr occupation."[51] He had reconciled the rivalries of France and Germany, while clearing the way for the reestablishment of a true European equilibrium. His admiration for the French had strengthened:

> The deeper Englishmen and Frenchmen penetrate into each other's nature, the more they will find they have common; the deeper Englishmen and German go, the greater the divergence of faith and spirit which will be revealed between them.[52]

But he intended to continue to pressure France for the "rapid evacuation of Cologne and to a sensible alleviation of the conditions in the territories still remaining occupied."[53]

Chamberlain believed he had mastered his anti-German bias, and he was now determined to civilize the Germans with full and equal partnership in the League of Nations. He felt he had been successful

because, in part, he had been able to strike a common chord with
Stresemann: "quite a pleasant companion, at any rate as pleasant as
anybody can be who speaks so ugly a language as German."[54]

The British believed that the most important section of the Treaty
lay in Article 4. Legal expert Hurst explained that if France were to
violate the treaty by attacking Germany

> she would find herself opposed immediately by a combination of
> Great Britain, Belgium and Italy as well as Germany: were
> Germany to attack France, she would find herself immediately
> opposed by a combination of Great Britain, Italy and Belgium as
> well as France.[55]

The British were satisfied that they had resolved the issue of French
security, the "root cause of European instability and unrest" and had
returned Germany to the family of nations.[56]   They had successfully
counterpoised their power between France and Germany, avoiding the
sort of military commitment that had existed before the First World
War.[57]   The British had once again achieved freedom of action.   The
Locarno agreement enlarged their options should a danger to British
security occur, but it still allowed them to judge what action they
should take.[58]

But Britain's reluctance to assume a broader, more active role in
the enforcement of peace was shortsighted.   Air power had weakened
the country's defensive perimeter, opening the country to attack from
bases in western Germany.   The perpetual demilitarization of the
Rhineland was, therefore, as important to them as it was to the French,
who regarded the Locarno treaty as inadequate substitution for a
guarantee treaty.   Locarno merely defined the circumstances when war
was legitimate: 1. self-defense, 2. action against a disturber of the
peace, and 3. defense of the Covenant of the League.   Enforcement was
now more difficult, especially the use of military force.   Furthermore,
in prescribing an obligation to arbitrate, the Locarno treaty could delay
taking action.

Not all agreed with this pessimistic assessment. Henri Fromageot,
the Quai d'Orsay's legal expert, pointed out that France still had
a perfect right to undertake appropriate counter-measures on its own
against German violation without waiting for League action:

In this case the guarantor does not take part in the deliberations of the Council of the League, but according to Article 16 of the Covenant, the other guarantors must have a favorable vote to act themselves. If the majority favors intervention, *all* the guarantors *must* act.[59]

Sir Cecil Hurst backed him up, arguing that a sudden attack

may call for instant measures of defense and support. In such a case the guarantee is to operate at once if the guaranteeing power is satisfied that an attack in breach of the Treaty of Locarno has been made.[60]

THE LOCARNO SETTLEMENT did nothing to change the current military balance. As before, France maintained its security with the size of its army and the determination to use it. The treaty would only take effect when Germany entered the League. The French hoped that such membership would make Germany a guarantor of the peace settlement. Briand emphasized that the "only basis of membership of the League was respect for treaties."[61]

The French had also wanted to shake Germany's association with the Soviet Union. They remained convinced that the Treaty of Rapallo contained secret military clauses. Bringing Germany solidly into the Western camp would make it more difficult for Germany to shift allegiances, "to have," as Briand put it, "one foot in the League of Nations and one foot in another camp in which the sentiments were very different."[62]

Briand knew that France could no longer perpetuate the post-war status quo, that it had to tolerate some revision of the Treaty of Versailles, including modification of Germany's eastern frontiers. This could hopefully be done peacefully, reasonably, and through the League of Nations.[63] But Briand feared that the French would not realize that things had changed, and that they would blame him for their loss of influence. They would point at him and claim that they "were already secure in their existing alliances under the Treaty of Versailles, and that there was no reason to alter that state of affairs."[64] Briand wished the Locarno pact would salve Europe's wounds to allow for solution of the difficult problems ahead.[65]

Locarno marked an end of the forward position the French had on the Rhine. But the French had already lost their taste for pushing around the Germans, and were more interested in solving domestic problems. This inward vision had an important effect on the country's willingness to furnish direct assistance to its eastern allies. After the Ruhr episode, French military policy had become more defensive, and France was no more eager to go to war for Danzig than were the British. From Berlin, Ambassador D'Abernon saw that France's post-war alliances would "cease to be the main protection, and in the process of time will probably fade away."[66]

The British expected the Locarno treaty to stabilize the situation created by the Treaty of Versailles.[67] But they also accepted it as the basis for change. They had less fear than the French that the Germans would upset the European balance of power. Consequently, they were more concerned with restraining French action than preventing German revision, especially in eastern Europe where they had little presence and scant interest. British responsibility extended only to the frontiers between France, Belgium, and Germany. This view had remained unchanged since the Paris Peace Conference and would continue unchanged for the next decade and a half.[68]

The "Allies" negotiated the Locarno treaty from a position of strength because Germany was still disarmed. But the victor powers had less power over their former enemy now than before—a situation due more to Germany's general recovery than the benefits of the Locarno agreement.

France lacked the resources and will to continue occupying Germany. Britain lacked the will and the means to intervene abroad. Both had to adjust to a reconstructed Germany. D'Abernon said the Locarno pact ended the system of one-sided alliances and restored a necessary balance of power by obliging Britain and Italy to commit all their moral and material weight to whatever side was deemed to be the innocent one in any Franco-German conflict.

> In this way the Pact was designed and destined to reassure France and Belgium against the peril of any renewed attack from Germany. Similarly, it reassured a disarmed Germany against any abuse of power by a fully-armed France and its numerous allies.[69]

Security agreements, grand designs, pacts, protocols, and treaties of guarantee had been discussed continuously since the end of the war. German determination to revise the Paris settlement had dogged all these efforts. German will and power stood in the way of any treaty of arbitration. The experienced politicians, who negotiated the Locarno agreement, knew this. They had pondered the settlement for almost ten months before bringing it to term. Their desire to liquidate the tensions of the First World War created the "Locarno Spirit." The agreement's weakness was less in the way it was phrased than in the way it would be enforced.

If there arose a myth that Locarno had established a new age of peace, there was something wrong with the myth. The Germans had never regarded the Treaty of Versailles as legitimate. Stresemann viewed any agreement as a stepping stone for further revision. Thus the lessening of tension was a means to an end, not an end in itself, the Locarno agreement only methodologically being a new departure in the politics of the Weimar government. Stresemann wanted the evacuation of the Second and Third Zones of the Rhineland, he wanted the retrocession of Malmédy, Eupen, and St. Vith, he wanted the return of Danzig and the Corridor, which, he thought, could be done without depriving Poland of access to the sea. "But don't tell Count Skrzynski," he admonished French embassy counsellor André de Laboulaye.[70] Colonial mandates: New Guinea, Togo, Cameroons, and Samoa were also on Stresemann's shopping list. "I need some territories to which to send the nationalists," he quipped.[71]

The German foreign office was full of men who thought as he did. These were the same men who had so willingly embraced expansionism under the kaiser. Stresemann had won their approval through his diplomatic skill and his ability to convince many in the Reichstag of his commitment to a greater Germany. Stresemann promoted the evacuation of foreign troops from the Rhineland without disarmament conditions. He helped weaken the Treaty of Versailles by recognizing the demilitarization of the Rhineland and promising to continue paying reparations. He explained German ambitions in the east with double-talk:

> I have no notions of decisions to be reached by war. What I have
> in mind is that when conditions arise which indicate that European
> peace or the economic consolidation of Europe is threatened by

developments in the East, and when it is realized that this entire
non-consolidation of Europe appears to have its origins in
impossible frontier-lines in the East, that Germany might succeed
with her claims, if she had previously effected a political
understanding with all the World Powers who would have to
decide the matter, and established a common interest with her
opponents.[72]

Stresemann resisted bragging about his success for fear of
alarming Britain and France.[73] If he had moments of doubt over his
achievement, other Germans felt cheated. These believed that the
general renunciation of the use of force weakened the determination to
regain lost territories.[74] Stresemann's critics attacked the Locarno
agreement for its failure to mention the *immediate* withdrawal of allied
troops from the Rhineland. They jumped on Stresemann for tying
Germany's hands in agreeing to join the League. Diplomats, like
Ambassador Konstantin von Neurath, believed that Stresemann had
fallen under the influence of Chamberlain and Lord D'Abernon.[75]
President Hindenburg denounced the agreement for its intrinsic
inequality, for leaving the Germans disarmed without comparable
disarmament by Britain and France, for recognizing a demilitarized
zone in the Rhineland, but demanding no corresponding neutralization
of Alsace-Lorraine.[76] "The Locarno soup was dished up to us by
Herr Stresemann and must be eaten now," he groused.

The Reichspräsident promised to attack the agreement "to the best
of his constitutional ability."[77] But, when the Reichstag approved the
treaty, by a vote of 292 to 177, Hindenburg dutifully appended his
signature, and, in an about face, began to criticize the Nationalists for
persisting in their opposition.[78] By then, the Nationalists had already
withdrawn from the cabinet. They had failed to prevent ratification,
but their continued opposition would help bring down Luther's
government.

The German menace still kept the French awake at nights. Briand
refrained from expressing his doubts about German intentions publicly,
even in the Chamber of Deputies.[79] He, however, told his associates of
"the well known and disturbing boldness and fertile imagination of the
German minister of foreign affairs" whose goals contradicted the
agreement founded on the respect of treaties.[80] Briand weathered his

share of criticism, one of the severest attacks coming from his old nemesis, Raymond Poincaré. "Belgium and France", Poincaré wrote,

> are no longer capable of adequate judgment in case of a flagrant violation. In return for a few concessions, we got from the Reich a pledge which will be worth as much as the German mentality.[81]

But most Frenchmen were tired of the cold war with Germany, they were concerned with domestic issues and wanted to get on with their mundane lives. The National Assembly passed the treaty by a comfortable majority.

In Britain, the treaty sailed through Commons with only 13 negative votes. The Liberal and Labour parties had reproached the foreign secretary, however, for his lackluster efforts to consult the Dominions, and MacDonald said he was disappointed the treaty omitted definite provisions concerning disarmament.[82]

Chamberlain came home a conquering hero. He was dubbed a Knight of the Garter—only three commoners had received that honor since Castlereagh in 1814[83]—and his wife was decorated with the Grand Cross of a Dame of the British Empire. (It is unknown whether Chamberlain induced the Treasury to cover Ivy's Locarno travel expenses.) The day the treaty was signed, George V wrote in his diary, "I pray this may mean peace for many years. Why not forever?"[84] The question then appeared reasonable.

Notes and Sources:

1. On 12 October, he told Chamberlain and Briand that the League of Nations should be based on the principle of "an equality of armaments" sufficient to meet a country's needs. *British Foreign Office Documents*: FO. 840/1, file 7. No. 15.

2. Gustav Stresemann, *Gustav Stresemann, His Diaries, Letters, and Papers* (London: Macmillan, 1935-1940), II, 179-180.

3. *British Foreign Office Documents*: FO. 840/1, file 9. No. 10.

4. Stresemann, *Gustav Stresemann, His Diaries, Letters, and Papers*, 180.

5. *British Foreign Office Documents*: FO. 840/1, file 8. No. 23.

6. *Ibid.*, file 8. No. 1.

7. *Ibid.*, file 9. No. 10.

8. *Ibid.*, file 9. No. 10.

9. To which Tyrrell replied, "Never imagined you could warble so sweetly, but to you all things seem possible now." *Ibid.*, file 9. No. 1.

10. Charles Petrie, ed., *The Life and Letters of the Right Hon. Sir Austen Chamberlain*, II, 289.

11. *British Foreign Office Documents*: FO. 840/1, file 9. No. 9.

12. Chamberlain to Tyrrell, 16 October 1925. *Ibid.*, file 9. No. 25.

13. It was decided that the treaty would be signed in London on 1 December "during the course of a single meeting." *League of Nations Treaty Series*, vol. LIV, 297. Nonetheless, contrary to the usual diplomatic practice, the treaty would bear the name of the place where it was negotiated, not where it was signed.

14. *British Foreign Office Documents*: FO. 840/1, file 8. No. 4.

15. Gustav Stresemann, *Gustav Stresemann, His Diaries, Letters, and Papers*, II, 188-9.

16. Georges Suarez, *Briand, sa vie, son oeuvre, avec son journal et des nombreux documents inédits*, VI, 129.

17. Charles Petrie, ed., *The Life and Letters of the Right Hon. Sir Austen Chamberlain*, II, 290.

18. *Ibid.*, 290.

19. Harold Nicolson, *King George The Fifth*, 409.

20. Charles Petrie, ed., *The Life and Letters of the Right Hon. Sir Austen Chamberlain*, II, 290.

21. Chamberlain generously agreed to allow the official text of the treaty to be in French. *British Foreign Office Documents*: FO. 840/1, file 8, No. 4.

22. *League of Nations Treaty Series*, vol. LIV, 1926-1927, 295.

23. *British Foreign Office Documents*: FO. 840/1, file 7. No 3.

24. *League of Nations Treaty Series,* vol. LIV, 293.

25. *British Foreign Office Documents*: FO. 840/1, file 7. No. 3.

26. Manfred J. Enssle, *Stresemann's Territorial Revisionism, Germany, Belgium, and the Eupen-Malmédy Question 1919-1929* (Wiesbaden: Franz Steiner, 1980), 190-1.

27. *League of Nations Treaty Series,* vol. LVI, 329-339, 343-351.

28. According to Sir Cecil Hurst, however, the relationship was clearly established by having the guarantee treaties come into force simultaneously with the arbitration conventions. Also, any French action against Germany "would fall either under Article 16 or under Article 15, paragraph 7, of the Covenant and would therefore be in strict conformity with Article 2 of the Treaty of Locarno." *British Foreign Office Documents*: FO. 840/1, file 9. No. 33.

29. In 1919, they had tried to become a part of Germany, or Austria, but the Czechs, supported by the French, insisted on maintaining Bohemia's historic frontier. The Czechoslovak Germans in retaliation refused to send representatives to the national parliament in Prague. The ban was broken in 1925, when the German Agrarians and the German Christian Socialists, the two leading Sudetenland parties, agreed to participate. The German Social Democrats, however, still continued their boycott. Hugh Seton-Watson, *Eastern Europe Between the Wars, 1918-1941* (New York: Harper and Row, 1962), 279, 414; *Annual Register 1925*, 188.

30. *Ministère des Affaires Étrangères,* série Y (Internationale), vol. 28, 100-4.

31. Piotr S. Wandycz, *France and her Eastern Allies, 1919-1925: French-Czechoslovak-Polish Relations from the Paris Peace Conference to Locarno,* 360-1.

32. *Ministère des Affaires Étrangères,* série Y (Internationale), vol. 28, 107-8.

33. *League of Nations Treaty Series,* vol. LIV, 361.

34. *British Foreign Office Documents*: FO. 840/1, file 2. No. 13.

35. Viscount D'Abernon, *The Diary of an Ambassador,* III, 194.

36. *Ministère des Affaires Étrangères,* série Z (Tchécoslovaquie), vol. 69, 112-3.

37. *League of Nations Treaty Series,* vol. LIV, 355.

38. *Documents on British Foreign Policy,* first series, XXVII, 770-771.

39. Georges Bonnet, *Quai d'Orsay,* 79.

40. In January 1921, Poland and Romania concluded an anti-Soviet defensive pact in which they promised to protect each others' frontiers, including Romanian ownership of Bessarabia, whose loss the Russians never recognized. When Chicherin visited Warsaw in September 1925, he made sure the Poles recognized this. *British Foreign Office Documents*: FO. 840/1, file 6. No. 1.

41. Lithuania by the acquisition of Vilna and Czechoslovakia by the claims on Teschen.

42. *British Foreign Office Documents*: FO. 840/1, file 7. No. 8.

43. Chamberlain to Tyrrell, 14 October 1925, *Ibid.*, file 8. No. 13.

44. *Ibid.*, file 6. No. 13.

45. *Documents on British Foreign Policy*, first series, vol. XXV, 944.

46. *Ibid.*, 944-5.

47. *Ministère des Affaires Étrangères*, série Z (Grande-Bretagne), vol. 89, 192.

48. *Survey of International Affairs 1925*, II, 29.

49. Piotr S. Wandycz, *France and her Eastern Allies, 1919-1925: French-Czechoslovak-Polish Relations from the Paris Peace Conference to Locarno,* 360.

50. Leopold Amery, *My Political Life*, II, 303.

51. *Ibid.*, 301.

52. Charles Petrie, ed., *The Life and Letters of the Right Hon. Sir Austen Chamberlain*, I, 28.

53. *British Foreign Office Documents*: FO. 840/1, file 8. No. 13.

54. *Ibid.*, file 7. No. 9.

55. *Ibid.*, file 9. No. 33.

56. *Documents on British Foreign Policy*, Series Ia, I, 6.

57. Leopold Amery, *My Political Life*, II, 301-2.

58. *Documents on British Foreign Policy*, Series Ia, I, 15.

59. Jules Laroche, *Au Quai d'Orsay avec Briand et Poincaré*, 214.

60. *British Foreign Office Documents*: FO. 840/1, file 9. No. 33.

61. *Ibid.*, file 5. No. 4.

62. *Ibid.*, file 5. No. 4.

63. Georges Bonnet, *Quai d'Orsay*, 81.

64. *British Foreign Office Documents*: FO. 840/1, file 8. No. 1.

65. *Ministère des Affaires Étrangères*, série Y (Internationale), vol. 28, 114.

66. Viscount D'Abernon, *The Diary of an Ambassador*, III, 194.

67. *British Foreign Office Documents*: FO. 840/1, file 9. No. 33.

68. Leopold Amery, *My Political Life*, II. 304.

69. Viscount D'Abernon, *The Diary of an Ambassador*, III, 199.

70. 28 November 1925. *Ministère des Affaires Étrangères*, série Y (Internationale), vol. 691, 254-5.

71. *Ibid.*, 255.

72. Gustav Stresemann, *Gustav Stresemann, His Diaries, Letters, and Papers* II, 220-1.

73. Thimme in Hans Gatzke, *European Diplomacy*, 85.

74. Stresemann tried to assure them otherwise on 26 October 1925, at the Dresden Press Club. *Ibid.*, 196-202.

75. John Heineman, *Hitler's Foreign Minister: Konstantine von Neurath, Diplomat and Statesman*, 29.

76. Andreas Dorpalen, *Hindenburg and the Weimar Republic*, 96. Stresemann once told the British ambassador that Hindenburg, "like most military men,...is skeptical as to the efficacity of any alternative to war." Viscount D'Abernon, *The Diary of an Ambassador*, III, 169.

77. Andreas Dorpalen, *Hindenburg and the Weimar Republic*, 96.

78. *Ibid.*, 97.

79. Manfred J. Enssle, *Stresemann's Territorial Revisionism, Germany, Belgium, and the Eupen-Malmédy Question 1919-1929*, 112-3.

80. 29 November 1925. *Ministère des Affaires Étrangères*, série Y (Internationale), vol. 691, 258.

81. Jules Laroche, *Au Quai d'Orsay avec Briand et Poincaré*, 215.

82. *Annual Register*, 1925, 111.

83. The other two were also foreign ministers: Edward Grey and Arthur Balfour.

84. Norman Rose, *Vansittart: Study of a Diplomat* (New York: Holmes and Meir, 1978), 387.

CHAPTER 13

THE LOCARNO SPIRIT

BY TEMPERING the injustices of the Versailles treaty, the Locarno accord had allowed Britain to escape making a security alliance with France and paved the way for the participation of Germany in the councils of Europe. Austen Chamberlain thought a strong, affluent Germany was necessary to promote British prosperity, to contain Bolshevik Russia, and to bolster the peacekeeping mission of the League of Nations.[1] He deemed that the disarmament of Germany dictated by the Treaty of Versailles had been unreasonable, not to mention unenforceable, and he favored allowing Germany a reasonable increase of its military power.

Briand, on the other hand, refused to believe that the Locarno pact had ended the need for close supervision of German armaments and was reluctant to make concessions.[2] He was particularly alarmed by Chamberlain's efforts to thin out the number of allied troops in the Rhineland. Like Poincaré, he believed that Franco-German reconciliation should produce positive results before any significant troop withdrawals. Briand complained that the Germans wanted everything at once: they wanted revision of the Danzig corridor; they wanted return of Eupen and Malmédy; they wanted an immediate end to the occupation of the Rhineland; they wanted reacquisition of the Saar and union with Austria.[3] On 19 January 1926, he informed the Foreign Affairs Committee of the Chamber of Deputies that he opposed early evacuation of the Rhineland; that is, before the 1935 date specified in the Treaty of Versailles.

To Briand, Locarno was justifiable in that it helped commit the British to shield France from attack, but it was a far cry from the sort of prewar Anglo-French military cooperation that he had wanted restored. Despite his professed Europeanism, he intended to strengthen the peacetime alliance system that his country had built with the nations of eastern Europe. Briand favored reconciliation with Germany, but his Locarno policy seemed dictated more by necessity than choice. He knew, however, that keeping the Locarno spirit alive was essential for Anglo-French cooperation. He was aware of the political risks Chamberlain had taken to get the British government to accept the agreement. (Many in the cabinet had opposed tying Britain's hands with any kind of security commitment. These, indeed, had a hard time considering their country part of Europe.) But Briand feared that demonstrating too much opposition to an early withdrawal of troops from the Rhineland might give Chamberlain's critics ammunition to abandon the Locarno guarantees altogether.[4] He, therefore, explained to Chamberlain that, although France had to protect the railways and discourage armament violations, he was willing to agree to a Rhineland troop withdrawal, beginning with a contingent of 6,000 soldiers, but he pointed out that there were limits to French generosity. After all, his country could not be expected to convoke the Locarno powers each time a violation occurred.[5]

Chamberlain was also sensitive to Briand's position, and he refrained from pushing his policy of concessions too forcefully. To Stresemann, he explained that it would be difficult even for an Englishman to continue appeasing Germany in the face of "a continuous and clamorous demand for further relief, as if each new concession served only to whet their insatiable appetite."[6]

Stresemann, however, felt he had nothing to lose by sticking to his guns. If there were to be a postponement of early evacuation, he wanted compensation by having the French army of occupation reduced in size. He accused Briand of intransigence, which, he said, came from ill-will and ill-health. Stresemann threatened to resign and torpedo the whole Locarno policy if he did not get his way.[7] Chamberlain, though, refused to be bluffed and continued to back Briand's refusal to withdraw troops. Consequently, a decision on the matter was deferred to the following year.

But Briand wanted to show he was still acting in good faith, and he said he was prepared to surrender French rights to the inspection of

German sites for violations of the Treaty of Versailles by allowing disbanding of the Allied Control Commission.[8] The Commission had been ineffective for some time, and Briand hoped by making such a concession he could facilitate the assumption of permanent supervisory authority over the Rhineland by the League of Nations. He hoped that German entrance into the League would help contain German power and insisted that the German application for membership, submitted on 8 February 1926, be considered at the earliest possible time. (Under the current rules of procedure, that was at a special meeting in March.) He also supported the German claim for permanent membership in the League Council as soon as they joined.[9] In this way he played on Stresemann's sense of importance.[10]

The prospect of taking his place at the high table with the other western powers did not distract Stresemann from seeking to strengthen the cooperation Germany had established with the Soviet Union at Rapallo over three years before.[11] To Chamberlain and Briand, he minimized the importance of this connection by pretending that he merely wanted to keep the Communists in bounds.[12]

Chamberlain was prepared to believe him. The British foreign secretary considered that an additional agreement between Moscow and Berlin might actually facilitate Anglo-German cooperation by encouraging Germany "to realize that her interests were best served by facing west rather than east."[13] Briand, however, viewed any rekindling the Rapallo agreement as dangerous and tried to get Chamberlain to join him in a protest. Chamberlain refused, and Briand went ahead anyway, even though he doubted whether it could now have much effect.[14]

Briand told Stresemann that the German-Soviet agreement was an affront to the Locarno spirit and a slight to the League of Nations and warned that such a move could further delay settling the question of troop reductions in the Rhineland.[15] Stresemann continued to insist that the agreement constituted "no new departure from [the] policy of Locarno but rather the logical completion of the treaties concluded there."[16]

The Treaty of Berlin, signed on 24 April 1926, pledged the German and Soviet governments:

> to remain sensitive to each other's concerns in a friendly way in order to bring about an understanding concerning all common

political and economic questions about which they are both
concerned.[17]

But the signatories also agreed to stay neutral should either be attacked
by a third party, and they pledged to avoid participation in any
economic or financial boycott directed against the other.[18] Thus the
agreement negated the obligations Germany would assume under
Articles XVI and XVII of the League Covenant.[19] The contradiction
did not escape the French.

Chamberlain, however, explained this undertaking as a mere
gesture of cooperation,

> an undertaking that Germany will consider without prejudice any
> complaint by a member of the League that Russia has been guilty
> of an act of aggression.[20]

The British foreign secretary did not think that the agreement
threatened European security because Germany and the Soviet Union
were still militarily weak. He further reasoned that Germany would
always prefer an association with the West because it had more to gain
by doing so. But among Foreign Office experts, Chamberlain's
interpretation seemed to be a minority position.

Miles Lampson and F. Maxse felt the Treaty of Berlin posed a
new challenge to the balance of power. They called, prophetically, the
Berlin-Moscow axis the potential "first step to yet another partition of
Poland." What was worse, they feared Britain could now do very little
to keep this from happening,

> for any opposition offered by us to the signature of this convention
> would almost certainly be useless and quite certainly strengthen the
> hands of the extremists (right and left) in Germany and play
> straight into the hands of the Soviet Government. The latter is a
> very present danger--the other dangers have at least a time element
> which may enable us to stave them off.[21]

Chamberlain, though, was still blinded by the splendor of his
achievement at Locarno.

On 29 July 1926, he told Briand that European relations were now
on a new footing.

We have, I hope, I believe, eliminated the danger of the revision of the western frontiers of Germany, consecrated at Versailles, so that they will never become the cause of a new war; and, if we have not yet been able to obtain the same certainty of stability in the east of Europe, we have, at least, sensibly diminished the menace, which in that area existed for peace.[22]

He boasted that British and French cooperation had made this possible and remarked, that if this cooperation continued, the two countries could accomplish anything.

GERMANY JOINED the League on 10 September 1926, and, as expected, became a member of the Council at the same time. Briand gave a warm speech of welcome; Stresemann replied in the same spirit. But later that day, the German foreign secretary showed a different face. In a a speech he gave to members of the local German colony at the Café Bavaria, he remarked that Germany's membership in the League showed the absurdity of blaming Germany for having started the war. He declared that Germany had the same right and capacity of other countries to administer colonial territory.[23] And he emphasized that he intended to work for the reestablishment of German sovereignty over all its national territory.

The occupation of German territory is absolutely incompatible with the principle of the absolute equality of rights of nations in the League of Nations, [and our duty is to work without rest to assure this to future generations] even if Germany must endure heavy financial burdens."[24]

The reference to "financial burdens" expressed German willingness to make economic concessions to France in exchange for French political concessions to Germany.

On 17 September, Stresemann met Briand at Thoiry, a small village outside Geneva in the foothills of the French Juras. Stresemann had solicited this private get-together, proposing that the two meet at Ferney-Voltaire, the first village across the frontier. But Ferney lacked a good restaurant while the Auberge des Chasseurs at Thoiry had a respectable menu of trout, chicken, duck, and partridge.[25]

Stresemann began by reminding Briand of his remarks at Locarno, when Briand had said that he wanted his contribution to history to be the rapprochement between France and Germany.[26] Stresemann agreed with the sentiment but alleged that this could come about only after Germany had regained its sovereignty, including the early reacquisition of the Saar, the withdrawal of the military control commission, the total allied evacuation of the Rhineland, retrocession of Eupen and Malmédy, and a revision of the Dawes plan.[27] Stresemann also wanted the liquidation of French ownership of German railroad bonds, replacing the arrangement with something "roomier", perhaps a Franco-German bond secured on other Dawes plan revenues, or the German mark and various international securities.[28]

Briand stated his own conditions. He wanted the continued payment of reparations, the granting of economic benefits,[29] the necessity for progress on the problem of security,[30] and the reduction of the high level of German armaments. And he insisted the German government control its military,

> I have a feeling that the Reichswehr is doing all manner of things of which you have no knowledge. I don't consider that too tragic. The military is the same everywhere. But our policy must not suffer for it.[31]

He listed the concessions that France had made to Germany since the signing of the Locarno pact: the withdrawal of troops from the Rhineland, the evacuation from certain military bases, the relaxation of inspection and control.

Stresemann confessed that he had never had these points spelled out to him such detail.[32] But he dismissed Briand's fears of a revival of German militarism by blaming it on a few reactionary generals and extreme nationalist politicians. He claimed that Germany's membership in the League had given him confidence to confront these nationalists anew and a desire to convince the German people of the advantages of League membership.[33] He described those favoring union with Austria as being obsessed with a "primordial interest."[34] Returning to his main theme, he emphasized that, "if peace between the two countries is to be erected on a sure footing," the Rhineland and the Saar must be evacuated.[35] Stresemann was convinced that France could no longer hold the line on the occupation of Germany.

Briand viewed the Thoiry meeting as "something of a preface" to future negotiations,[36] which would be held only after the experts at the

Quai d'Orsay had prepared the way.[37] Briand thought that his conversation with Stresemann revealed the mutual interest France and Germany had in examining various questions that troubled their relations, questions that should be considered together and not one at a time.[38] Briand claimed he was impressed by Stresemann's cordiality.

> It is always easy to have this temperamental man become enthusiastic for some promising (féconde) idea, but it is more difficult to keep him going steadily in a straight line. One can do it, but on condition that one does not become winded.[39]

But he realized the futility of trying to reconcile Germany to a position of military inferiority.[40] Briand suspected that Stresemann was trying to take advantage of France's current financial predicament in dangling before him the prospect economic concessions.[41] Ever since Poincaré had again become premier, on 22 July 1926, Briand had to be careful to do nothing that gave the appearance he might compromise French security. But Poincaré prefered concentrating on strengthening the French economy leaving Briand the problem of how to dampen down the revisionist lust of the Germans. A strong foreign policy demanded a strong economy. Briand knew that France had to maintain its military edge to offset Germany's much larger population and greater industrial potential. Yet any help that the Germans would provide France economically would contain a political price, which might be higher than France could afford. Stresemann did not believe in generosity for its own sake. The mercantilistic fervor which guided French and German economic relations since 1871 would continue until cooled by the ashes of another war.

After Thoiry, Stresemann told a *Journal de Genève* reporter that the French had made a big mistake in heaping scorn on Germany after the war. The English had been more courteous.[42] He stated that the League of Nations was the only organization that the Germans would allow to have anything to do with the control of disarmament once the foreign troops had left Germany. And he warned that as long as they remained in the Rhineland unpleasant incidents would continue.[43]

> We are at the mercy of the stupidity of [French] generals who amuse themselves by organizing manoeuvres in the Palatinate the same day when Germany is admitted to the League of Nations. That cannot continue![44]

Jacques Seydoux, a Quai d'Orsay political/economic affairs expert, observed that Germany's intentions at Thoiry were no different from those at Locarno: Germany was trying to modify existing treaties, and

> constantly looked for ways to undermine the Treaty of Peace and it took all the energy of the French delegation and England to head it off.[45]

The French knew, though, that they could not always rely on such British energy.

FRANCE SHORED up its diplomatic strength by signing a treaty of friendship with Romania in 1926 and one with Yugoslavia in 1927. But the eastern European alliance system hardly proved to be a bulwark against German revisionism. Both Romania and Yugoslavia had reasons to appease Germany: the Romanians wanted German support against the Soviet Union, and the Yugoslavs wanted German support against Italy. Furthermore, France had no significant trade with either country and provided neither with significant military assistance. France could no longer enforce the Treaty of Versailles let alone the treaties of the Trianon and St. Germain.

The final report of the Allied Control Commission, which had ceased operation in January 1926, made it clear that France lacked the ability to prevent German revisionism without strong support from other countries.[46] Although the report stated that German armaments had been reduced, compulsory military service eliminated, and military bases and Rhineland fortifications had been dismantled, it pointed out that the German General Staff continued to exist; that civilian forces, like the police, had become more militarized; and that non-authorized auxiliary military forces were flourishing.[47] It said that prohibited weapons continued to be manufactured and military expenditures to rise.[48]

> The circumstance of a rapid material disarmament of a country which is not occupied by its conquerors is only moral disarmament of the country.... The military traditions of Germany were too well established and too brilliant, and during the period of the war, this nation had fought with too much energy and too much success, to

question its warrior-like qualities and be suddenly converted to the ideal of peace.[49]

In short, Germany had never been disarmed, had no intention of disarming, avoided allied control of its weaponry, and, despite protestations of compliance, continued to violate the military clauses of the Treaty of Versailles with relative impunity. The judgement was little different from what the inspector general of the French army had said two years before that disarmament of Germany was only a distant hope.[50] In bequeathing its task to the League of Nations, the Commission expressed the forlorn hope that disarmament become more solid and lasting.[51]

German violations naturally continued. The French noted an increase in the cooperation between the German Foreign Ministry and the army chiefs in violating the Weimar laws, which prohibited foreign trade in war materials.[52] German diplomats often arranged the contracts and expedited the export of equipment to Germany. This was especially true in the Netherlands where many armaments companies had German directors.[53] The Germans figured that the French would tolerate these violations as long as Germany paid reparations and pretended to honor the current equilibrium.[54]

Briand followed the Thoiry discussions with the conclusion of an agreement on the early evacuation of troops from the Rhineland, making complete withdrawal contingent on German respect for the territorial and political clauses of the Treaty of Versailles. Briand wanted to create a permanent disarmament control mechanism in the demilitarized zone, but Stresemann insisted that there was no longer any reason for France to feel insecure and reiterated that, as long as the occupation lasted, there could never be a true detente between their two countries. The occupation, he said, hung like an "iron curtain" between Germany and France.[55]

> A great deal is said in France about security, particularly French security.... I have never seen a formula providing a stronger guarantee of security between two neighboring states than the Locarno treaty between Germany and France.[56]

He criticized the British for failing to get the French to agree to an immediate and complete evacuation, remarking that Chamberlain "played France's game through and through." Stresemann complained that Chamberlain had given him "no cards to play with" and that he had made the solution of reparations and other problems so much more difficult.[57] Stresemann promised that with "a rectification on the Polish front, Europe could have peace for a hundred years."[58]

THE SENTIMENTAL REALIST.

Scene—In Rhineland.

Germany. "MUST YOU STAY?"

M. Briand (recalling the Locarno spirit). "I LOVE YOU TOO MUCH TO THINK OF LEAVING YOU JUST YET."

The Sentimental Realist. *Aristide Briand, in this Bernard Partridge cartoon* (Punch, September 10, 1928), *plays the part of an unwelcome guest, who knows it's time to leave, but can't, his presence not tolerated, his charms falling on deaf ears.*

British military planners calculated that Germany would not be a serious military threat for at least ten years. Reassured, the government continued its appeasement. Sir Horace Rumbold, the current British ambassador in Berlin, spoke for many of his colleagues when he favored a return to splendid isolationism. Rumbold stated that the time had come to admit "that it is not now sensible to imagine that we have the power...of enforcing an observance of any but our most vital requirements."[59]

Chamberlain had wanted reconciliation with Germany, he wanted to eliminate the possibility of France again punishing Germany with another Ruhr-style invasion, but at the same time he hoped the Locarno agreement would not lead to a drastic loss of French influence. French power, though, continued to decline.

After the war, the French army had kept itself in readiness for an immediate attack on Germany should there be a threat to peace. According to General Edmond-Alphonse Buat, chief of the General Staff:

> Only an offensive plan permits France to profit from the real advantage that has been given her by the Treaty of Versailles to prevent Germany from simultaneously massing its forces as it did in 1914; only [the offensive] can prevent the heavy sacrifices of a long, drawn out war.[60]

Buat demanded that the standing army (*unités de couverture*) be able to "to paralyze the enemy in depriving it of the Ruhr and to penetrate rapidly into Germany to prevent [the Germans] from mobilizing the bulk of their forces."[61] He said that even though France might count on outside support, it had to be capable of fighting alone.[62] It, therefore, needed a peacetime army of 45 divisions, or about 675,000 men.[63]

But this offensive policy began to change towards the end of the occupation of the Ruhr. In 1924, a new conscription law increased the army's reliance on the reserves by reducing the length of military service to 18 months, about half of what it had been. Reserves were incapable of the rapid mobilization the General Staff advocated.[64] The withdrawal of troops from the Rhineland, the decline of the birth rate, and the flagging industrial output—especially in such essential commodities as coal, copper, aluminium, steel, lead, and oil—reinforced the desire for a strategy that would allow France to dispense with a large standing army and conserve its resources by blunting, rather than, initiating an attack.

A series of permanent fortifications were built along the country's eastern and northern frontiers.[65]   This super trench, known as the Maginot Line, was intended to funnel a German attack into Belgium where the hilly Ardennes, the Meuse river, and the northern canals would slow it down, allowing time for mobilizing the reserves and the resources of the empire, allowing time for intervention from the forces of the Locarno allies.[66]   The French figured that a German attack on Belgium would automatically guarantee British participation, as had been the case in 1914. The logic of delay thus prevailed over the logic of enterprise.

WHILE THE LOCARNO TREATY contributed to a change in French military policy, it brought the Germans new sources of strength. So much industrial investment flowed into the country that the Germans paid no reparations from their country's basic resources. From 1924 to 1931, Germany paid 2 billion 6 hundred thousand dollars in reparations, but received over 6 billion dollars in loans. Much of this difference was earmarked for the modernization of industry so that, by the end of the decade, Germany was second only to the United States in world industrial production, and its increasing population—250 people per square kilometer compared to only 70 for France—enjoyed a material prosperity greater than before.[67]   Some French half-seriously suggested that the excess German population be shipped off to a distant colony.[68]

The British policy of appeasement and the spectacular German recovery convinced Briand of the necessity of getting the United States more involved in European affairs. On 6 April 1927, on the tenth anniversary of U.S. entry into the war, he appealed to the American people to join France in renouncing war as an instrument of national policy.[69]   As a first step, he wanted to induce Washington's participation in the forthcoming Disarmament Conference, sponsored by the League of Nations.

President Coolidge praised the work of pacification, but was unwilling to do more than send an observer.[70]   Secretary of State Frank Kellogg explained that he could never agree to have any restriction placed on our using any of our resources whether in men or materials with risk that if we suffered to exceed those limits we might be declared an aggressor nation.[71]

The Americans suspected that the French had already arranged the agenda of the Disarmament Conference in their favor.[72]

The reduction of armaments, however, was an issue that had the enthusiastic support of the American people.[73] And Kellogg knew that he had put a positive face on America's refusal to join the League's disarmament work. He, therefore, concentrated on Briand's proposal for a Franco-American entente, but puffed it up into a general, more nebulous, scheme to outlaw war altogether.[74]

To the French, Kellogg's proposal was, at worst, dangerous, and at best, superfluous. Briand feared that the scheme could weaken France's treaty system, but he feared rejecting it might give the impression he favored war. He, therefore, decided to try to make Kellogg's plan conform to French interests. Briand agreed to become a co-sponsor, providing the declaration allow "defensive wars" and that it avoid sanctions against violation.

At a ceremony held in Paris on 27 August 1928, fifteen states endorsed the Kellogg-Briand Peace Pact. All the signatories were members of the League of Nations except the United States. Eventually almost every sovereign state in the world took this pledge, which had no effect on European security.[75]

Notes and Sources:

1. Cf. Foreign Ministry memo, 8 November 1926. *Ministère des Affaires Étrangères*, série Z (Grande-Bretagne), vol. 89, 104-119.

2. 29 July 1926. *Ibid.*, (Grande-Bretagne}, vol. 58, 78-9.

3. *DBFP*, series Ia, II, 289.

4. *MAE*, série Z (Grande-Bretagne), vol. 58, 31.

5. 6 August 1926. *Ibid.*, 84-9.

6. *DBFP*, series Ia, II, 781.

7. Jon Jacobson, *Locarno Diplomacy, Germany and the West, 1925-1929*, 117.

8. Stresemann maintained that the Commission had nothing to control since Germany had fulfilled all its obligations. *MAE*, série Z (Grande-Bretagne), vol. 130, 90.

9. Membership in the Assembly took a simple majority, but becoming a permanent member of the Council required a unanimous vote from that body's permanent and non-permanent members. Still, with the sponsorship of the Locarno powers, the nomination would not seem to present any trouble.

10. The British ambassador in Berlin wrote that Stresemann was "in high spirits" and curious to see what the Geneva atmosphere was really like. Viscount D'Abernon, *The Diary of an Ambassador*, III, 224.

11. *MAE*, série Z (Russie), vol. 333, 67

12. Von Schubert to Viscount D'Abernon (*DBFP*, series Ia, I, 567), and Leopold von Hoesch to Philippe Berthelot (*MAE*. série Z, vol. 333, 26.)

13. *DBFP*, series Ia, I, 596.

14. *MAE*, série Z (Russie), vol. 333, 96.

15. *Ibid.*, 607.

16. Stresemann's answer to the French protest came on Sunday 18 April on a stop-over in Stuttgart while he was on way back to Berlin from a vacation in Italy. *DBFP*, series Ia, I, 640.

17. *"in freundshaftlicher Fühlung miteinander bleiben, um über alle ihre beiden Länder gemeinsam berühreden Fragen politischer und wirtschftlicher Art eine Verständigung herbeizuführen."* *LNTS*, LIII, 389. The official version was in Russian and German.

18. In a separate letter of explanation attached to treaty, Stresemann emphasized that, if the League of Nations directed any of its efforts against the USSR, Germany would energetically oppose such measures, including the imposition of sanctions under Articles XVI and XVII. He emphasized that Germany had made specific reservations about carrying out its functions under the League Covenant, when Germany signed the Treaty of Locarno. He insisted that Germany alone would determine whether the USSR should be branded an aggressor. *Ibid.*, 394-5.

19. *MAE*, série Z (Russie), vol. 333, 111-2.

20. To Ambassador French Ambassador de Fleuriau. *DBFP*, series Ia, I, 742.

21. *DBFP*, series Ia, I, 567.

22. *MAE*, série Z (Grande-Bretagne), vol. 58, 76-7

23. *Les Cahiers de l'Histoire* (Paris: Librarie Le Griffon, 1961), no. 9, 118.

24. *MAE*, série Z (Allemagne), vol. 398, 82-4.

25. Suarez, VI, 219-29, and Stresemann, *Vermächtnis*, III, 17-23. Stresemann and Briand were accompanied only by Oswald Hesnard the French press attaché at the Berlin embassy, who acted as translator.

26. *MAE*, série Z (Allemagne), vol. 398, 197-8.

27. *Ibid.*, (Allemagne), vol. 400, 54.

28. *MAE*, série Z, (Allemagne), vol. 398, 55-6, 79-80, 214-5.

29 The close relationship between French economic policy and its foreign policy in the post-Locarno era is treated in Edward David Keeton, *Briand's Locarno Policy, French Economics, Politics, and Diplomacy* (New York: Garland Publishing, 1987).

30. *MAE*, série Z, (Allemagne), vol. 400, 65.

31. Gatzke, 58.

32. *MAE*, série Z, (Allemagne), vol. 398, 56.

33. *Ibid.*, 215.

34. *Ibid.*, 215.

35. *Ibid.*, (Allemagne), vol. 400, 198.

36. *Ibid.*, 80.

37. *Ibid.*, 68-9.

38. *Ibid.*, 68.

39. *Ibid.*, 58.

40. *DBFP*, series Ia, II, 418-9.

41. *MAE*, série Z (Allemagne), vol. 400, 64-5.

42. *Ibid.*, 198.

43. Subsequently the French tried to minimize such incidents by disassociating the French military authorities from the most controversial aspects of their occupation policy--the establishment of military bordellos. These establishments had offended French as well as Germans. The influential *Ligue française pour le relevement de la moralité publique* (League for the Improvement of Public Morality) stepped pressure for the elimination of these establishments, claiming that it be done to further the national interest, "in the spirit that has been created by the Locarno accords." *MAE*, série Z (Rive gauche du Rhin), vol. 192, 72. 112.

44. 5 October 1926. *MAE*, série Z (Allemagne), vol. 400, 198.

45. *Ibid.*, 64.

46. Foch had directed the dismantling of all German fortifications that the French army found inessential, specifically the forts of Blehler, Rheinhed, Asterstein, Arzheim, and Rheinbeck, plus the fortifications of Plettenberg, Ehrenbreitstein, and Glockenberg. *Ibid.*, série Z (Allemagne), vol. 161, 3.

47. *Resumé et conclusions: Rapport final de la commission militaire de contrôle en Allemagne* (28 February 1927). *MAE*, série Z (Allemagne), vol. 132, 215-222.

48. *Ibid.*, 215-220.

49. *Ibid.*, série Z (Allemagne), vol. 130, 68.

50. *Ibid.*, série Z (Allemagne), vol. 132, 226.

51. *Ibid.*, 227.

52. *MAE*, série Z (Allemagne), vol. 161, 221-3. See also: Gaines Post, Jr., *The Civil-Military Fabric of Weimar Foreign Policy* (Princeton, N.J.: Princeton University Press, 1973), 209.

53. *MAE*. série Z (Allemagne), vol. 132, 150-1.

54. British and French military attachés routinely reported the extent of the illegal activities of the Germans, the presence of paramilitary units, the manufacture of machine-gun carriages, the production of castings for anti-aircraft guns, of shell cases for field, costal and naval artillery, of rifle barrels, and even of poison gas. Cf: *DBFP*, series Ia, V, 513, 588, 592-5; series Ia, VI, 213-6, 302-5. Also *MAE*, série Z (Allemagne), vol. 161. The Quai d'Orsay archives have 81 files on arms and control of disarmament from July 1918 to December 1929, seven of these dating since January 1927 when the Allied Control Commission ceased to exist.

55. *DBFP*, series Ia, I, 260.

56. *Documents on International Affairs*, 1928, 34.

57. Lockhart Diaries, 83. Chamberlain for the time being was willing to accept the continued presence of the French army in the Rhineland. *DBFP*, series Ia, IV, 19.

58. Lockhart Diaries, 83.

59. Dated 19 December 1928. *DBFP*, series Ia, V, 589.

60. Report of the Minister of War, 8 November 1921. *MAE*, série Y (Internationale) vol. 504, 138.

61. *Ibid.*, 139.

62. Belgium could mobilize 12 divisions in a month, but needed help to do so. Britain could have three divisions ready in three weeks, another 2 to 3 after two months. The United States 2 to 3 divisions, perhaps as many as 4, within a month. *Ibid.*, 139-40.

63. Considering that the German army remained at its present strength: 100,000 men in the regular forces, another 150,000 in the militarized police.

64. The 1928 law would reduce the time of service further to one year.

65. Cf: Judith M. Hughes, *To the Maginot Line: The Politics of French Military Preparedness in the 1920's* (Cambridge, Mass.: Harvard University Press, 1971).

66. Richard D. Challener, *The French Theory of the Nation in Arms, 1886-1939* (New York: Columbia University Press, 1955), 220-4.

67. The United States had 42.2 percent; Germany 11.6 percent; Britain: 9.4 percent; France, 6.6 percent; Russia, 4.3 percent; and Italy, 3.3 percent.

68. *MAE*, série Z (Allemagne), vol. 400, 80.

69. Suarez, *Briand*, VI, 259.

70. *DBFP*, series Ia, I, 35.

71. Suarez, Briand, VI, 259.

72. *DBFP*, series Ia, I, 481

73. *SIA*, 1928, 10-16.

74. *Ibid.*, 16-26.

75. Cf. *DIA*, 1928, 1-14.

TEA TIME

WITH THE PASSING of time most Germans minimized the destruction they had caused during the war, and they came to look upon reparations as punishment, not restitution. Nonetheless, they continued to pay. In 1929, they managed to get the Dawes Plan revised, however.[1] The Young Plan, put into effect on June 7, ended German payment of occupation costs and foreign control of German economic affairs. Stresemann made it clear that Germany's acceptance of the new plan was conditional on the complete evacuation of allied troops from the Rhineland. While Briand made evacuation conditional on German acceptance, the final result was the same. With no foreign troops on German soil and no likelihood of foreign intervention, the payment of reparations became subject almost entirely to German good will.

The withdrawal of allied troops from the two remaining zones began in September 1929 to be completed nine months hence. The Germans could hardly wait and began celebrating early. Those in the Rhineland became so boisterous that Philippe Berthelot feared they might awaken "passions contrary to the pacification of spirits that was the normal development of the policy coming from the Treaty of Locarno."[2] He asked the German government to impose restraint and promote an attitude that "will correspond to that observed in 1871 when our territory was freed, this being accomplished with as much calm as dignity."[3] This advice made the Germans suspect that the French were looking for ways to continue the occupation.[4]

Briand renewed his promise that the French army would leave on schedule, if not before. In fact, the withdrawal began as soon as an inventory of buildings and furniture had been completed.[5] Von Schubert assured Briand that the German authorities would do their utmost to avoid incidents and give the Rhinelanders instructions to act with moderation.[6] On 5 September 1929, Briand celebrated the tenth anniversary of the League of Nations with an important speech on the need for European unity. He proposed that the peoples of Europe form some sort of federal bond, which would give them the solidarity to meet any grave emergency. Although the association was to be "primarily economic," political and social ties could also be established without affecting national sovereignty. The proposal was vague and showed that France was still trying to control Germany through some sort of multi-national organization.

The Germans opposed anything that might frustrate the cause of revisionism, especially anything concerning the eastern frontiers. Great Britain also opposed Briand's scheme for fear that European federalism would undermine its independence and its ties with the Commonwealth. And Italy denounced federalism as a device for the spread of Bolshevism. Thus the cause of European unity died almost as fast as it had been created. It would remain dormant until after another world war.

The evacuation of the Rhineland was the last major achievement of Stresemann's foreign policy. His health had so declined that, in November 1928, his doctor forbade him to work more than three hours a day. But the reduced work load had little long-term effect, and rumors circulated that he was "finished".[7] He died on 3 October 1929. He was only 51. As the eulogies poured in, the British and French tried to figure out what effect his death would have on the future course of German policy, especially in the light of a current surge in the militancy and strength of rightist parties. The ultra-nationalist Nazi party had made impressive gains in recent municipal and local elections, capturing control of the Munich city council. British Ambassador Horace Rumbold explained their attraction: "among the more sober party orchestras they have the magnetic attraction of a jazz band."[8]

The British hoped their foreign policy would help cure the imperfections existing in their society. They felt that the restoration of German prosperity and the protection of German unity against France to be essential for British prosperity. Since the ill-fated invasion of the Ruhr, the British no longer feared French hegemony, but they realized that French security would have to be protected.

MacDonald had tried to do this through the Geneva Protocol; Chamberlain thought he had accomplished it with the Locarno Treaty. Anglo-French cooperation suffered in the process. The Entente Cordiale no longer existed even though the British assumed that they would come to the aid of France should France be attacked by Germany.

The French deplored British detachment from continental affairs. Failing to get Britain and the United States to honor the promises made at the Paris Peace Conference, the French had taken an increasingly hard-line on the enforcement of the Treaty of Versailles, especially on reparations. Most French statesmen favored a policy of accountability. But the contradiction of wanting German reparations, but not German recovery, had prevented them from developing a coherent foreign policy and led to the ill-fated invasion of the Ruhr and the subsequent alienation of Great Britain and the United States.

During the last half of the twenties, tension among the states of Europe declined, but a peaceful future did not seem assured. By 30 June 1930—five years before the time specified in the Treaty of Versailles—no foreign soldiers remained on German soil. The Rhineland was still demilitarized, but France and Great Britain no longer had the will nor desire to ensure that it remain so. The French knew that without Anglo-French cooperation their attempt to moderate the power of Germany could not succeed.

Robert Vansittart, the permanent under-secretary of state for foreign affairs, feared the effects of German revisionism. Germany, he said, wanted to annex Austria, drastically change the frontiers with Poland, and become again a world power, complete with colonies and mandates. Even under moderate leaders, Germany would be

> sorely tempted to apply the old methods of diplomacy if she finds the new ones of arbitration and conciliation eventually ineffective for changing the status quo to her purpose.[9]

Vansittart also worried that Italy would try to supplant French and British power in the Mediterranean.[10] He suspected Mussolini might turn to Germany for support.[11] He further feared that the Soviet Union would always remain outside the European community of nations, its ambitions as aggressive those of as tsarist Russia, "incurable by any process of arbitration or conciliation."[12]

Vansittart's memorandum followed in the example of the 1907 *tour d'horizon* of Eyre Crowe, who had given a similarly pessimistic appraisal of German intentions. Crowe had questioned whether Germany was capable of living within the context of the balance of power.

This is the opinion of those who see in the whole trend of Germany's policy conclusive evidence that she is consciously aiming at the establishment of a German hegemony, at first in Europe, and eventually in the world.[13]

He also warned against any policy of appeasement.

Crowe had been Vansittart's mentor when permanent under-secretary of the Foreign Office from 1919-1925. Both men believed that Great Britain had a mission to hold states to rules of civilized behavior. Vansittart feared that Britain was shrinking from that task, becoming more isolationist, its people losing their capacity of self-preservation. He did not advocate a return to an alliance system, nor did he think that Britain could do the job on its own. He believed that European security could only be fully guaranteed, if the United States took over the role of holder of the balance of power, once exercised by Great Britain. But although America possessed the strength, it lacked the will. Vansittart said that the United States lived in a world of illusion "as long as filmland is open to her."[14] He predicted that Britain's next war would be with Germany and that the United States would do nothing to stop it until it had already begun.

France and Britain struggled to adjust to the forces of revisionism, but had no common policy to combat them. The French wanted to maintain the status quo and preserve the peace settlement, while Britain was content to maintain an equilibrium by functioning as the holder of the balance of power until the United States could be induced from its "palatial tub" to assume the international peacekeeping responsibilities commensurate with its strength and position. Vansittart said that British had to continue to maintain their economic and military strength to avoid giving the impression that they were "living at tea time."[15]

But the feared tea-break lasted for another decade. When Anglo-French cooperation was finally resurrected at the end of the thirties, the alliance came too late to prevent war. The French, despite an acute awareness of the dangers of a ressurgent Germany, were unable to build an effective policy without the British, who, plagued by class and political division and wishful thinking, continued their dubious policy of appeasement. The French, uncomfortable but resigned, followed the British lead suspecting, but not fully understanding how dangerous that policy had become.

Notes and Sources:

1. The Young Plan created a new Bank of International Settlements at Basel, for the handling of German annuities, replacing the Reparation Commission and the Reichsbank supervisory committee, established by the Dawes Plan. For the first time, a terminal date was set, all payments ending in 1988, and the value of the entire amount was capitalized at 9.25 billion dollars, a rather significant reduction from the 33 billion dollars the Reparation Commission set in 1921. *SIA*, 1929, 150-66.

2. *MAE*, série Z (1930-1940), vol. 258 (Rive gauche du Rhin), 56.

3. *Ibid.*, 56.

4. *Ibid.*, 144-8.

5. *Ibid.*, 156.

6. *Ibid.*, 191.

7. *DBFP*, series Ia, V. 448, 479.

8. *Ibid.*, series Ia, VII, 261.

9. Memorandum dated May 1, 1930. DBFP, series Ia, VII, 837. The While the National Socialists, "under the leadership of the half-mad and ridiculously dangerous demagogue Hitler," were uncompromisingly hostile "to the peace settlement and the policy of fulfillment." *Ibid.*, 837.

10. *Ibid.*, 839.

11. *Ibid.*, 842.

12. *Ibid.*, 848.

13. *British Documents on the Origins of the War*, III, Appendix A, 414.

14. *DBFP*, series Ia, VII, 849.

15. *Ibid.*, 843.

TREATY BETWEEN FRANCE AND GREAT BRITAIN

Assistance to France in the Event of Unprovoked
Aggression by Germany

ARTICLE 1

In case the following stipulations relating to the Left Bank of the Rhine contained in the Treaty of Peace with Germany signed at Versailles the 28th day of June, 1919, by the British Empire, the French Republic, and the United States of America among other Powers:

"Article 42. Germany is forbidden to maintain or construct any fortifications either on the left bank of the Rhine or on the right bank to the west of a line drawn 50 kilom. to the east of the Rhine.

"Article 43. In the area defined above the maintenance and assembly of armed forces, either permanently or temporarily, and military manoeuvres of any kind, as well as the upkeep of all permanent works for mobilisation, are in the same way forbidden.

"Article 44. In case Germany violates in any manner whatsoever the provisions of Articles 42 and 43, she shall be regarded as committing a hostile act against the Powers signatory of the present Treaty and as calculated to disturb the peace of the world."

may not at first provide adequate security and protection to France, Great Britain agrees to come immediately to her assistance in the event of any unprovoked movement of aggression against her being made by Germany.

ARTICLE 2
The present Treaty, in similar terms with the Treaty of even date for the same purpose concluded between the French Republic and the United States of America, a copy of which Treaty is annexed hereto, will only come into force when the latter is ratified.

ARTICLE 3
The present Treaty must be submitted to the Council of the League of Nations and must be recognized by the Council, acting if need be by a majority, as an engagement which is consistent with the Covenant of the League; it will continue in force until on the application of one of the Parties to it the Council, acting if need be by a majority; agrees that the League itself affords sufficient protection.

ARTICLE 4
The present Treaty shall before ratification by His Majesty be submitted to Parliament for approval.

It shall before ratification by the President of the French Republic be submitted to the French Chambers for approval.

ARTICLE 5
The present Treaty shall impose no obligation upon any of the Dominions of the British Empire unless and until it is approved by the Parliament of the Dominion concerned.

The present Treaty shall be ratified, all shall, subject to Articles 2 and 4, come into force at the same time as the Treaty of Peace with Germany of even date comes into force for the British Empire and the French Republic.

In Faith Whereof the above-named Plenipotentiaries have signed the present Treaty, drawn up in the English and French languages.

Done in duplicate at Versailles, on the twenty-eighth day of June, 1919.

(Bearing the seals of David Lloyd George, Arthur James Balfour, Georges Clemenceau, and Stéphen Pichon.)

CHIEFS OF STATE, HEADS OF GOVERNMENT AND FOREIGN MINISTERS, 1919-1929

BRITAIN

Chief of State:

King George V (6 May 1910-20 Jan. 1936)

Date	*Prime Minister*	*Secretary for Foreign Affairs*
6 Dec. 1916	David Lloyd George	Arthur Balfour
(Oct. 1919)		George Curzon
23 Oct. 1922	Andrew Bonar Law	George Curzon
22 May 1923	Stanley Baldwin	George Curzon
22 Jan. 1924	Ramsay MacDonald	Ramsay MacDonald
4 Nov. 1924	Stanley Baldwin	Austen Chamberlain
5 Jun. 1929	Ramsay MacDonald	Arthur Henderson

FRANCE

President of the Republic:
>Raymond Poincaré (17 Jan. 1913)
>Paul Deschanel (18 Feb. 1920)
>Alexandre Millerand (23 Sep. 1920)
>Gaston Doumergue (13 Jun. 1924-13 Jun. 1931)

	President of the Council of Ministers	*Minister of Foreign Affairs*
16 Nov. 1917	Georges Clemenceau	Stéphen Pichon
20 Jan. 1920	Alexandre Millerand	Alexandre Millerand
24 Sep. 1920	Georges Leygues	Georges Leygues
16 Jan. 1921	Aristide Briand	Aristide Briand
15 Jan. 1922	Raymond Poincaré	Raymond Poincaré
8 Jun. 1924	Frédéric François-Marsal	Edmond Lefebvre du Prey
14 Jun. 1924	Édouard Herriot	Édouard Herriot
17 Apr. 1925	Paul Painlevé	Aristide Briand
28 Nov. 1925	Aristide Briand	Aristide Briand
19 Jul. 1926	Édouard Herriot	Édouard Herriot
23 Jul. 1926	Raymond Poincaré	Aristide Briand
29 Jul. 1929	Aristide Briand	Aristide Briand
3 Nov. 1929	André Tardieu	Aristide Briand

GERMANY

State President:

Friedrich Ebert (11 Feb. 1919-28 Feb. 1925)
Paul von Hindenburg (26 Apr. 1925-2 Aug. 1934)

	Chancellor	Secretary of State for Foreign Affairs
13 Feb. 1919	Philipp Scheidemann	Ulrich von Brockdorff-Rantzau
21 Jun. 1919	Gustav Bauer	Hermann Müller
28 Mar. 1920	Hermann Müller	Adolf Köster
25 Jun. 1920	Konstantin Fehrenbach	Walther Simons
10 May 1921	Joseph Wirth	Friedrich Rosen
(Oct. 1922)		Joseph Wirth
(Jan. 1922)		Walter Rathenau
(Jun. 1922)		Joseph Wirth
22 Nov. 1922	Wilhelm Cuno	Fredric Hans von Rosenberg
13 Aug. 1923	Gustav Stresemann	Gustav Stresemann
30 Nov. 1923	Wilhelm Marz	Gustav Stresemann
15 Jan. 1925	Hans Luther	Gustav Stresemann
17 May 1926	Wilhelm Marx	Gustav Stresemann
28 Jun. 1928	Hermann Müller	Gustav Stresemann

ITALY

Chief of State:
King Victor Emmanuel III (29 JUL 1900-9 MAY 1946)

	Premier	*Minister of Foreign Affairs*
29 Oct. 1917	Vittorio Orlando	Sidney Sonnino
21 Jun. 1919	Francisco Nitti	Tommaso Tittoni
Nov. 1919)		Vittorio Scialoja
15 Jun. 1920	Giovanni Giolitti	Carlo Sforza
1 Jul. 1921	Ivanoe Bonomi	Tomasi Della Toretta
25 Feb. 1922	Luigi Facta	Carlo Schanzer
30 Oct. 1922	Benito Mussolini	Benito Mussolini
(Sep. 1929)		Dino Grandi

SOVIET UNION

	Premier	*Commissar for Foreign Affairs*
8 Nov. 1917	Vladimir Lenin	Leon Trotsky
(Mar. 1918)		Georgi Chicherin
Jan. 1924	Alexei I. Rykov	Georgi Chicherin

* State power was of course really controlled by Josef Stalin, the Secretary-General of the Communist Party. Stalin held no other post until 1940 when he at last officially assumed the headship of the government.

EUROPEAN BALANCE OF POWER [1]

1921	Britain	France	Germany	Italy	USSR
Population (000s)	42,769	38,798	59,859[2]	37,974	132,000[3]
Males aged 15-24 (000s)	3,730	3,134	6,350[4]	3,573	14,595[5]
Regular Army	201,127	462,000	100,000[6]	250,000	1,595,000
Colonial Army	84,200	251,000	00	25,000	00
Navy	121,600	25,500	15,000	41,000	----
Air Force	30,880	22,600	----	----	----
Dread-noughts	39	22	6[7]	8	8
Steel Production (000s m.t.)	3,762	3,099	9,997	700	220
Coal (000s m.t.)	165,871	28,960	236,962	1,143	9,520
Electric Energy (000 k. h.)	8,410	6,500	17,000	4,690	520

1925	Britain	France	Germany	Italy	USSR
Population (000s)	43,783	40,228[8]	63,181	39,693	132,008
Regular Army	158,257	419,176	100,000	326,000	260,000
Colonial Army	65,307	265,873	00	26,567	00
Navy	100,787	25,500	15,000	46,000	----
Air Force	36,000	32,886	----	24,512	----
Dread-noughts	22	12	4/	8	5
Steel (000 m.t.)	7,504	7,464	12,195	1,786	1,868
Coal (000 m.t.)	247,078[9]	48,091	272,533	1,197	16,520
Electric (000 k.h.)	12,110	11,140	20,330	6,450	2,930
Motor Vehicles	167,000	177,000	49,000	49,600	----
1929	Britain	France	Germany	Italy	USSR
Population (000s)	45,741	41,020	63,603	41,169	153,956
Regular Army	147,732	317,076	99,121	251,270	562,000
Colonial Army	65,755	150,910	none	50,580	none
Navy	98,800	25,500	15,000	46,000	----
Air Force	32,500	36,800	----	22,981	---
Dread-noughts	20	8	3/	7	5
Steel (000 m.t.)	9,791	9,716	16,245	2,122	4,854
Coal (000 m.t.)	262,046	54,977	337,895	1,006	40,067

Electric Engery (000 k.h.)	16,980	15,600	30,660	9,630	6,220
Sulphuric Acid (000 metric tons)	930	1,032	1,704	835	265
Motor Vehicles	239,000	254,000	128,000	55,200	2,200
Students in Universities	59,474	73,600	121,183	44,940	

Notes and Sources:

  1.   The statistics have been culled from the appropriate editions of the *Statesman's Year-Book* and the League of Nations, *Armaments Year-Book* as well as *European Historical Statistics*.

  2.   In 1919.

  3.   In 1923.

  4.   In 1925. The French figure for the same age group (in 1926) was 3,392,000. Or to put it another way, since the time period is rougly half a decade later than 1921: in the male age group 20 to 29, Germany had 5,553,000 while France only 3,292,000. France benefitted somewhat by immigration, but there still existed an enormous, alarming disadvantage for France in its capacity to field an army to counter a German threat.

  5.   In 1920.

  6.   The size of the Reichswehr, revealed in these figures, is the amount of manpower allowed the Germans by the Treaty of Versailles, consequently the figures are misleading. The Germans probably never reduced their armed forces below 350,000 men.

  7.   These were all pre-dreadnought battleships possessing little fighting value. All were completed between 1904 and 1908, none possessing more than 4 eleven-inch guns.

  8.   In 1926.

  9.   In 1926, the year of the General Strike, the annual output fell to 128 million metric tons. The industry recovered, but no year surpassed the all time high of 280 million reached in 1923 thanks to the Ruhr invasion.

LOCARNO TREATY OF MUTUAL GUARANTEE

Between Germany, Belgium, France, Great Britain, and Italy

The President of the German Reich, His Majesty the King of the Belgians, the President of the French Republic, His Majesty the King of the United Kingdom of Great Britain and Ireland and of the British Dominions beyond the Seas, Emperor of India, His Majesty the King of Italy;

Anxious to satisfy the desire for security and protection which animates the peoples upon whom fell the scourge of the war of 1914-18;

Taking note of the abrogation of the treaties for the neutralisation of Belgium, and conscious of the necessity of ensuring peace in the area which has so frequently been the scene of European conflicts;

Animated also with the sincere desire of giving to all the signatory Powers concerned supplementary guarantees within the framework of the Covenant of the League of Nations and the treaties in force between them;

Have determined to conclude a treaty with these objects, and have appointed as their plenipotentiaries:

Who, having communicated their full powers, found in good and due form, have agreed as follows:—

ARTICLE 1

The high contracting parties collectively and severally guarantee, in the manner provided in the following articles, the maintenance of the territorial *status quo* resulting from the frontiers between Germany and Belgium and between Germany and France and the inviolability of the said frontiers as fixed by or in pursuance of the Treaty of Peace signed at Versailles on the 28th June, 1919, and also the observance of the stipulations of articles 42 and 43 of the said treaty concerning the demilitarised zone.

ARTICLE 2

Germany and Belgium, and also Germany and France, mutually undertake that they will in no case attack or invade each other or resort to war against each other.

This stipulation shall not, however, apply in the case of—

1. The exercise of the right of legitimate defence, that is to say, resistance to a violation of the undertaking contained in the previous paragraph or to a flagrant breach of articles 42 or 43 of the said Treaty of Versailles, if such breach constitutes an unprovoked act of aggression and by reason of the assembly of armed forces in the demilitarised zone immediate action is necessary.

2. Action in pursuance of article 16 of the Covenant of the League of Nations.

3. Action as the result of a decision taken by the Assembly or by the Council of the League of Nations or in pursuance of article 15, paragraph 7, of the Covenant of the League of Nations, provided that in this last event the action is directed against a State which was the first to attack.

ARTICLE 3

In view of the undertakings entered into in article 2 of the present treaty, Germany and Belgium and Germany and France undertake to settle by peaceful means and in the manner laid down herein all questions of every kind which may arise between them and which it may not be possible to settle by the normal methods of diplomacy:

Any question with regard to which the parties are in conflict as to their respective rights shall be submitted to judicial decision, and the parties undertake to comply with such decision.

All other questions shall be submitted to a conciliation commission. If the proposals of this commission are not accepted by the two parties, the question shall be brought before the Council of the

League of Nations, which will deal with it in accordance with article 15 of the Covenant of the League.

The detailed arrangements for effecting such peaceful settlement are the subject of special agreements signed this day.

ARTICLE 4

1. If one of the high contracting parties alleges that a violation of article 2 of the present treaty or a breach of articles 42 or 43 of the Treaty of Versailles has been or is being committed, it shall bring the question at once before the Council of the League of Nations.

2. As soon as the Council of the League of Nations is satisfied that such a violation or breach has been committed, it will notify its finding without delay to the Powers signatory of the present treaty, who severally agree that in such case they will each of them come immediately to the assistance of the Power against whom the act complained of is directed.

3. In case of a flagrant violation of article 2 of the present treaty or of a flagrant breach of articles 42 or 43 of the Treaty of Versailles by one of the high contracting parties, each of the other contracting parties hereby undertakes immediately to come to the help of the party against whom such a violation or breach has been directed as soon as the said Power has been able to satisfy itself that this violation constitutes an unprovoked act of aggression and that by reason either of the crossing of the frontier or of the outbreak of hostilities or of the assembly of armed forces in the demilitarised zone immediate action is necessary. Nevertheless, the Council of the League of Nations, which will be seized of the question in accordance with the first paragraph of this article, will issue its findings, and the high contracting parties undertake to act in accordance with the recommendations of the Council provided that they are concurred in by all the members other than the representatives of the parties which have engaged in hostilities.

ARTICLE 5

The provisions of article 3 of the present treaty are placed under the guarantee of the high contracting parties as provided by the following stipulations:—

If one of the Powers referred to in article 3 refuses to submit a dispute to peaceful settlement or to comply with an arbitral or judicial decision and commits a violation of article 2 of the present treaty or a breach of articles 42 or 43 of the Treaty of Versailles, the provisions of article 4 shall apply.

Where one of the Powers referred to in article 3 without committing a violation of article 2 of the present treaty or a breach of articles 42 or 43 of the Treaty of Versailles, refuses to submit a dispute to peaceful settlement or to comply with an arbitral or judicial decision, the other party shall bring the matter before the Council of the League of Nations, and the Council shall propose what steps shall be taken; the high contracting parties shall comply with these proposals.

In faith whereof the above-mentioned plenipotentiaries have signed the present treaty.

Don at Locarno, the 16th October, 1925. (Signed) LUTHER, STRESEMANN, EMILE VANDERVELDE, A. BRIAND, AUSTEN CHAMBERLAIN, BENITO MUSSOLINI.

THE GENERAL PACT FOR THE RENUNCIATION OF WAR

The President of the German Reich, The President of the United States of American, His Majesty The King of the Belgians, The President of the French Republic, His Majesty The King of Great Britain, Ireland and the British Dominions beyond the Seas, Emperor of India, His Majesty The King of Italy, His Majesty The Emperor of Japan, The President of the Republic of Poland, The President of the Czechoslovak Republic,

Deeply sensible of their solemn duty to promote the welfare of mankind;

Persuaded that the time has come when a frank renunciation of war as an instrument of national policy should be made to the end that the peaceful and friendly relations now existing between their peoples may be perpetuated;

Convinced that all changes in their relations with one another should be sought only by pacific means and be the result of a peaceful and orderly process, and that any signatory Power which shall hereafter seek to promote its national interests by resort to war should be denied the benefits furnished by this Treaty;

Hopeful that, encouraged by their example, all the other nations of the world will join in this humane endeavour and by adhering to the present Treaty as soon as it comes into force bring their peoples within the scope of its beneficent provisions, thus uniting the civilised nations of the world in a common renunciation of war as an instrument of their national policy;

Have decided to conclude a Treaty and for that purpose have appointed... as their respective Plenipotentiaries, who having communicated to one another their full powers found in good and due form have agreed upon the following articles:

ARTICLE I. The High Contracting Parties solemnly declare in the names of their respective peoples that they condemn recourse to war for the solution of international controversies, and renounce it as an instrument of national policy in their relations with one another.

ARTICLE II. The Hight Contracting Parties agree that the settlement or solution of all disputes or conflicts of whatever nature or of whatever origin they may be, which may arise among them, shall never be sought except by pacific means.

ARTICLE III. The present Treaty shall be ratified by the High Contracting Parties named in the Preamble in accordance with their respective constitutional requirements, and shall take effect as between them as soon as all their several instruments of ratification shall have been deposited at Washington.

This Treaty shall, when it has come into effect as prescribed in the preceding paragraph, remain open as long as may be necessary for adherence by all the other Powers of the world. Every instrument evidencing the adherence of a Power shall be deposited in Washington and the Treaty shall immediately upon such deposit become effective as between the Power thus adhering and the other Powers parties hereto.

It shall be the duty of the Government of the United States to furnish each Government named in the Preamble and every Government subsequently adhering to this Treaty with a certified copy of the Treaty and of every instrument of ratification or adherence. It shall also be the duty of the Government of the United States telegraphically to notify such Goverments immediately upon the deposit with it of each instrument of ratification or adherence.

In Faith Whereof the respective Plenipotentiaires have signed this Treaty in the French and English languages, both texts having equal force, and hereunto affix their seals.

Done at Paris the twenty-seventh day of August in the year of one thousand nine hundred and twenty-eight.

I. ARCHIVES

A. France:
Ministre des Rélations Extérieures, Quai D'Orsay, Paris VIIème Archives du Ministère des Affaires Étrangères.

Série Z, Europe, 1918-1929 (Allemagne, Grand Bretagne, Italie, Petite Entente, Saint-Siège, Tchécoslovaquie, Russie)
Série Y, International, 1918-1940 (Conférence de Cannes, Conférence de Gênes, Conférence de Londres, Conférence de Washington)
Rive Gauche du Rhin, Europe, 1918-1929

B. Great Britain:
Public Record Office, Kew, Surrey TW9 4DU, Records of the Foreign Office:
General Correspondence
Confidential Print
Archives of Conferences
Personal Papers (Austen Chamberlain, Robert Crewe, Eyre Crowe, George Curzon, William Tyrrell)

II. PUBLISHED DOCUMENTS

A. Belgium:

Académie Royale de Belgique, *Documents diplomatiques belges, 1920-1940.*
La politique de sécurité extérieure, I, 1920-1924. Brussels: Commission
Royale d'Histoire, 1964.

B. France:

Assemblée Nationale, *Journal official, débats parlementaires (Chambre des
Députés); Journal officiel, débats parlementaires (Sénat)*
Constitutions et Documents Politiques, Maurice Duverger, ed. Paris: Presses
Universitaires de France, 1960.
Ministre des Affaires Étrangères, *Annuaire diplomatique et consulaire de la
république française.* Paris: Berger-Levrault Librarie, 1918-1930;
Documents diplomatiques. Paris: Imprimerie Nationale, 1920-1929.
Ministre de Guerre, *Annuaire officiel de l'armée française, troupes
métropolitaines et troupes coloniales.* Paris: Librarie Militaire Berger-
Levrault, 1921-1929.

C. Germany:

Auswärtiges Amt, *Akten zur Deutschen auswärtigen Politik, 1918-1945.*
Bonn, 1949--; *Das Kabinett Cuno 22 November 1922 bis 12 August
1923,* ed. Karl-Heinz Harbeck. Boppard Am Rhein, Harald Boldt, 1968.

D. Great Britain:

British and Foreign State Papers. London: H.M. Stationary Office, 1919-29.
British Documents on the Origins of the War, 1898-1914, G.P. Gooch and
Harold Temperly, eds. London: HMSO, 1926-38.
*Documents Illustrating the Hostile Activities of the Soviet Government and
Third International against Great Britain. Command Document* 2874.
Documents on British Foreign Policy 1919-1939, E.L. Woodward and Rohan
Butler, eds. London: HMSO, 1946--.
Foreign Office. Peace Handbooks, *Handbooks Prepared Under the Direction
of the Historical Section of the Foreign Office.* London: HMSO, 1920.
Report of the 17th Conference of the Labour Party. London: British Labour
Party, 1918.

E. Italy:

Benito Mussolini, *Opera Omnia,* XII-XXIV. Firenze: La Fenice, 1953-58.

I documenti diplomatici italiani, 1922-1935, Settima Serie, I & II. Rome: Instituto Poligrafico dello Stato, 1953-55.

F. League of Nations:

Armament's Year-Book. Geneva: League of Nations, 1924-1930.

Economic Fluctuation in the United States and the United Kingdom, 1918-1922. Geneva: League of Nations, 1942.

International Economic Conference Geneva, May 1927. Geneva: Imprimerie Kundig, 1927.

Official Journal. Geneva: League of Nations, 1920-1929.

The Problem of the Coal Industry. Geneva: League of Nations, 1929.

Protocol for the Pacific Settlement of International Disputes. New York: Carnegie Endowment for International Peace, 1924.

The Reduction of Armaments. New York: American Association for International Concilation, 1923.

Treaty Series. London: Harrison and Sons, 1920-1931.

World Production and Prices, 1925-1933. Geneva: League of Nations, 1934.

G. Soviet Russia:

Jane Degras, ed., *The Communist International 1919-1922,* London: Frank Cass, 1971; *Soviet Documents on Foreign Policy,* London: Oxford University Press, 1951.

Documents Illustrating the Hostile Activities of the Soviet Government and Third International against Great Britain. Command Document 2874.

Helmut Gruber, ed., *International Communism in the Era of Lenin, A Documentary History.* New York: Fawcett World Library, 1967.

H. United States:

Bureau of U.S. Foreign and Domestic Commerce, *German Reparations, Budget, and Foreign Trade.* Washington, D.C.: Government Printing Office, 1922.

Conference on the Limitation of Armament, Senate Documents, Vol. 9, 67th Congress, 2nd Session 1921-1922, Raymond Leslie Buell,ed. Washington, D.C.: Government Printing Office, 1922.

Congressional Record. Washington. D. C., 1920-29.

Department of Commerce, *American Underwriting of Foreign Securities.* Washington, D.C.: Government Printing Office, 1928-1931; *Balance of*

International Payments of the United States, 1926-1933. Washington,
  D.C.: Government Printing Office, 1927-1933; *Historical Statistics of
  the United States*. Washington, D.C.: Department of Commerce, 1950; *A
  New Estimate of American Investments Abroad*. Washington, D.C.:
  Government Printing Office, 1931.
Foreign Relations of the United States, 1919-1929. Washington, D. C.:
  Government Printing Office, 1930-44.
Statistical Abstract of the United States 1920-1929. Washington, D.C.:
  Government Printing Office, 1920-1929.

I. Other:

Comments by the German Delegation on the Conditions of Peace. New York:
  American Association for International Conciliation, 1919.
André Gauthier, *Les chansons de nôtre histoire*. Paris: Waleffe, 1967.
International Conciliation, European Security. New York: Carnegie
  Endowment for International Peace, 1925.
Paul Mantoux, *Les délibérations du Conseil des Quatres*, I. Paris: Centre
  National de la Recherche Scientifique, 1955.
*Reply of the Allied and Associated Powers to the Observations of the German
  Delegation on the Conditions of Peace*. New York: American
  Association for International Conciliation, 1919.
*The Treaty of St. Germain, A Documentary History of its Territorial and
  Political Clauses*, Nina Almond and Ralph Lutz, eds. Stanford, Calif.:
  Stanford University Press, 1935.

III. MEMOIRS, SPEECHES, PERSONEL PAPERS, CONTEMPORARY ACCOUNTS

Henry T. Allen, *My Rhineland Journal*. Boston: Houghton Mifflin, 1923.
Leopold Amery, *My Political Life*. London, 1955.
Earl of Avon, *The Memoirs of Anthony Eden, Facing the Dictators*. Boston:
  Houghton Mifflin, 1962.
Jacques Bainville, *Journal, 1919-1926*. Paris: Plon, 1949.
Ray Stannard Baker, *Woodrow Wilson, Life and Letters*, 8 Vols. Garden City:
  Doubleday, Page & Co., 1927-1939.
Jacques Bardoux, *De Paris à Spa, la bataille diplomatique pour la paix
  française*. Paris: F. Alcan, 1921.
Bernard M. Baruch, *The Making of the Reparation and Economic Sections of
  the Treaty*. London and New York: Harper & Brothers, 1920.

Lord Beaverbrook (William Maxwell Aitken), *Men and Power, 1917-1918.* New York: Duell, Sloan and Pearce, 1957.

William Bolitho, *Leviathan.* London: Chapman and Dodd, 1923.

Georges Bonnet, *Quai d'Orsay.* Isle of Man: Times Press, 1965; *Vingt ans de vie politique.* Paris: Fayard, 1969.

Stephen Bonsal, *Unfinished Business.* New York: Doubleday, Doran, 1944.

Léon Bourgeois, *Le traité de paix de Versailles.* Paris: Akan, 1919.

Vera Brittain, *Testament of Youth.* New York: Macmillan, 1934.

Ulrich Karl Brockdorff-Rantzau, *Dokumente.* Charlottenburg: Deutsche Verlagsgesellschaft für Politik und Geschichte, 1919.

Joseph Caillaux, *Mes mémoires,* 3 Vols. Paris: Plon, 1947.

Viscount Cecil (Edgar Algernon Gascoyne-Cecil), *A Great Experiment.* New York: Oxford University Press.

Austen Chamberlain. *The Life and Letters of the Right Hon. Sir Austen Chamberlain,* Sir Charles Petrie, ed. London: Cassell, 1940.

Georges Clemenceau, *The Grandeur and Misery of Victory.* New York: Harcourt, Brace, 1930; *Au soir de ma pensée.* Paris: Plon, 1930.

Étienne Clémentel, *La France et la politique économique interalliée.* Paris: Carnegie Foundation for International Peace, 1931.

Calvin Coolidge, *The Talkative President, The Off the Record Press Conferences of Calvin Coolidge,* Howard H. Quint, and Robert H. Ferrell, eds. Amherst: University of Massachusetts Press, 1964.

Viscount D'Abernon, *The Diary of an Ambassador,* 3 Vols. Garden City, New York.: Doubleday, Doran, 1929-31.

Josephus Daniels, *The Wilson Era: Years of War and After, 1917-1923.* Chapel Hill: University of North Carolina, 1946.

Léon Daudet, *Député de Paris, 1919-1924.* Paris: B. Grasset, 1933.

Charles G. Dawes, *A Journal of Reparations.* London: Macmillan, 1939.

Xenia J. Eudin and Harold H. Fisher, *Soviet Russia and the West, 1920-1927.* Stanford: Stanford University Press, 1957.

Ferdinand Foch, *Mémoirs pour servir à l'histoire de la guerre de 1914-1918.* Paris: Plon, 1931.

André François-Poncet, *De Versailles à Potsdam, la France et le problème allemand contemporain.* Paris: Flammarion, 1948.

Rear Admiral Cary T. Grayson, *Woodrow Wilson, An Intimate Memoir.* New York: Holt Rinehart and Winston, 1960.

George Grosz, *A Little Yes and a Big No.* New York: Dial Press, 1946.

Raffaele Guariglia, *Ricordi, 1922-1946.* Naples: Scientifiche Italiane, 1950.

Maurice Hankey, *The Supreme Council at the Paris Peace Conference*.
    London: Allen and Unwin, 1963.
Gabriel Hanotaux, *Carnets, 1907-1925*, Georges Dethan, ed. Paris:
    A. Pedone, 1982; *Le traité de Versailles du 28 Juin 1919: L'Allemagne*
et   L' Europe. Paris: Alcan, 1919.
Herbert Hoover, *The Memoirs of Herbert Hoover: The Cabinet and the
    Presidency, 1920-1933*. New York: Macmillan, 1952.
Nicolas Horthy. *The Confidential Papers of Admiral Horthy*. Budapest:
    Corvina, 1965.
Edward M. House and Charles Seymour, eds., *What Really Happened at
    Paris: The Story of the Peace Conference, 1918-1919, by American
    Delegates*. New York: Charles Scribner's Sons, 1921.
Joseph Joffre, *Mémoires du Maréchal Joffre*, 2 Vols. Paris: Plon et Nourrit,
    1938.
Louis Klotz, *De la guerre à la paix, souvenirs et documents*. Paris: Payot,
    1924.
Robert Lansing, *The Big Four and the Others of the Peace Conference*.
    Boston: Houghton, Mifflin, 1921; *The Peace Negotiations*. Boston:
    Houghton Mifflin, 1921.
Jules Laroche, *Au Quai d'Orsay avec Briand et Poincaré*. Paris: Hachette,
    1957.
Vladimir I. Lenin, *Collected Works*, Vol. 31. Moscow: Progress Publishers,
    1977.
David Lloyd George, *Lloyd George Family Letters, 1885-1936* Kenneth O.
    Morgan, ed. New York: Oxford University Press, 1973; *Memoirs of the
    Peace Conference*, I. New Haven: Yale University Press, 1939; *The
    Truth about Reparations and War Debts*. London: Heinemann, 1932;
    The Truth about the Peace Treaties, 2 Vols. London: V. Gollancz Ltd.,
    1938; *War Memoirs*, V. London: Nicholson and Watson, 1933.
Edward House, *The Intimate Papers of Colonel House*, Charles Seymour, ed.
    Boston: Houghton Mifflin, 1918.
Bruce Lockhart, *The Diaries of Sir Bruce Lockhart*, Kenneth Young, ed. New
    York: St. Martin's Press, 1973; *Retreat from Glory*. New York:
    Putnams, 1934.
Louis Loucheur, *Carnets Secrets, 1908-1932*, Jacques de Launay, ed.
    Brussels and Paris: Brepols, 1962.
Harold Macmillan, *Winds of Change, 1914-1939*. New York: Harper and
    Row, 1966.
Ivan Maisky, *Journey into the Past*. London: Hutchinson, 1962.

Louis-Étienne Mangin, *La France et le Rhin, hier et aujourd'hui*. Geneva: Éditions du Milieu du Monde, 1945.

David Hunter Miller, *The Drafting of the Covenant, II*. New York: G. P. Putnam's Sons, 1928; *My Diary at the Conference of Paris, III*. New York: Appeal Printing Company, 1928.

Jean-Jules Henri Mordacq, *Clemenceau au soir de sa vie 1920-1929*. Paris: Plon, 1933; *Le ministère Clemenceau, journal d'un témoin*, 4 Vols. Paris: Plon, 1930-1931.

Konstantine D. Nabokov, *The Ordeal of a Diplomat*. London: Duckworth, 1921.

Pietro Nenni, *Storia de quattro anni, 1919-1922*. Rome: Einaudi, 1946.

Harold Nicholson, *Peacemaking 1919*. New York: Grosset and Dunlap, 1965.

Gustav Noske, *Von Kiel bis Kapp*. Berlin: Verlag für Politik und Wirtschaft, 1920.

Vittorio Orlando, *Memorie, 1915-1919*, ed. Rodolfo Mosca. Milan: Rizzoli, 1960.

Joseph Paul-Boncour, *Entre deux guerres, souvenirs sur la troisième république*. Paris: Plon, 1945.

Raymond Poincaré, *Au service de la France: neuf années de souvenirs*, 10 Vols. Paris: Plon-Nourrit, 1926-1933.

Wather Rathenau, *Tagbuch, 1907-1922*, Harmut Pogge von Strandmann, ed. Düsseldorf: Droste, 1967.

Lord Riddell, *Intimate Diary of the Peace Conference and After*.

Alexander Ribot, *Journal et correspondances inédites, 1914-1922*. Paris: Plon, n.d..

Viscount Rothermere, *My Campaign for Hungary*. London: Eyre and Spottiswood, 1939.

August de Saint-Aulaire, *Confession d'un vieux diplomate*. Paris: Flammarion, 1953.

Hans Von Seeckt, *Deutschland zwischen West und Ost*. Hamburg: Hanseatische Verlaganstalt, 1933; *Gedanken eines Soldaten*. Berlin: Verlag für Kulturpolitik, 1929.

Jacques Seydoux, *De Versailles au Plan Young, réparations, dettes interalliéennes*. Paris: Plon, 1932.

Gustav Stresemann, *Gustav Stresemann, His Diaries, Letters, and Papers*. London: Macmillan, 1935-1940.

Georges Suarez, *Briand, sa vie, son oeuvre, avec son journal et des nombreux documents inédits*, 6 vols. Paris: Plon, 1938-1952.

André Tardieu, *La paix*. Paris: Payot, 1921.

Margaret Thatcher, *The Downing Street Years*. New York: Harper Collins,
      1993.

Leon Trotsky, *My Life*. New York: Pathfinder, 1970; *The Trotsky Papers
      1917-1922*. The Hague: Mouton, 1971.

Lord Robert Vansittart, *Lessons of My Life*. New York: Alfred A. Knopf,
      1943.

John Wheeler-Bennett, *Information on the Problem of Security 1917-1926*
      London: Allen and Unwin, 1927.

Wythe Williams, *The Tiger of France, Conversations with Clemenceau*. New
      York: Sloan and Pearce, 1949.

Edith Bolling Wilson, *My Memoir*. Indianapolis: Bobbs-Merrill, 1938.

Woodrow Wilson, *War and Peace, Presidential Messages, Addresses and
      Public Papers, 1917-1924*. New York: Harper, 1927; *The Public
      Papers of Woodrow Wilson*, Vol. 1. New York: Harper, 1927; *Messages
      and Papers of the Presidents, XVIII*. New York: Bureau of National
      Literature, n.d.

IV. NEWSPAPERS, PERIODICALS, ANNUALS, BIBLIOGRAPHIES

Annual Register. London: Longmans, Green, 1918-1930.

Guides to Research and Research Materials, 1918-1945 (Wilmington,
      Delaware: Scholarly Resources, Inc., 1991) Revised Editions: i. Sidney
      Aster, ed. *British Foreign Policy*; ii. George W. Baer, ed., *International
      Organization*; iii. Alan Cassels, ed., *Italian Foreign Policy*; iv. Christof
      M. Kimmich, ed., *German Foreign Policy*; v. Robert J. Young, ed.,
      French Foreign Policy

*Flight; Flight and Aircraft Engineering; Illustrated London News;
      L'Illustration; Jane's All the World's Aircraft; Jane's Fighting Ships;
      League of Nations Year-Book*. Geneva: League of Nations, 1921-1929;
      *Manchester Guardian; National Catholic Reporter; New Statesman and
      Nation; New York Times, The Observer; Punch, Revue des Deux
      Mondes; Simplicissimus, Spectator, Time; The* (London) *Times, The New
      York Times, Whitaker's Almanak*. London: Whitaker, 1918-1929.

V. GENERAL HISTORIES

Édouard Bonnefous, *Histoire politique de la Troisième République, L'après-
      guerre 1919-1924*. Paris: Presses Universitaire de France, 1959.

Denis W. Brogan, *The Development of Modern France*, Vol. II. New York: Harper and Row, 1966.

Les cahiers de l'histoire, No 9. Paris: Librarie Le Griffon, 1961.

Jacques Chastenet, *Histoire de la Troisième République, Jours inquiets et jours sanglants*. Paris: Hachette, 1955.

Erich Eych, *A History of the Weimar Republic*, I & II. Cambridge, Mass.: Harvard University Press, 1962.

Basil Liddell Hart, *The Real War*. Boston: Atlantic-Little Brown, 1930.

Alfred F. Havighurst, *Britain in Transition, The Twentieth Century* Chicago: University of Chicago Press, 1979; *Twentieth-Century Britain*. New York: Harper and Row, 1962.

Georges and Janine Hémeret, *Les présidents, République française*. Paris: Socadi, 1985.

History of the 20th Century, Vols. I-III. London: BPC Publishing Co., 1970.

Eric Hobsbawm, *The Age of Extremes, A History of the World, 1914-1991*. New York; Pantheon Books, 1994.

Henry Kissinger, *Diplomacy*. New York: Simon and Schuster, 1994.

Wm. Laird Kleine-Ahlbrandt, *Twentieth Century European History*. St. Paul: West Publishing Co., 1993.

George H. Mayer and Walter O. Forster, *The United States and the Twentieth Century*. Boston: Houghton Mifflin, 1958.

Koppel Pinson, *Modern Germany, Its History and Civilization*. New York: Macmillan, 1966.

Harold W. V. Temperly, ed., *A History of the Peace Conference* I. London: Oxford University Press, 1920.

Francis P. Walters, *A History of the League of Nations*, I. London: Oxford University Press, 1952.

VI. BIOGRAPHY AND BIOGRAPHIC MONOGRAPHS

Thomas A. Bailey, *Wilson and the Great Betrayal*. Chicago: Quadrangle Books, 1963.

Michael Balfour, *The Kaiser and His Times*. Boston: Houghton Mifflin, 1964.

James Barros, *Office without Power: Secretary-General Sir Eric Drummond 1919-1933*. Oxford: Clarendon Press, 1979.

André Beauguitte, *Le Chemin de Cocherel*. Paris: Alphonse Lemerre, 1960.

Lord Beaverbrook (William Maxwell Aitken), *The Decline and Fall of Lloyd George*. London: Collins, 1963.

Hans Peter Berglar-Schröer, *Wather Rathenau: seine Zeit, sein Werk: seine Persönlichkeit*. Breman: Schünemann, 1970.

Donald Graeme Boadle, *Winston Churchill and the German Question in British Foreign Policy, 1918-1922*. The Hague: Martinus Nijhoff, 1973.

Rolf Brandt, *Albert Leo Schlageter: Leben und Sterben eines deutschen Helden*. Hamburg: Hanseatische Verlagsanstalt Aktiengesellschaft, 1926.

Henry L. Bretton, *Stresemann and the Revision of Versailles; A Fight for Reason*. Stanford: Stanford University Press, 1953.

Gordon Brook-Shepherd, *The Last Habsburg*. New York: Waybright and Talley, 1968.

Geoffrey Bruun, *Clemenceau*. Cambridge, Mass.: Harvard University Press, 1943.

Winston Churchill, *Great Contemporaries*. New York: G. P. Putnan, 1937.

Joel Colton, *Léon Blum, Humanist in Politics*. New York: Knopf, 1966.

Pierre Crabitès, *Benes, Statesman of Central Europe*. London: G. Routledge, 1935.

Colin Cross, *Philip Snowden*. London: Barnie and Rockliff, 1966.

Gregor Dallas, *At the Heart of a Tiger, Clemenceau and His World 1841-1929*. New York: Carroll and Graf, 1993.

Issac Deutscher, *The Prophet Armed, Trotsky: 1879-1921*. New York: Oxford University Press, 1959; *Stalin, A Political Biography*. New York: Oxford University Press, 1967.

Andreas Dorpalen, *Hindenburg and the Weimar Republic*. Princeton, N.J.: Princeton University Press, 1964.

M. K. Dziewanowski, *Joseph Pilsudski, A European Federalist, 1918-1922*. Stanford: Hoover Institution Press, 1969.

Marvin L. Edwards, *Stresemann and the Greater Germany, 1914-1918*. New York: Bookman Associates, 1963.

Max Egremont, *Balfour: A Life of Arthur James Balfour*. London: Collins, 1980.

Klaus Epstein, *Matthias Erzberger and the Dilemma of German Democracy*. Princeton: Princeton University Press, 1959.

Cyril Falls, *Marshal Foch*. London: Blachie, 1939.

Louis Fischer, *The Life of Lenin*. New York: Harper and Row, 1964.

Michael G. Fry, *Lloyd George and Foreign Policy*. Montreal: McGill-Queen's University Press, 1977.

Martin Gilbert, ed., *Lloyd George*. Englewood Cliffs, N.J.: Prentice Hall, 1968.

Betty Glad, *Charles Evans Hughes and the Illusions of Innocence; A Study in American Diplomacy.* Urbana: University of Illinois Press, 1966.

Claus Guske, *Das politische denken des Generals von Seecht.* Hamburg: Matthiesen, 1971.

Roy F. Harrod, *The Life of John Maynard Keynes.* London: Macmillan, 1951.

Irving Howe, *Leon Trotsky.* New York: Viking Press, 1978.

Sisley Huddleston, *Poincaré: a Biographical Portrait.* Boston: Little, 1924.

Wilhelm Hügenell, *Schlageter.* Munich: Verlag der Deutschvölkischen Buchhandlung, 1923.

Henry M. Hundman, *Clemenceau the Man and His Time.* New York: Fredrick A. Stokes, 1919.

Hampden Jackson, *Clemenceau and the Third Republic.* New York: Collier Books, 1962.

L. Kemechey, *'Il Duce', The Life and Work of Benito Mussolini.* New York: Richard R. Smith, 1930.

Michael Kinnear, *The Fall of Lloyd George, the Political Crisis of 1922.* London: Macmillan, 1973.

Harry Klemens Kessler, *Walther Rathenau; His Life and Work.* New York: H. Fertig, 1969.

Joachim von Kürenberg, *The Kaiser.* New York: Simon and Schuster, 1955.

Jean Lacouture, *Léon Blum.* New York: Holmes and Meier, 1982.

Basil Henry Liddell Hart, *Foch, the Man of Orléans.* Boston: Little, Brown, 1932.

Louis Paul Lochner, *Herbert Hoover and Germany.* New York: Macmillan, 1960.

Robin Bruce Lockhart, *Ace of Spies.* New York: Stein and Day, 1968.

Ruddock F. Mackay, *Balfour, Intellectual Statesman.* New York: Oxford University Press, 1985.

William R. Manchester, *The Last Lion, Winston Spencer Churchill: Visions of Glory, 1874-1932.* Boston: Little, Brown, 1983; *The Arms of Krupp.* Boston: Little, Brown, 1968.

David Marquand, *Ramsay Macdonald.* London: Jonathan Cape, 1977.

Jean Martet, *Le tigre.* Paris: A. Michel, 1930.

Keith Middlemas and John Barnes, *Baldwin, A Biography.* New York: Macmillan, 1970.

Paolo Monelli, *Mussolini.* New York: Vanguard, 1954.

Kenneth O. Morgan, *British Prime Ministers in the Twentieth Century.* New York: St. Martin's Press, 1977.

Harold Nicolson, *Curzon: The Last Phase 1919-1925, A Study in Post-War Diplomacy*. New York: Harcourt, Brace and Co., 1939; *King George the Fifth, His Life and Reign*. New York: Doubleday, 1953.

Frank Owen, *Tempestuous Journey: Lloyd George: His Life and Times*. London: Hutchinson, 1955.

Alan Palmer, *The Kaiser, Warlord of the Second Reich*. New York: Scribners, 1978.

Dexter Perkins, *Charles Evans Hughes and American Democratic Statesmanship*. Boston: Little, Brown, 1956.

Sir Charles Petrie, *The Chamberlain Tradition*. New York: Fredrick A. Stokes, 1938.

Merlo J. Pusey, *Charles Evans Hughes*. New York: Columbia University Press, 1963.

Carl Eric Roberts, *Stanley Baldwin, Man or Miracle?* New York: Greenberg, 1937.

Norman Rose, *Vansittart: Study of a Diplomat*. New York: Holmes and Meier, 1978.

Owen Rutter, *Regent of Hungary: The Authorized Life of Admiral Horthy*. London: Rich and Cowan, 1939.

David Schub, *Lenin*.

George Seldes, *Sawdust Caeser*. New York: Harper and Brothers, 1935.

Leonard Shapiro and Peter Reddaway, eds., *Lenin: The Man, the Theorist, the Leader*. New York: Praeger, 1967.

Gene Smith, *When the Cheering Stopped, The Last Years of Woodrow Wilson*. New York: Morrow, 1964.

Michel Soulié, *La vie politique d'Edouard Herriot*. Paris: Armand Colin, 1962.

Boris Souvarine, *Stalin, A Critical Survey of Bolshevism*. New York: Longmans, Green, 1939.

Alan J. P. Taylor, ed., *Lloyd George, Twelve Essays*. New York: Atheneum, 1971.

D. R. Thorpe, *The Uncrowned Prime Ministers*. London: Darkhorse, 1980.

Karl Tschuppik, *Ludendorff, The Tragedy of a Military Mind*. Boston: Houghton, Mifflin, 1934.

Henry Ashby Turner, Jr., *Stresemann and the Politics of the Weimar Republic*. Princeton, N.J.: Princeton University Press, 1963.

John Wheeler-Bennett, *Hindenburg: The Wooden Titan*. New York: St. Martin's Press, 1967.

Georges Wormser, *La république de Clemenceau*. Paris: Presses
     Universitaires de France, 1961.
Gordon Wright, *Raymond Poincaré and the French Presidency*. Stanford
     University, Calif.: Stanford University Press, 1942.
Peter Wulf, *Hugo Stinnes: Wirtschaft und Politik, 1918-1924*. Stuttgart:
     Klett-Cotta, 1979.
George Malcom Young, *Stanley Baldwin*. London: Rupert Hart-Davis, 1952.
Sydney H. Zebel, *Balfour; A Political Biography*. Cambridge, Eng.:
     University Press, 1973.

VII. MONOGRAPHS AND SPECIAL STUDIES

A. Economic and Social Questions:

Derek H. Aldcroft, *The Inter-War Economy: Britain, 1919-1939*. New York:
     Columbia University Press, 1970.
Denise Artaud, *La question des dettes interalliées et la reconstruction de
     l'Europe, 1917-1929*. Paris: Librarie Honoré Champion, 1978.
Heinrich Bennecke, *Wirtschaftliche Depression und politischer Radikalismus*.
     Munich:Günter Olzog, 1970.
Philip Mason Burnett, *Reparation at the Paris Peace Conference from the
     Standpoint of the American Delegation*. New York: Columbia
     University Press, 1940.
Frank Dunstone Graham, *Exchange, Prices and Production in Hyper-
     Inflation: Germany, 1920-1923*. Princeton: Princeton University Press,
     1930.
Samuel J. Hurwitz, *State Intervention in Great Britain, A Study of Economic
     Control and Social Response, 1914-1919*. New York: Columbia
     University Press, 1949.
Bruce Kent, *The Spoils of War: The Politics, Economics and Diplomacy of
     Reparations 1918-1932*. Oxford: Clarendon Press, 1989.
John Maynard Keynes, *The Economic Consequences of the Peace*. New York:
     Harcourt, Brace and Rowe, 1920; *A Revision of the Treaty: Being a
     Sequel to the Economic Consequences of the Peace*. New York:
     Harcourt, Brace, 1922.
Michel Lescure, *Les banques, l'état et le marché Immobilier en France à
     l'époque contemporaine, 1820-1940*. Paris: Éditions de l'École des
     Hautes Etudes en Sciences, 1982.
Charles S. Maier, *Recasting Bourgeois Europe*. Princeton, N.J.: Princeton
     University Press, 1975.

Etienne Mantoux, *The Carthaginian Peace or the Economic Consequences of Mr. Keynes*. London: Oxford University Press, 1946.

Harold G. Moulton, *Germany's Capacity to Pay: A Study of the Reparation Problem*. New York: McGraw-Hill, 1923.

Wilhelm Röpke, *L'économie mondiale aux XIXe et XXe Siècles*. Geneva: Droz, 1959.

Dan Silverman, *Reconstructing Europe after the Great War*. Cambridge, Mass.: Harvard University Press, 1982.

Gustav Stolper, *German Economy, 1870-1940, Issues and Trends*. New York: Reynal and Hitchcock, 1940.

Marc Trachtenberg, *Reparation in World Politics*. New York: Columbia University Press, 1980.

Étienne Weill-Raynal, *Les rèparations allemandes et la France*, 3 Vols. Paris: Nouvelles Éditions Latines, 1947-49.

B. International Relations:

John Spencer Bassett, *The League of Nations, A Chapter in World Politics*. New York: Longmans, Green: 1928.

Raymond Leslie Buell, *The Washington Conference*. New York: Appleton, 1922.

Edward H. Carr, *German-Soviet Relations Between the Two World Wars, 1919-1939*. Baltimore: Johns Hopkins Press, 1951.

W. P. and Z. K. Coates, *A History of Anglo-Soviet Relations, 1917-1942*. London: Lawrence and Wishart, 1943.

Gordon Craig and Felix Gilbert, eds., *The Diplomats, 1919-1939*, I. New York: Atheneum, 1963.

Jacques de Launay, *Secrets diplomatiques, 1914-1918*. Paris: Brepols, 1963.

Robert Dell, *The Geneva Racket, 1920-1939*. London: Robert Hale, 1941.

Carol Fink, *The Genoa Conference: European Diplomacy, 1921-1922*. Chapel Hill: University of North Carolina Press, 1984.

Gerald Freund, *Unholy Alliance, Russian-German Relations from the Treaty of Brest-Litovsk to the Treaty of Berlin*. New York: Harcourt, Brace and Co., 1957.

Hans W. Gatzke, ed., *European Diplomacy Between Two Wars, 1919-1939*. Chicago: Quadrangle, 1972.

Paul Helmreich, *From Paris to Sèvres, the Partition of the Ottoman Empire at the Peace Conference of 1919-1920*. Columbus: Ohio State University Press, 1974.

Jon Jacobson, *Locarno Diplomacy, Germany and the West, 1925-1929*.
Princeton: Princeton University Press, 1972.

Jan Karshi, *The Great Powers and Poland, 1919-1945, From Versailles to Yalta*. New York: University Press of America, 1985.

Robert Klein, *The Idea of Equality in International Politics, The Tension Between the Concept of Great-Power Primacy and the Concept of Sovereign Equality*. Annemasse: Les Presses de Savoie, 1966.

Henri Lichtenberger, *The Ruhr Conflict*. Washington: Carnegie Endowment for International Peace, 1923.

Sally Marks, *The Illusion of Peace: Europe's International Relations, 1918-1933*. New York: St. Martin's Press, 1976.

Arno J. Mayer, *Politics and Diplomacy of Peacemaking, Containment and Counterrevolution at Versailles 1918-1919*. New York: Knopf, 1967; *Political Origins of the New Diplomacy, 1917-1918*. New Haven: Yale University Press, 1959.

Charles L. Mee, Jr., *The End of Order, Versailles 1919*. New York: E. P. Dutton, 1980.

J. Saxon Mills, *The Genoa Conference*. London: Hutchinson, 1923.

Kurt Rosenbaum, *Community of Fate, German-Soviet Diplomatic Relations, 1922-1928*. Syracuse, New York: Syracuse University Press, 1965.

Royal J. Schmidt, *Versailles and the Ruhr: Seedbed of World War II*. The Hague: Martinus Nijhoff, 1968.

Harold Temperly, *A History of the Peace Conference of Paris*. London: H. Frowde, 1920-24.

Adam Ulam, *Expansion and Coexistence*. New York: Praeger, 1974.

Piotr Stefan Wandycz, *France and Her Eastern Allies, 1919-1925: French-Czechoslovak-Polish Relations from the Paris Peace Conference to Locarno*. (Minneapolis: The University of Minnesota Press, 1962); *The Twilight of French Eastern Alliances, 1926-1936: French-Czechoslovak-Polish Relations from Locarno to the Remilitarization of the Rhineland*. Princeton, N.J.: Princeton Univerasity Press, 1988.

C. War and Military Policy:

B. Bond, *British Military Policy between the Two World Wars*. London, 1984.

Gordon Craig, *The Politics of the Prussian Army, 1640-1945*. New York: Oxford University Press, 1964.

John Ehrman, *Cabinet Government and War, 1890-1940*. Cambridge: Cambridge University Press, 1958.

Bernard Fitzsimons, ed., *Weapons and Warfare*. New York: Columbia House, 1978.

Tony Gibbons, *The Complete Encyclopedia of Battleships*. New York: Cresent Books, 1983.

Judith M. Hughes, *To the Maginot Line: The Politics of French Military Preparations in the 1920's*. Cambridge, Mass.: Harvard University Press, 1971.

S. J. Lewis, *Forgotten Legions: German Infantry Policy, 1918-1941*. New York: Praeger, 1985.

Basil Liddell Hart, *The Real War, 1914-1918*. Boston: Little, Brown: 1930.

Edward N. Luttwak, *The Political Uses of Sea Power*. Baltimore: The Johns Hopkins University Press, 1974.

Salvador de Madariaga, *Disarmament*. New York: Coward-McCann, 1929.

Arthur J. Marder, *From the Dreadnought to Scapa Flow, V. Victory and Aftermath*. New York: Oxford University Press, 1970.

Philippe Masson, La marine française et la mer noire, 1918-1919. Paris: Publications de la Sorbonne, 1982.

Barry R. Posen, *The Sources of Military Doctrine: France, Britain, and Germany between the World Wars*. Ithaca: Cornell University Press, 1984.

Pierre Renouvin, *L'armistice de Rethondes*. Paris: Hachette, 1968.

Stephen Roskill, *Naval Policy Between the Wars, The Period of Anglo-American Antagonism 1919-1929*. London: Collins, 1968.

David Spires, *Image and Reality: The Making of the German Officer, 1921-1933*. Westport, Conn.: Greenwood, 1984.

John Wheeler-Bennett, *The Nemesis of Power*. New York: Viking Press, 1967.

D. France:

Malcolm Anderson, *Conservative Politics in France*. London: Allen and Unwin, 1974.

Jean-Pierre Auclert, *La grande guerre des crayons*. Paris: Robert Laffont, 1981.

Jacques Bariéty, *Les relations franco-allemandes après la première-guerre mondiale: 10 novembre 1918-10 jamvier 1925: de l'exécution à la négotiation*. Paris: Éditions Pedone, 1977.

Claude Billanger, et al., eds., *Histoire générale de la presse française, De 1871 à 1940*. Paris: Presses Universitaires de France, 1972.

Michael J. Carley, *Revolution and Intervention: The French Government and the Russian Civil War, 1917-1919*. Buffalo: McGill-Queens University Press, 1983.

Richard D. Challener, *The French Theory of the Nation in Arms, 1886-1939*. New York: Columbia University Press, 1955.

Ebba Dahlin, *French and German Public Opinion on Declared War Aims, 1914-1918*. London: Oxford University Press.

Colin Dyer, *Population and Society in Twentieth Century France*. New York: Holmes and Meier, 1978.

Paul-Marie de la Gorce, *The French Army, A Military-Political History*. New York: George Braziller, 1963.

Edward David Keeton, *Briand's Locarno Policy: French Economics, Politics, and Diplomacy 1925-1929*. New York: Garland, 1987.

Jere Clemens King, *Foch Versus Clemenceau, France and German Dismemberment, 1918-1919*. Cambridge: Harvard University Press, 1960; *Generals and Politicians, Conflict Between France's High Command, Parliament and Government, 1914-1918*. Berkeley: University of California Press, 1951.

Les cahiers de l'histoire, La IIIe République. Paris: Librairie Le Griffon, 1961.

Walter A. McDougall, *France's Rhineland Diplomacy, The Last Bid for a Balance of Power in Europe*. Princeton, N.J.: Princeton University Press, 1978.

Harold G. Moulton and Cleona Lewis, *The French Debt Problem*. New York: Macmillan, 1925.

Jacques Néré, *The Foreign Policy of France from 1914 to 1945*. London: Routledge, 1975.

Gaéan Pirou, *Les doctrines économiques en France depuis 1870*. Paris: Armand Colin, 1952.

Vincent Joseph Pitts, *France and the German Problem: Politics and Economics in the Locarno Period 1924-1929*. New York: Garland, 1987.

Steven A. Schuker, *The End of French Predominance in Europe, The Financial Crisis of 1924 and the Adoption of the Dawes Plan*. Chapel Hill: University of North Carolina Press, 1976.

William I. Shorrock, *From Ally to Enemy: the Enigma of Fascist Italy in French Diplomacy 1920-1940*. Kent, Ohio: Kent State University Press, 1988.

D. Stevenson, *French War Aims Against Germany 1914-1919*. Oxford: Clarendon Press.

Jean Touchard, *La gauche en France depuis 1900*. Paris: Seuil, 1977.

Gordon Wright, *Raymond Poincaré and the French Presidency*. New York: Octagon Books, 1967.

E. Germany:

James W. Angell, *The Recovery of Germany*. New Haven, Conn.: Yale University Press, 1929.

Werner T. Angress, *Stillborn Revolution: The Communist Bid for Power in Germany, 1921-1923*. Princeton: Princeton University Press, 1963.

Benoist-Méchin, *Histoire de l'armée allemande*. Paris: Albin Michel, 1964.

Helmut Böhme, *An Introduction to the Social and Economic History of Germany: Politics and Economic Change in the Nineteenth and Twentieth Centuries*. Oxford: Blackwell, 1978.

Richard Breitman, *German Socialism and Weimar Democracy*. Chapel Hill: The University of North Carolina Press, 1981.

Charles B. Burdick and Ralph H. Lutz, eds., *The Political Institutions of the German Revolution of 1918-1919*. New York: Praeger, 1966.

Francis Ludwig Carsten, *The Reichswehr and Politics 1918-1933*. London: Oxford University Press, 1966.

Rudolf Coper, *Failure of a Revolution, Germany in 1918-1919*. Cambridge: Cambridge University Press, 1955.

James M. Diehl, *Paramilitary Politics in Weimar Germany*. Bloomington: Indiana University Press, 1977.

Manfred J. Enssle, *Stresemann's Territorial Revisionism, Germany, Belgium, and the Eupen-Malmédy Question, 1919-1929*. Weisbaden: Franz Steiner, 1980.

Jean-Claude Favez, *Le Reich devant l'occupation franco-belge de la Ruhr en 1923*. Geneva: Librarie Droz, 1969.

David Felix, *Walther Rathenau and the Weimar Republic, The Politics of Reparations*. Baltimore: The Johns Hopkins Press, 1971.

Fritz Fischer, *Germany's Aims in the First World War*. New York: Norton, 1967.

Bruce B. Frye, *Liberal Democrats in the Weimar Republic: The History of the German Democratic Party and the German State Party*. Carbondale: Southern Illinois University Press, 1985.

Hans Ernest Fried, *The Guilt of the German Army*. New York: Macmillan, 1942.

Hans W. Gatzke, *Stresemann and the Rearmament of Germany*. Baltimore: The John Hopkins Press, 1954.

Walter Goerlitz, *History of the German General Staff, 1657-1945*. New York: Praeger, 1959.

The Reichswehr and the German Republic 1919-1926. Princeton: Princeton University Press, 1957.

Robert P. Grathwol, *Stresemman the DNVP, Reconciliation or Revenge in German Foreign Policy 1924-1928*. Lawrence, Kansas: The Regents Press, 1980.

Claus Guske, *Das politische Denken des Generals von Seeckt: Ein Beitrag zur Diskussion des Verhältnises Seeckt-Reichswehr-Republik*. Lübeck: Matthiesen Verlag, 1971.

John Hiden, *Germany and Europe 1919-1939*. London: Longman, 1993.

Edward L. Homze, *Arming the Luftwaffe, The Reich Air Ministry and the German Aircraft Industry 1919-39*. Lincoln: University of Nebraska Press, 1976.

Richard N. Hunt, *The Creation of the Weimar Republic*. Lexington, Mass.: Heath, 1969.

Christoph Kimmich, *The Free City, Danzig and German Foreign Policy, 1919-1934*. New Haven: Yale University Press, 1968; *Germany and the League of Nations*. Chicago: University of Chicago Press, 1976.

Karsten Laursen and Jorgen Pedersen, *The German Inflation 1918-1923* Amsterdam: North-Holland Publishing Co., 1964.

Alma Luchau, *The German Delegation at the Paris Peace Conference*. New York: Fertig, 1971.

Ralph H. Lutz, *The Causes of the German Collapse in 1918* Stanford: Stanford University Press, 1934.

Anthony James Nicholls, *Weimar and the Rise of Hitler*. New York: St. Martin's Press, 1968.

Gaines Post, Jr., *The Civil-Military Fabric of Weimar Foreign Policy*. Princeton, N.J.: Princeton University Press, 1973.

Norman J. G. Pounds, *The Ruhr, A Study in Historical and Economic Geography*. Bloomington, Ind.: Indiana University Press, 1952.

Rationalization of German Industry. New York: National Industrial Conference Board, 1931.

Fritz K. Ringer, ed., *The German Inflation of 1923*. New York: Oxford University Press, 1969.

A. J. Ryder, *The German Revolution of 1918, A Study of German Socialism in War and Revolt*. Cambridge: Cambridge University Press, 1967.

Wolfe Schnokel, *Dream of Empire, German Colonialism, 1919-1945.* New
    Haven: Yale University Press, 1964.

Richard M. Watt, *The Kings Depart, The Tragedy of Germany: Versailles and
    the German Revolution.* New York: Simon and Schuster, 1968.

John Willett, *Art and Politics in the Weimar Period: The New Sobriety, 1917-
    1933.* New York: Pantheon, 1978.

Z. A. B. Zeman, ed., *Germany and the Russian Revolution, 1915-1918.* New
    York: Oxford University Press 1958.

F. Great Britain:

Corelli Barnett, *The Collapse of British Power.* New York: Morrow, 1972.

Christopher John Bartlett, *British Foreign Policy in the Twentieth Century.*
    New York: St. Martin's Press, 1989.

Francis Ludwig Carsten, *Britain and the Weimar Republic.* London, 1984.

Lewis Chester, Stephen Fay, and Hugo Young, *The Zinoviev Letter.*
    Philadelphia: J. B. Lippincott, 1968.

John Connell, *The 'Office', The Story of the British Foreign Service, 1919-
    1951.* New York: St. Martin's Press, 1958.

Michael L. Dockrill and J. Douglas Goold, *Peace without Promise: Britain
    and the Peace Conferences, 1919-23.* Hamden, Conn.: Anchor, 1981.

Patricia A. Gajda, *Postscript to Victory: British Policy and the German-
    Polish Borderlands, 1919-1925.* Washington: University Press of
    America, 1982.

Leslie Gardiner, *The British Admiralty.* London: William Blackwood, 1968.

Martin Gilbert, *The Roots of Appeasement.* London: Weidenfeld and
    Nicholson, 1966.

John Howes Gleason, *The Genesis of Russophobia in Great Britain, A Study of
    the Interaction of Policy and Opinion.* New York: Octagon Books,   1972.

Michael Eliot Howard, *The Continental Commitment: The Dilemma of British
    Defense Policy in the Era of the the Two World Wars.* London, 1974.

Lorna S. Jaffe, *The Decision to Disarm Germany, British Policy Towards
    Postwar German Disarmament, 1914-1919.* Boston: Allen and Unwin,
    1985.

John Maynard Keynes, *The Economic Consequences of Mr. Churchill.*
    London: Woolf, 1925.

Stephen E. Koss, *The Rise and Fall of the Political Press in Britain, The
    Twentieth Century.* Chapel Hill: The University of North Carolina
    Press, 1984.

Arthur Marwick, *The Deluge, British Society and the First World War*. Boston: Little, Brown, 1965.

B. S. McBeth, *British Oil Policy, 1919-1939*. London: Frank Cass, 1985.

B.J.C. McKercher, *The Second Baldwin Government and the United States, 1924-1929: Attitudes and Diplomacy*. New York: Cambridge University Press, 1984.

Kenneth O. Morgan, *Consensus and Disunity, The Lloyd George Coalition Government, 1918-1922*. Oxford: Clarendon Press, 1979.

Charles Loch Mowat, *Britain Between the Wars, 1918-1940*. Chicago: University of Chicago Press, 1961.

Anne Orde, *Great Britain and International Security, 1920-1926*. London: Royal Historical Society, 1978; *British Policy and European Reconstruction after the First World War*. Cambridge: Cambridge University Press, 1991..

G. C. Peden, *Keynes, the Treasury and British Economic Policy*. London, 1988.

V. H. Rothwell, *British War Aims and Peace Diplomacy, 1914-1918*. Oxford: Clarendon Press, 1971.

G. Schmidt *The Politics and Economics of Appeasement: British Foreign Policy in the 1930s*. Oxford: Oxford University Press, 1986.

Seth Tillman, *Anglo-American Relations at the Paris Peace Conference of 1919*. Princeton, N.J.: Princeton University Press, 1961.

John Turner, *Lloyd George's Secretariat*. New York: Cambridge University Press, 1980.

Richard Ullman, *Anglo-Soviet Relations, 1917-1921*. Princeton: Princeton University Press, 1961.

David Walder, *The Chanak Affair*. London: Macmillan, 1969.

G. Italy:

Alan Cassels, *Mussolini's Early Diplomacy*. Princeton: Princeton University Press, 1970.

Alexander DeGrand, *Italian Fascism, Its Origins and Development*. Lincoln: University of Nebraska Press, 1983.

Charles E. Delzell, ed., *Mediterranean Fascism*. New York: Harper and Row, 1970.

William S. Halperin, *Mussolini and Italian Fascism*. Princeton, N.J.: Van Nostrand, 1964.

Cedric Lowe and F. Marzari, *Italian Foreign Policy 1870-1940*. London: Routledge and Paul, 1975.

Maxwell H. Macarteny and Paul Cremona, *Italy's Foreign and Colonial Policy 1914-1937*. London: Oxford University Press, 1938.

Carlo Sforza, *Contemporary Italy*. New York: Dutton, 1944.

Denis Mack Smith, *Mussolini's Roman Empire*. New York: Penguin Books, 1977.

J. A. Thayer, *Italy and the Great War, Politics and Culture*. Madison: University of Wisconsin Press, 1964.

H. Soviet Union:

Arthur E. Adams, ed., *Readings in Soviet Foreign Policy*. Boston: D. C. Heath, 1961.

Franz Borkenau, *The Communist International*. London: Faber and Faber, 1938.

John Bradley, *Allied Intervention in Russia*. New York: Basic Books, 1968; *Civil War in Russia, 1917-1920*. New York: St. Martin's Press, 1975.

Eber M. Carroll, *Soviet Communism and Western Opinion, 1919-21*. Chapel Hill: University of North Carolina Press, 1965.

Kathryn Wasserman Davis, *The Soviets at Geneva: The USSR and the League of Nations, 1919-1933*. Westport, Conn.: Hyperion Press, 1977.

Louis Fischer, *Russia's Road from Peace to War, Soviet Foreign Relations, 1917-1941*. Westport, Conn.: Greenwood Press, 1969.

Ruth Fischer, *Stalin and German Communism, A Study in the Origins of the State Party*. Cambridge, Mass.: Harvard University Press, 1948.

History of the Communist Party of the Soviet Union (Bolsheviks), Short Course. New York: International Publishers, 1939.

James W. Hulse, *The Forming of the Communist International*. Stanford: Stanford University Press, 1964.

George F. Kennan, *Russia and the West under Lenin and Stalin*. Boston: Little, Brown and Company, 1961; *Russia Leaves the War*. Princeton: Princeton University Press, 1961.

Michael Kettle, *Russia and the Allies, The Allies and the Russian Collapse, March 1917-March 1918*. Minneapolis: University of Minnesota Press, 1981.

Lionel Kochan, *Russia and the Weimar Republic*. Westport, Conn.: Greenwood Press, 1978.

Max Laserson, ed., *The Development of Soviet Foreign Policy in Europe, 1917-1942*. New York: The Carnegie Endowment for International Peace, 1943.

Günther Nollau, *International Communism and World Revolution, History and Methods*. New York: Fredrick Praeger, 1961.

Richard Pipes, *The Formation of the Soviet Union, Communism and Nationalism, 1917-1923*. Cambridge: Harvard University Press, 1964.

Leonard Schapiro, *The Communist Party of the Soviet Union*. New York: Vintage Books, 1971.

John M. Thompson, *Russia, Bolshevism, and the Versailles Peace*. Princeton, N.J.: Princeton University Press, 1966.

Jan F. Triska and Robert M. Slusser, *The Theory, Law, and Policy of Soviet Treaties*. Stanford: Stanford University Press, 1962.

Adam B. Ulam, *The Bolsheviks*. New York: Collier Books, 1968; *Communism and Coexistence, Soviet Foreign Policy, 1917-73*. New York: Praeger, 1974.

Teddy J. Uldricks, *Diplomacy and Ideology: The Origins of Soviet Foreign Relations, 1917-1930*. Beverly Hills, Calif.: Sage, 1979.

Zygmunt L. Zaleski, *Le dilemme russo-polonais, L'alliance franco-russe et la Pologne, Les deux conceptions de l'ordre et de la liberté*. Paris: Payot, 1920.

I. United States:

Hamilton Fish Armstrong, *Peace and Counter Peace, From Wilson to Hitler*. New York: Harper and Row, 1971.

Ray Stannard Baker, *Woodrow Wilson and the World Settlement*. Garden City, New York: Doubleday, 1923.

Denna Frank Fleming, *The United States and the League of Nations, 1918-1920*. New York: G. P. Putnam's Sons, 1932.

Norman A. Graebner, ed., *An Uncertain Tradition: American Secretaries of State in the Twentieth Century*. New York: McGraw-Hill, 1961.

Melvyn P. Leffler, *The Elusive Quest: America's Pursuit of European Stability and French Security, 1919-1933*. Chapel Hill: University of North Carolina Press, 1979.

Keith L. Nelson, *Victors Divided, America and the Allies in Germany, 1918-1923*. Berkeley: University of California Press, 1975.

David F. Trask, *The United States and the Supreme War Council, American War Aims and Inter-Allied Strategy, 1917-1918*. Middletown, Conn.: Wesleyan University Press, 1961.

John Chalmers Vinson, *Referendum for Isolation: Defeat of Article Ten of the League of Nations Covenant*. Athens: University of Georgia Press, 1961.

Edmund Wilson, *Shores of Light*. New York: Farrar, Straus and Young, 1952.

J. Lesser Powers:

Eva Susan Balogh, *The Road to Isolation: Hungary, the Great Powers, and the Successor States, 1919-1920*. Ann Arbor: University Microfilms International, 1980.

Vlacev Benes, *Poland*. New York: Praeger, 1970.

Stephen Bonsal, *Suitors and Suppliants: The Little Nations at Versailles*. New York: Prentice-Hall, 1946.

J. W. Bruegel, *Czechoslovakia Before Munich*. London: Cambridge University Press, 1973.

Anna M. Cienciala and Titus Komarnick, *From Versailles to Locano: Keys to Polish Foreign Policy, 1919-1925*. Lawrence: University Press of Kansas, 1984.

Barbara Jelavich, *History of the Balkans, Twentieth Century*. New York: Cambridge University Press, 1983.

Gyula Juhàsz, *Hungarian Foreign Policy, 1919-1945*. Budapest: Akadémiai Kiado, 1979.

David Owen Kieft, *Belgium's Return to Neutrality*. Oxford: Clarendon Press, 1972.

Ernst Heinrich Kossmann, *The Low Countries, 1780-1940*. New York: Oxford University Press, 1978.

Ivo Lederer, *Yugoslavia at the Paris Peace Conference, A Study in Frontier Making*. New Haven: Yale University Press, 1938.

Carlile A. MacCartney, *Hungary and Her Successors: The Treaty of Trianon and its Consequences, 1919-1937*. London: Oxford University Press, 1937.

Sally Marks, *Innocent Abroad, Belgium at the Paris Peace Conference of 1919*. Chapel Hill: University of North Carolia Press, 1981.

Jane Kathryn Muller, *Belgian Foreign Policy Between Two Wars, 1919-1940*. New York: Bookmann Associates, 1951.

Edmond Paris, *Le Vatican contra L'Europe*. Paris: Fischbacher, 1959.

Hugh Seton-Watson, *Eastern Europe Between the Wars, 1918-1941*. New York: Harper and Row, 1962.

James T. Shotwell and Max E. Laserson, *Poland and Russia, 1919-1945*. New York: Carnegie Endowment for World Peace, 1945.

Daniel H. Thomas, *The Guarantee of Belgian Independence and Neutrality in European Diplomacy, 1830's to 1930's*. Kingston, R.I.: D. H. Thomas, 1983.